Digital Impact

THE
TWO SECRETS
TO
ONLINE MARKETING
SUCCESS

Vipin Mayar
Geoff Ramsey

WILEY

John Wiley & Sons, Inc.

Published by John Wiley & Sons, Inc., Hoboken, New Jersey.
Published simultaneously in Canada.

For general information on our other products and services or for technical support, please contact our Customer Care Department within the United States at (800) 762-2974, outside the United States at (317) 572-3993 or fax (317) 572-4002.

Wiley also publishes its books in a variety of electronic formats. Some content that appears in print may not be available in electronic books. For more information about Wiley products, visit our website at www.wiley.com.

Library of Congress Cataloging-in-Publication Data:

Ramsey, Geoff, 1959–
    Digital impact : the two secrets to online marketing success / Geoff Ramsey, Vipin Mayar.
        p. cm.
    Includes index.
    ISBN 978-0-470-90572-2 (cloth); ISBN 978-1-118-08774-9 (ebk);
ISBN 978-1-118-08775-6 (ebk); ISBN 978-1-118-08776-3 (ebk)
        1. Internet marketing.   2. Electronic commerce.   I. Mayar, Vipin, 1962– II. Title.
    HF5415.1265.R358 2011
    658.8'72—dc22

                                                                        2011005630

Printed in the United States of America

10 9 8 7 6 5 4 3 2 1

CONTENTS

ACKNOWLEDGMENTS

The authors would like to extend their gratitude to the many who have helped shape, support, and streamline the process of writing this book.

GEOFF

A number of eMarketer staff provided assistance to help us present the latest and most relevant data and information, but I'd especially like to thank Tracy Tang, a master researcher who can find anything; Dana Hill, who took on the role of chart production manager; and Nicole Perrin, who helped pull together key trends for the mobile chapter. Special thanks also go to my dear friend and business partner Terry Chabrowe, and eMarketer President Lisa Church, who were both so understanding as I redirected more and more of my time and attention toward the book this past year. Finally, I am thankful for my family—my wife Kimberley, three sons Graham, Liam, and Kieran, and daughter Kaitlyn—who all had to put up with my early morning, late night, weekend, and holiday schedule changes as this project progressed.

VIPIN

My special thanks to Laurie Peterson for doing the heavy lifting on a couple of chapters. To my wife, Ranjana, and my three kids—Vinay, Ajay, and Anika—thank you all for understanding that I was not crazy getting up at 4 A.M. every day, and for giving me a lot of personal time on weekends to write. Finally, I'd like to thank McCann Worldgroup for providing a stimulating work environment that motivated me to develop and complete this book.

Last but not least, both of us would like to personally thank and honor Mia Amato who helped edit, organize, and manage the entire process of writing this book.

PART I

CHAPTER 1

Introduction

"The 2010s will be the Data Decade. Companies that
understand how to harness it will win. Those that don't
will perish. The same goes for marketers."
— *Steve Rubel, Senior VP, Director of Insights,
Edelman Digital* (Advertising Age, *January 4, 2010)*

In an era of constantly evolving
technologies and platforms, companies large and small need a bulletproof
game plan for their digital marketing programs. *Digital Impact* answers
that need by providing readers with a complete set of guidelines, along
with practical strategies, for both engaging consumers online and ensuring
maximum return on investment.

But you can stop reading this book now—unless you fundamentally
identify with the two common challenges facing digital marketers today:

1. Lack of adequate metrics and measurement systems to drive marketing
   performance.
2. Frustration with how to effectively engage online consumers, who
   have short attention spans, face abundant choices, and are increasingly
   resistant to advertising messages.

In this book, we'll explore solutions to both of these big challenges in
considerable depth and explain two core strategies you can use to address
them in every online channel you employ. You'll learn:

1. The seven most important digital marketing metrics every marketer
   should know.
2. How to establish the right measurement system for your organization.

3. How to break through advertising clutter and engage with consumers on a deeper and more personalized level.
4. How to calculate a return on investment (ROI) for social media and other new media initiatives.
5. How to integrate offline and online marketing approaches for the best possible outcomes.

Along the way, we'll show you how to plan, execute, and optimize every facet of your online marketing programs. Even if you use only a few online channels today or have not yet explored some of the more complex measurement systems out there, you will find a variety of tips, tactics, and strategies that will help you move your business—and your career—forward.

Our more than 30 years of combined experience in digital marketing is supplemented here with insights by dozens of top-tier marketing professionals interviewed for this book. We bring you statistics, best practices, and practical advice culled from McCann Worldgroup's global analytic practices and from hundreds of other sources aggregated by eMarketer, the digital intelligence firm co-founded by author Geoff Ramsey in 1996. You'll benefit from all we have learned—and much more. All the cards will be on the table; there will be no smoke and mirrors, no sleight of hand.

That's not how it all got started, of course.

The Magic of Measurement and Engagement

GEOFF: Many people ask me how I got into the research business with my company, eMarketer.

I like to tell them this story. I was 15, living in the college campus town of East Lansing, Michigan. I was determined to turn my love for performing magic tricks as a hobby into a career. I had managed to get the occasional paid gig—a child's birthday party, a Lion's Club meeting, a Boy Scout event—but it was difficult to get sufficient steady work to even pay for the cost of the magic tricks I bought, and there was certainly no money for advertising in the local newspaper.

I began looking for an arrangement where I could get paid for doing my magic on a regular, weekly basis. I eventually came up with a plan to offer my magical services to the owners of local, fine-dining restaurants, who would pay me to entertain their dinner guests. I would perform what is called "table-top" magic, during the period between ordering the food and waiting for it to arrive or while waiting for dessert or the check. There was only one problem. How would I convince the managers that my entertainment offering would have a material impact on their businesses? This question was all the more challenging considering that I was, for all outward appearances, a typical, bumbling, pimple-faced teenager.

Then I had an idea—to devise a small survey, an evaluation if you will—that I would hand out after each magic session at a guest's table. There would be three simple questions:

1. Did you enjoy having the magician at your table? (scale of 1 to 5)
2. Would this entertainment encourage you to return to this restaurant? (scale of 1 to 5)
3. Would you be likely to tell others about having a magician entertain you at this restaurant?

To create and mass-produce these little surveys, I resorted to the only technology available at the time: an old-fashioned manual typewriter, mimeograph paper (the kind that got your hands smeared with blue ink), and scissors to cut three sets of surveys off of each page.

I was able to convince a couple of restaurant managers to pay me the grand sum of $30 cash each night for about two hours of service during the busy dinner shift. Payment, however, would be predicated on receiving positive feedback from the surveys.

The results were fantastic. Not only were the diners enthusiastic about the whole magic experience, the managers could see their marketing goals being achieved:

1. The patrons were delighted to have a magician appear at their table—and this experience positively affected their feelings toward the restaurant (increased brand favorability ratings!).
2. The diners said that having a magician personally greet them at their table would definitely encourage them to return to the restaurant (increased brand loyalty and intent to purchase!).
3. The diners were excited about telling their friends and family about the restaurant and their special experience there (viral marketing and peer-to-peer endorsements!).

Little did I realize back then that I had two powerful forces working in my favor. First, people really enjoyed my magic; I was able to entertain and *engage* them. Second, the measurement of those interactions, although crude by today's standards, allowed me to prove my worth to the restaurant managers and continuously improve my performances based on the survey feedback.

The restaurant owners, of course, were investing in experiential marketing. Their $30 payments were coming back to them in the form of happier clients who were more likely to return and perhaps bring in new customers. Everyone involved was a winner, including me. Now let's turn our attention from the analog to the digital world.

Digital Impact: The Secrets of Performance Measurement and Magnetic Content

What are the secrets to digital marketing success?

There are probably a thousand and one answers to that question, and yet we propose there are just two key principles for achieving the impact you want from your online marketing efforts. They are Performance Measurement and Magnetic Content. Together, they represent a powerful, one-two punch to ensure your digital marketing gets the job done, proves itself, and improves over time.

In a Sea of Data, Be the Pilot

VIPIN: Ever since I can remember, I was really good at numbers and math. I especially enjoyed doing calculations in my head. Before Blackberrys and PDAs, I had trained my mind to remember phone numbers. I would have my friends test my memory, and I always felt a strong sense of accomplishment when they would ask, "How do you do that?"

When direct marketing was taking off in the 1980s, I was completely intrigued by the analytics behind these campaigns. For the first time, I saw my five years of rigorous engineering and quantitative courses being put to use in my marketing work. I remember building my first predictive model for a large cable company to identify consumers with a high propensity to buy Pay-Per-View movies. There was nothing special about the methodology of the model, except that it worked and drove really high response and close rates. I knew then that this area of marketing science, analytics, and technology driving marketing results was the space in which I wanted to make my career.

I have since then spent the past 20 years working with numerous Fortune 500 companies, consulting on metrics, uncovering data-driven insights, and building dashboards and models for all types of programs, including estimating ROI for marketing mix optimization. Essentially, I've been helping to drive true improvements in marketing performance for my clients.

What I see today is that marketers are drowning in an ocean of metrics. Through my measurement work at McCann, I have witnessed marketing executives being held up to increasingly high standards of proving the effectiveness of their spend—with metrics that relate directly to the bottom line.

A New Approach to Performance Measurement

The first secret centers on marketing Performance Measurement. The Internet allows for far greater measurement possibilities than any other media. But that's not enough. In fact, it's too much. If you are like most marketers, you are struggling to keep up with the array of metrics choices. There are far too many metrics. Just in social media alone there are more than 100 metrics to choose from.

Far too often you find that you are measuring the wrong things or in the wrong ways. Too many marketers, for example, are still using the highly flawed click-through-rate (CTR) as the primary metric for their online marketing efforts. Others are struggling to find the right metrics for linking social media mentions to purchases or grasping at methods to put a dollar value on a Facebook "friend" that might yield comparative ROI to some other channel. And then there is consumer "engagement," a marketing objective popularized in new media circles, which suffers not only from a lack of measurement protocols but also from a lack of agreement on the definition for what it is!

The executive suite is also demanding ROI on branding initiatives, even as the marketing industry struggles with new methods to calculate the value of a branding experience (Figure 1.1). Never before has marketing been held up to such a high standard to prove itself—and to drive accountable performance with metrics that relate directly to the bottom line. Along with this relentless drive toward marketing performance comes an unprecedented focus on data and analytics. Marketers now have numbers coming out their ears and may feel they need a PhD in statistics to merely do their job.

What marketers really need is a fresh strategy and a set of clearer guidelines for Performance Measurement and metrics in the digital space. In this book, you will find these guidelines. With the use of new data management and analytics capabilities, it is now possible for marketers to track the complete digital footprint of consumers to gain a 360-degree view of their interactions, preferences, and behaviors, often right down to the purchase level. Success ultimately involves tracking performance over time and then optimizing the inputs of media and messaging to the outputs of sales, cost-per-lead, or some other bottom-line metric of your choice. You'll get there faster once you understand that there are really only six or seven key metrics you can use to drive performance for entire campaigns.

Figure 1.1

Priorities for the C-suite

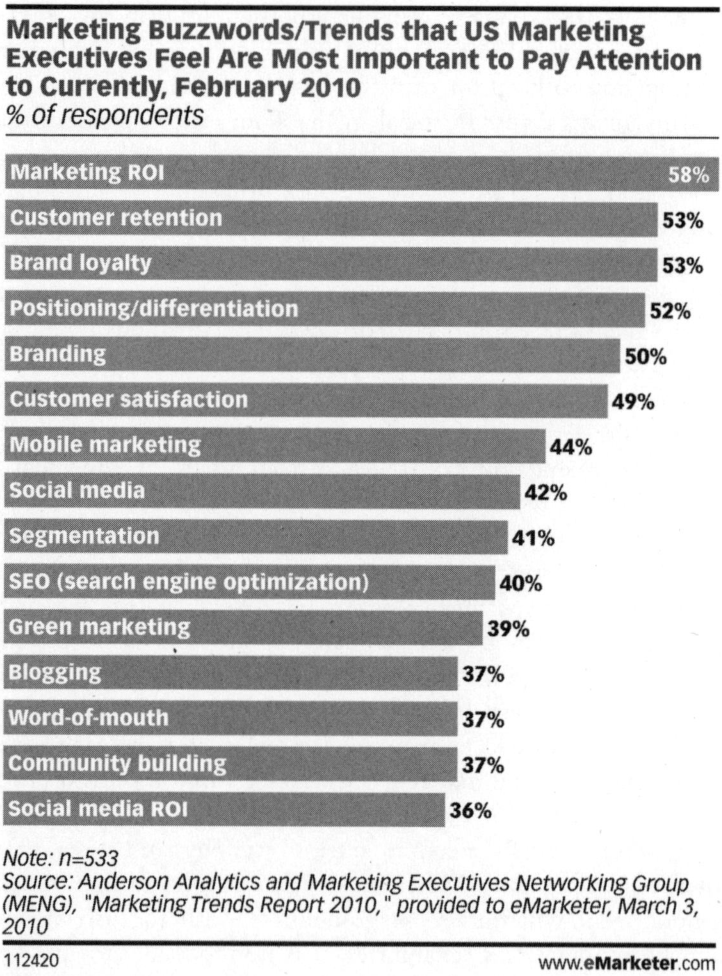

Marketing Buzzwords/Trends that US Marketing Executives Feel Are Most Important to Pay Attention to Currently, February 2010
% of respondents

Marketing ROI	58%
Customer retention	53%
Brand loyalty	53%
Positioning/differentiation	52%
Branding	50%
Customer satisfaction	49%
Mobile marketing	44%
Social media	42%
Segmentation	41%
SEO (search engine optimization)	40%
Green marketing	39%
Blogging	37%
Word-of-mouth	37%
Community building	37%
Social media ROI	36%

Note: n=533
Source: Anderson Analytics and Marketing Executives Networking Group (MENG), "Marketing Trends Report 2010," provided to eMarketer, March 3, 2010

112420   www.**eMarketer**.com

Magnetic Content: A New Way to Think about Engagement

The second secret has nothing to do with metrics but everything to do with turning the entire conventional advertising model upside down. It involves systematically creating content and messaging—that may, or may not be, classified as "advertising" per se—that is unique, useful, well-executed and fun, such that it resonates with consumers in deeper, more meaningful ways than ever before. It's designed to attract consumers, rather than shout for their attention. It's also more effective and cost-efficient. Buying frequency becomes less important than creating compelling content that will draw the consumer in. Targeting becomes less of a headache when it's a two-way street: instead of constantly examining the inbound traffic for online leads, you make it easier for potential consumers to use their own considerable web research skills to beat a path to *you*.

Rather than *interrupting* consumers with ads, it's about *attracting* them, *engaging* them—with some kind of utility, entertainment, helpful information, or other valuable content that is actually welcomed by the consumer. We'll refer to this type of marketing communication as Magnetic Content, because it involves crafting content for consumers that attracts them like a magnet, as opposed to most ads today, which are seen as a distraction, or worse, a detraction.

Jim Stengel, the former global marketing officer of Procter & Gamble, a company that spends upwards of $8 billion globally on advertising, has consistently argued that marketers adopt a radical rethinking of their approach to connecting with consumers in the digital age. He has been a long-time proponent of the engagement movement, notably saying in 2006, "What's changed is that the engagement level we can have with our consumers is just so much higher. We can have a two-way dialogue, a relationship. That means we will need more brand-enhancing, consumer-enhancing dialogue in more of our businesses. It's a different skill set—with different capabilities—than we required in the past."

Yet, five years later, we still find less savvy marketers are using great new tools in bad, old-fashioned ways. Tweeting out a random message about a product feature or a two-for-one offer is as scattershot a strategy today as many mass-market network television ads were thirty years ago.

This book offers insights on how brands can create Magnetic Content that answers the vital marketing question, "What can I do for you, the consumer, that is unique, valuable, fun and compelling?" We will show you how innovative companies are blending digital channels for messaging, experiences and services that delight consumers and create a deeper, more intimate connection with them. And you'll learn about measurement systems that allow you to continuously optimize your marketing for maximum impact online for every channel that you use.

A Crash Course in the New Marketing Landscape

You would not need this book were it not for the radical shifts that technology, consumer behavior, social and cultural dynamics, and, of course, the Internet have wrought upon the marketing landscape.

Recognize that the Internet has become the hub—the starting or pivot point for marketers in all industries.

The Internet as "media hub" makes sense for a number of reasons, not the least of which is that the web has become a central place where consumers like to hang out and spend their time—and their money. When shopping or buying a product, a majority of consumers will look to the web as a primary influencer and as a decision tool. This is even true in the analogue world: go into any appliance store, for example, and you'll find prospective customers surfing the web on their smart phones in search of lower prices at competing stores or online outlets. ("I tried it out in the store, but I bought it on Amazon" is the bane of many a retailer.) In the business-to-business realm, your customer is probably familiar with online exchanges and can collect pricing data from your competitors around the globe.

For many product and service categories, the Internet is used by upwards of 80 percent of those considering a purchase. In addition, the web is unique in that it can impact every stage along the consumer buying cycle. It can be used to create awareness, interest, or consideration for a product (e.g., banners, video ads, online sponsorships); facilitate information-gathering (e.g., search, product or brand websites); enable a transaction (e-commerce); offer post-sales support (e.g., e-mail); reinforce brand loyalty (e.g., e-mail, social media); accelerate referrals (e.g., social media); and so on.

From a media measurement perspective, too, the Internet earns its place as the center of attention. The Internet promises far greater potential when it comes to measuring the impact of advertising and marketing. Indeed, its very interactivity creates built-in measurement possibilities galore!

Agencies are taking notice of the web's primacy, too. Every major ad agency holding company, in fact, is jockeying for the title of being the most digitally centric, that is, having the highest proportion of media dollars supporting digital initiatives. Agencies see their future growth in digital.

Let's next look at a fundamental marketing question: Where is your money and your competitors' money going today?

It's a Trillion-Dollar Marketing Pot

In the United States alone, marketers will shell out over $170 billion on advertising in 2011, according to eMarketer. But that sum is just a bite of the enchilada. Although advertising—placing advertisements on media properties—represents a $170 billion outlay, other marketing expenditures dwarf that figure.

In fact, ad media dollars comprise less than one-quarter of total marketing expenditures in the United States. In most organizations, the so-called below-the-line spending, which typically includes trade and consumer sales promotion, events marketing, public relations, and a variety of other nonmedia expenditures, represents the lion's share of spending.

When these nonmedia expenditures are included, the total marketing spending pie balloons to $700 billion to $900 billion, depending on which sources you trust. What's more, in just a year or two, the aggregate spending figure for marketing communications will pass the trillion-dollar mark. That's if you credit merchant bank Veronis Suhler Stevenson (VSS) and their estimated total communications spending in the United States at $878 billion in 2009, with projected growth to more than $1.4 trillion by 2014.

Research firm Outsell, using a more restricted definition, estimates that U.S. marketers spent $368 billion on advertising and marketing programs in 2010. Business-to-business spending, including in-person events, print media, online advertising, webinars, search engine optimization (SEO), and corporate websites was $129 billion in 2010, according to Outsell.

Outsell also estimates that marketers now invest more than $60 billion each year on building and maintaining their websites, almost as much as they spend, in aggregate, on television advertising.

Of course, like many marketers, you may not care what the aggregate figure is. Your concern is more focused on this question: How much money is *my* company spending on marketing, and how much is it wasting? Or even more to the point: How can I spend my marketing dollars so as to waste as little as possible? And within the particular scope of this book: How can I best spend my digital marketing dollars for the greatest possible impact?

To answer these questions, we offer our two solutions. Performance Measurement systems that do not task your resources, and are simple and easy to execute across channels, will answer the call for better marketing performance. Directing your creative efforts to focus primarily on Magnetic Content (for customer attraction) will give you a competitive edge in a consumer-driven digital marketplace.

The New Digital Consumer: Trends and Challenges for Marketers

Let's face it, you can't simply buy demographics, such as women 18 to 34, and hope to effectively and efficiently hit your prime audience target today. Fragmentation has exploded. The average American has hundreds of channel choices on their high definition television system. There are roughly 11,000 different choices in consumer and business magazines. The average radio listener in a given market can access more than two dozen local stations from the more than 10,000 commercial outlets on the broadcast band and can access many thousands more if you count satellite radio, blog radio networks, time-shifted podcasting, and Internet radio websites.

That's challenging enough, but in a web world, the number of media, entertainment, news, and communication choices is mind-boggling— millions, to be more specific. What's more, consumers, particularly teens and *millennials* (20-somethings born in 1980 or later), seem to effortlessly flit from one site or channel to the next, from social networking sites to mobile apps to YouTube videos, to Twitter and instant messaging—all in a matter of milliseconds. They will seamlessly switch not just channels within mediums, but across mediums—from their computer, to their cell phone, to their wide-screen TV. And, yes, they expect marketers to keep up with them throughout all this activity. Your problem—and your pain—is that your methods, and likely your advertising agency, can't keep up with these consumers or engage them fast enough to meet your goals. So, where can you find the digital consumer today?*

- More than 60 percent of all Internet users regularly visit social network sites, and well over three-quarters of teens and millennials do so.
- Well over half of Internet users regularly read blogs, and about 12 percent write them.
- Nearly 70 percent of all Internet users in the United States are active watchers of online video, and more than 90 percent of millennials stream and/or download videos.
- Nearly 15 percent of Internet users are Tweeting or participating in some other kind of microblogging activity.

The growth rates for these technologies and consumer activities have been nothing short of astounding. It's all the more amazing when you realize these new media platforms are in addition to—if not a partial replacement of—traditional media outlets, such as television, radio, magazines, and newspapers. Generally, a new medium does not replace the old; it just gets squeezed in. That's why daily consumer time spent with media has continued to rise over the past few years. In the United States, total time spent with media rose from 635 minutes to 660 minutes daily, from 2008 to

*All figures are from eMarketer.

2010. According to eMarketer, over the same time, television viewing rose by 10 minutes daily, even as web video viewing increased as well.

The Balance of Power Has Shifted Even More to the Consumer   Although all of these activities and new technologies are very exciting, they have fundamentally shifted the balance of power between the consumer and the marketer. Consumers have gained the upper hand with their unprecedented control of what they watch, when they watch it, and how they watch it—not to mention who they share it with. It is truly a consumer *on-demand* world. Getting your organization to recognize that advertisers no longer control the entirety of the message is a critical step to appreciating the importance of Magnetic Content.

Multitasking Means Divided Attention   The proliferation of media, content, and communication choices, particularly on the web and mobile devices, leads to an increasingly granular fragmentation of time (Figure 1.2). That means as a marketer you have to work harder to reach an ever smaller consumer audience that is often watching different things, on different devices, at different times, and even for different reasons.

Consumers of all demographics split their media time, such as by simultaneously watching television or listening to the radio while browsing online. We all know that younger generations take this to a higher level. Have you ever watched a teenager IM her friend while simultaneously browsing online, updating her Facebook page, playing a mobile game, and chewing gum? With the Internet, attentions are being divided, subdivided, and often subdivided again. As a result, at any given point in time, your carefully crafted, highly targeted ad message is likely attracting only 3.4 percent of the consumer's attention. That's a made-up statistic, but the point is clear: the more engaging your message, the more attention you'll get.

Filtering, Zapping, and Clicking Away Are Not Going Away   In an on-demand media world, the consumer can filter out, zap, eradicate, tune out, and generally obliterate ad messages faster than you can blink an eye. Truth be told, most consumers don't exactly like ads. Oh sure, they put up with them, and once in a Super Bowl moment, they actually enjoy them. And sometimes, though not nearly often enough, they can come at just the right time—when the consumer is actually in the market for the product advertised. But for the most part, consumers see ads as the necessary evil to get what they really want, which is great content. And particularly in digital channels, consumers can bypass ads easily, even if it's simply by ignoring a static banner ad.

Figure 1.2

Share of time spent with major media, 2008–2010

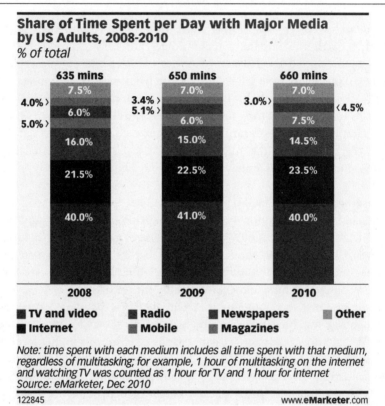

Share of Time Spent per Day with Major Media
by US Adults, 2008-2010
% of total

	2008	2009	2010
Total	635 mins	650 mins	660 mins
Other	7.5%	7.0%	7.0%
	4.0% / 5.0%	3.4% / 5.1%	3.0% / 4.5%
	6.0%	6.0%	7.5%
	16.0%	15.0%	14.5%
	21.5%	22.5%	23.5%
	40.0%	41.0%	40.0%

■ TV and video   ■ Radio   ■ Newspapers   ■ Other
■ Internet   ■ Mobile   ■ Magazines

Note: time spent with each medium includes all time spent with that medium, regardless of multitasking; for example, 1 hour of multitasking on the internet and watching TV was counted as 1 hour for TV and 1 hour for internet
Source: eMarketer, Dec 2010

122845   www.**eMarketer**.com

Erosion of Trust Erodes All Messaging—Including Yours Just to make matters worse for marketers, there's the declining trust issue. Over the past decade, consumer trust levels in marketers, advertising agencies, and marketing in general has continually drifted downward. It's likely no coincidence that this erosion of trust has occurred along with the rise of the Internet, which both empowers consumers and makes information about companies, products, and brands more transparent than ever before. We knew something was deeply wrong when, in 2005, popular marketing speaker and author Seth Godin published the book *All Marketers Are Liars*.

This dwindling of trust phenomenon is especially bad news for brand marketers because trust is central to a brand's equity. Consumer trust in a brand is what keeps it strong and growing. Social media, one of the newer channels for marketers, offers opportunities to burnish, encourage, mitigate, or restore brand trust on a global platform. But it can also accelerate a brand's demise.

A New Approach: The Two Secrets to Online Success

With these challenges in mind, eMarketer issued a report in June 2009 exploring many of these familiar problems in detail. The report relied heavily on interviews with experts from all sides of the online advertising industry, including marketers, digital agencies, market research firms, and a host of vendors in the digital space.

The two secrets described in this book represent a new approach to solving the two basic issues that were found to be the heart of the dilemma for marketers today. One major obstacle that marketers now recognize is their own tendency to measure only what can be easily measured, resulting in an overemphasis on direct response. Click-throughs on banner ads are simple to measure, and so are open rates on e-mails. On the other hand, when it comes to measuring the branding impact of social media efforts, most marketers remain completely stymied. They have also failed in their attempts to accurately measure a return on their digital media investments (ROI), despite spending large sums on branding initiatives.

The second most mentioned obstacle to improving performance, in the eMarketer report, was attributed to a lack of focus on digital data, from the level of chief marketing officer (CMO) and down! And this, in turn, was linked to a lack of understanding of "how digital works" from top-line management as well as creative staff.

By combining the most proven measurement techniques with the magnetized pull of engaging content, it is possible to find new customers and develop and nurture existing relationships that will grow your brand and sell your products. This book will help you concentrate on the right approaches and strategies that will create a real, lasting, and measurable difference in your marketing.

How This Book Is Organized

We realize that there are many aspects of web marketing that you will delegate and quite a few that you will wish to manage on your own. To make it easy to organize and educate your teams, this book is divided into three sections, or phases, by function.

In this first section, Phase I, we outline the two keys to your online marketing success and explain how this system, which we use ourselves, can be utilized and adapted to organizations large and small.

In Phase II, we present six chapters that deal with specific digital marketing channels:

- Search (Chapter 4)
- Online Display Ads (Chapter 5)
- E-mail Marketing (Chapter 6)
- Social Media (Chapter 7)
- Mobile (Chapter 8)
- Online Video (Chapter 9)

In each of these six chapters, and for each respective channel, we'll walk you through how to measure and optimize marketing efforts and engage with consumers. In addition, we will provide context and perspective about the consumer trends and best marketing practices related to each channel.

In Phase III, we help you manage the process. Two chapters concentrate on the nitty-gritty of measurement systems and metrics, including best practices and ways to drive online marketing performance:

- Integration across Online and Offline Channels (Chapter 10)
- Digital Dashboards (Chapter 11)

Finally, we help you integrate all key learnings in a final chapter called:

- Putting It All Together (Chapter 12)

We understand the pressures you face as a digital marketer today. Within this book you will find new tools, new strategies, and new approaches that will give you a critical edge to move your initiatives, your organization, and your marketing career, forward and into the future.

CHAPTER 2

Secret #1: The Right Approach to Performance Measurement

"If you cannot measure it, you cannot manage it."
—*Lord Kelvin*

If you think that strategizing the right measurement metrics is easy and can be handed off to someone else, it's time to wake up, smell the coffee, roll up your sleeves, and read this chapter on measurement. In this chapter we will:

- Provide a strategy and framework for building the right Performance Measurements for your marketing programs.
- Describe the seven critical performance metrics necessary for every digital marketer to master.
- Identify the one performance metric that is the most important one!

CEOs and CFOs of Fortune 1000 corporations are demanding that their marketing departments provide a clear return on investment for the millions they spend on advertising and marketing. Likewise, in small businesses, there is a growing need to account for every dollar spent. Across the board, we're all looking to measure and increase the value we get for our marketing programs.

"Marketers have been challenged to be more accountable by CEOs who are looking for shareholder return and value," said Bob Liodice, the president and CEO of the Association of National Advertisers, in an interview with eMarketer. "The challenge for marketing is 'Prove to me that marketing works. Prove to me that no matter how you slice it, the investments are paying back in both short- and long-term deliverables.'"

In fact, in countless surveys and studies over the past few years, marketing accountability/ROI has come up as a top-ranked priority for companies. Its importance is being driven by many factors: the proliferation of digital channels, the increasing microsegmentation of consumers, a growing torrent of marketing data available, a dramatic reduction in hardware costs for data processing, and, most important, the increased scrutiny on marketing returns.

This ROI obsession applies to all media. No medium or channel today can escape the crosshairs of marketing performance! Any medium that gets a budget better be prepared to prove its case. And no surprise here, the performance fixation has drawn disproportionate attention to more strategic measurement of digital channels. To be sure, this kind of scrutiny scares the pants off many marketers, as online measurement and intense data analytics are often considered as pleasant an experience as visiting a dentist for a root canal. We conceived this book with the intention of changing these perceptions and making the measurement discipline easier for marketers and general managers.

Today, marketers are drowning in metrics. Social media alone has a possible set of more than 100 ways to measure its impact! And every channel has its own unique set of metrics, making it very difficult for marketers to compare effectiveness across channels. When it comes to digital marketing, positioned as the most trackable of all media, the challenge is even greater. Digital media suffers from an overabundance of data, which creates confusion for marketers and overwhelms them.

A particularly telling statistic comes from a June 2008 survey by McKinsey & Company: some 80 percent of the 340 marketers surveyed said that their companies allocated their budgets across different media by either using subjective judgments or simply by repeating what they did the year before. Only a small minority of advertisers claimed to use quantitative analytical techniques to optimize their online marketing. Since that survey, we know there has been marginal progress in the area of measurement, yet most marketers are still flailing (and failing) when it comes to proper use of measurement and metrics.

One of the biggest barriers to an effective online measurement strategy is a lack of budget and resources (Figure 2.1). A 2010 global study by Econsultancy found this was the number one obstacle, even trumping organizational silos.

Similarly, according to a U.S.-based survey by the Lenskold Group, although 79 percent of marketers agreed that the need to measure, analyze, and report marketing effectiveness had increased in 2009, 59 percent said they were not budgeted for it.

We are stumped as to why businesses would place such a low-budget priority on the measurement of their marketing initiatives. It is particularly odd because

Figure 2.1
What keeps marketers from measuring online programs?

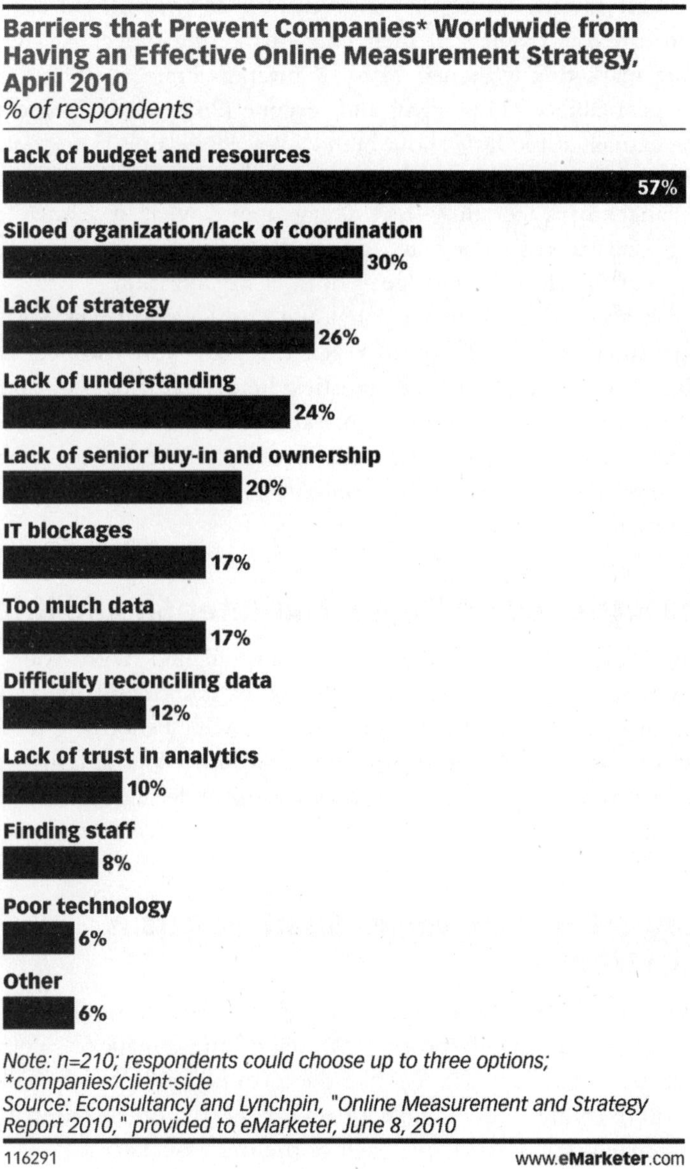

Barriers that Prevent Companies* Worldwide from Having an Effective Online Measurement Strategy, April 2010
% of respondents

Lack of budget and resources
57%

Siloed organization/lack of coordination
30%

Lack of strategy
26%

Lack of understanding
24%

Lack of senior buy-in and ownership
20%

IT blockages
17%

Too much data
17%

Difficulty reconciling data
12%

Lack of trust in analytics
10%

Finding staff
8%

Poor technology
6%

Other
6%

Note: n=210; respondents could choose up to three options;
*companies/client-side
Source: Econsultancy and Lynchpin, "Online Measurement and Strategy Report 2010," provided to eMarketer, June 8, 2010

116291   www.**eMarketer**.com

we know that most companies understand how important it is for marketing measurement to be tightly aligned with business strategy. In fact, in a survey by Spencer Stuart among 200 top-level executives, 35 percent said the best way to measure the effectiveness of their chief marketing officer (CMO) was to "make sure marketing is aligned with the business strategy." This was ranked even over profitability (29 percent) and revenue (25 percent). These same top executives actually cared little about brand awareness—only 5 percent believed it to be a good measure of a CMO's value.

Top management certainly isn't fuzzy about what it wants from the marketing department. They are demanding that it measures marketing success against the clear business goals of their organization.

Although you will need to set your own goals, we can help you measure the performance of your efforts to reach the goals you choose. And we're not talking about mountains of statistics here. Actually, you only need seven—that's right, seven—types of marketing metrics to measure almost all of your marketing campaigns. And there's one that we believe is absolutely *essential and should be used in **all** your campaigns*.

Let's get started!

Seven Metrics Every Digital Marketer Should Know

Once you have established the right goals, aligned with your business objectives, you are faced with the challenge of identifying the right set of metrics to measure the success of your programs. We'll be looking at two major categories of metrics and then organizing them into a logical framework. Yes, there is way to categorize metrics to make them understandable to anyone in your organization.

Category 1: Exposure versus Strategic versus Financial Metrics

The first step is to identify and categorize metrics according to the following three operative buckets: Exposure, Strategic, and Financial. These terms refer to the goals you have set. We like the term *buckets* because it's illustrative of what you're trying to do—collect data for specific organizational needs in a very organized way. Let's define each of the three buckets:

1. *Exposure*—metrics that typically relate to the short-term aspects of the campaign, such as the reach/frequency and engagement of digital marketing.

2. *Strategic*—metrics that capture strategic, longer-term marketing objectives of customer and brand growth.
3. *Financial*—metrics that quantify the return on investment, or financial outcomes, of the marketing activity.

Now, let's review each of these buckets in more detail.

Exposure metrics capture the immediate impact of a marketing spend, such as an increase in the number of visitors to a site, or click-through rates on search terms. Exposure metrics are often used as *diagnostics* because they provide an immediate and obvious view of the short-term aspects of the program. Are consumers noticing the ads? Are the messages reaching the right audience? Are they driving them to the right online destinations?

Strategic metrics are more forward-looking and are used to evaluate the effects of the marketing spend on strategic marketing dimensions, such as brand impact on favorability or consideration or customer impact on acquisition/retention and Net Promoter Score (NPS). Strategic metrics take longer to build and often require at least three months before their impact can be measured.

Finally, *Financial metrics* are the ones relating to financial performance, such as sales, market share, profits, or ROI. They are the ultimate consequence of the marketing effort. With marketing becoming more accountable, all programs should have financial metrics. The most important objective over time, at least for a large public firm, is to create movement in the stock price or to impact market capitalization. This kind of movement can be achieved with a successful branding campaign, as well as with direct-response or e-commerce efforts. For smaller, private firms, the ultimate objective might be to increase revenues and/or profits by a certain percentage. Or the goal might be to attain enough brand presence to attract new venture capital or assist an IPO.

According to a survey from the Winterberry Group, transactional data, focusing on online/offline purchase history, is the most important type of data for driving marketing performance (Figure 2.2).

Category 2: Primary versus Diagnostic Metrics

Another way to classify data is by function and usefulness, either as primary or as a diagnostic tool.

Primary metrics are used to gauge the overall success of your marketing programs and business. They are closely aligned to the overarching goal of the marketing spend. Typical primary metrics are sales, revenue, and key brand attributes. Often we find marketers are not focusing on the right primary metric—they end up compromising with an activity metric, because they're

Figure 2.2

Transactional data is ideal for measuring performance

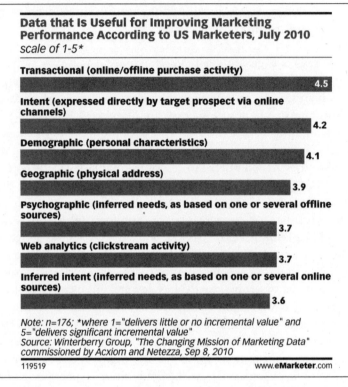

Data that Is Useful for Improving Marketing
Performance According to US Marketers, July 2010
scale of 1-5*

Transactional (online/offline purchase activity)
4.5

Intent (expressed directly by target prospect via online channels)
4.2

Demographic (personal characteristics)
4.1

Geographic (physical address)
3.9

Psychographic (inferred needs, as based on one or several offline sources)
3.7

Web analytics (clickstream activity)
3.7

Inferred intent (inferred needs, as based on one or several online sources)
3.6

Note: n=176; *where 1="delivers little or no incremental value" and 5="delivers significant incremental value"
Source: Winterberry Group, "The Changing Mission of Marketing Data" commissioned by Acxiom and Netezza, Sep 8, 2010
119519   www.**eMarketer**.com

usually easier to measure. For example, some marketers will use web traffic or click-through rates (CTR) as their primary metric, when their real goal is to build brand preference through engaging online content. Always make sure that you have carefully selected the right primary metric that truly reflects your ultimate marketing objective.

Diagnostic metrics help explain the primary metric. For example, lack of message clarity can explain why a print ad campaign is not breaking through and driving preference or sales. Or in the digital space, an ad unit's inability to drive clicks may help explain why you're not getting visitors to your site. Using the right set of diagnostic metrics is vital; without them, it is impossible to know the reason (or reasons) why you are seeing movement—or not seeing it—in your primary metric. Too many programs are implemented without due consideration to setting diagnostic metrics that can help explain the success or failure of an initiative.

How to Build Your Performance Metrics Framework

Now that we understand the two broad categories of metrics, let's build out the Performance Measurement framework based on these categories. Trust us, if you select two metrics from each of the three tiered buckets—one primary, and one diagnostic—you will have a complete measurement system. Establishing a primary metric as well as accompanying diagnostic metrics will provide a solid foundation for measuring any campaign or marketing initiative.

Figure 2.3 shows one way to visualize your framework and the linkages between all three levels.

Note that Figure 2.3 resembles the common marketing orientation—a classic sales funnel—only completely upside down. We believe this orientation more accurately represents how a marketing campaign is built over time. Exposure metrics provide a base and help you get a handle on your audience. Strategic metrics help you measure whether your tactics are working or not. Properly done, strategic metrics also inform you, on a continual basis, whether or not you are going to achieve what you've defined as your financial metrics goals. As far as overall organizational goals, the three buckets, or tiers, fall along a continuum, with exposure metrics being the least closely tied to business performance and ROI/financial outcomes being the most directly linked to business success.

Figure 2.3
Performance Measurement can be viewed as a pyramid

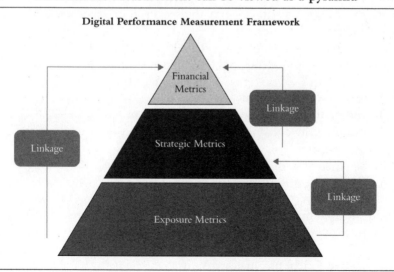

Digital Performance Measurement Framework

Source: Vipin Mayar.

In this pyramid, each set of metrics provides a foundation for the next higher tier. For the right measurement approach, not only should the metrics be right, but the linkages between them should also be clearly established. Of course, as you move up the pyramid, from exposure to financial metrics, the measurement process becomes more difficult.

Let's start with a common example: developing metrics for a destination site that seeks to engage consumers with Magnetic Content and with the objective of building brand preference, ultimately leading to an increase in sales. A metrics model in this case might select the following metrics for each level:

1. **Exposure metric**—Determine reach, by number of visitors who have interacted with the magnetic content on the branded website.
2. **Strategic metric**—Gauge levels of brand preference and look for increases in preference through surveys administered before and after the site visit.
3. **Financial (ROI/sales outcomes) metric**—Calculate change in sales and ROI based on the cost of the branded content.

This all looks familiar, right? Now let's hone in and focus on seven measurements that are proven to be effective, which we recommend for *all* marketers.

We believe there are indeed only seven metrics that are critical. Although many other metrics are available to marketers, it is these seven—which are appropriate for even the smallest business—that marketers should seek to master. You'll notice that they cover the spectrum of exposure, strategic, and financial metrics.

The selected seven metrics are based on the rationale that all digital campaigns have the following common objectives, regardless of the channel:

- To reach the right audience
- To engage the audience with relevant content
- To motivate the audience to take a desired action—registration, demo, conversion, etc.
- To be efficient with the spend
- To deliver a positive ROI

With these common goals in mind, the seven selected metrics align with these objectives:

1. Qualified Reach, or Qualified Visits
2. CTR

3. Brand perception lift
4. Engagement Score
5. End Action rate (end action can be acquisition, redemption, trial, purchase, or other conversion)
6. Efficiency metrics cost per X (X can be clicks, impressions, leads, orders, or engagement)
7. ROI

Let's dive into each of these seven metrics to get an understanding of how they work within our framework of exposure, strategic, and financial buckets.

The Best Exposure Metrics

Our example destination website chose as its exposure metric "reach"— the number of unique visitors and the number of visitors who "interacted" with the key content on site. Within the variety of ways one could examine site traffic or inside page wanderings, there can be an overflow of data, depending on how you define *interaction*. Will it be time spent on the site? Registration or sign-ups? Downloads? What really counts? This is a key issue, so let's now introduce the most important digital metric: Qualified Reach. We recommend this metric for all your marketing programs!

1. Qualified Reach, or Qualified Visits, Is the Better Way to View Traffic Reach and frequency have been used as the primary exposure metrics for traditional media for decades. The unresolved question, though, has been: *Do they apply to the Internet?* Because if they did, they would offer an apples-to-apples comparison across media.

We believe that reach and frequency, although highly relevant to marketers, are not adequate metrics for the Internet. They fail to capture the key "quality" ingredients of interaction and engagement, which are essential with digital channels.

However, we do believe a modified version of reach and frequency should apply to digital channels. The modified definition of reach is not simply the number of people who may have seen an advertising asset online. Rather, it is *the number of visitors who may have seen an advertisement or brand-related content online AND then choose to have some interaction with the branded content, such as a website, video, or ad.* We call this *Qualified Reach*. If the interaction occurs on the brand's website, we refer to it as *Qualified Visits*. In either case, the reach is "qualified" because it requires some measurable degree of engagement from the consumer, which in turn signifies some level of interest or intention. The key, therefore, is to elicit some kind of measurable behavior (engagement) that can serve as a proxy for the consumer's intention or interest. Qualified Reach and Qualified Visits are similar, the only difference being that Visits is used in the context of a site, whereas Reach can be anywhere. Both these metrics are critical diagnostic tactical metrics, and they go way beyond just measuring raw impressions. They are about ensuring that the impressions drive the right set of visitors who then go on to have a meaningful engagement with your branded content. Otherwise, you cannot be sure you have made a genuine impact.

Marketers are realizing there is a trade-off between aggregate audience reach and the quality of the engagement consumers have with the brand. We believe it is better to restrict your definition of reach to include only those consumers who, by their engagement, demonstrate some level of interest in your product or brand, for example, opening an e-mail, viewing your videos, or interacting with your mobile content. Many marketers agree it is worth sacrificing some reach to ensure a deeper level of engagement.

Why do we believe Qualified Reach is the most important metric? It captures two important dimensions that no other single metric does. It has quantity (number of individuals) and quality (have performed a desired interaction, which in turn suggests a degree of intention on the part of the consumer).

2. Click-Through Rates Still Have Their Uses   CTR is the most common metric used by online advertisers and in fact is the way most digital campaigns are measured. *We believe it should be used—but only as a diagnostic metric, as a somewhat crude and incomplete measure of consumer interest.*

CTR is calculated by dividing the number of users who clicked on an ad or a link by the number of times the ad or link was delivered (that is, impressions). For example, if an ad on a website content page was delivered to 100 viewers, or at least 100 times to repeat viewers, and it was clicked on 10 times by the audience who saw it, then the CTR is 0.1, or 10 percent.

CTR is the current, default standard for measuring the effectiveness of online advertisements. Huge sums of money are exchanged between advertisers and publishers based on the CTR for an ad unit. Conceptually, it represents the number of consumers who clicked on a specific ad unit to learn more about the topic. It is easily measurable by web analytics software and also provides quick insights into who is clicking the ads, what they do when they visit your website, and ultimately, if they complete an end action or convert.

What are the problems with CTRs? Why can't they be used a primary metric?

The CTR is by no means a perfect metric. According to several sources, the CTR currently hovers at the low rate of about 0.09 percent. Furthermore, panel measurement firm comScore reports that two-thirds of Internet users never click on display ads over the course of a month; moreover, only 16 percent of Internet users account for 80 percent of all clicks.

Many limitations and problems are associated with the CTR metric, most of which relate to the misuse and overuse by marketers. First, CTRs are best used for direct response initiatives, and yet many brand marketers rely on them extensively as well. This can be a problem because the effects of branding are best measured over a period of time—weeks, months, or even years—not the nanosecond of a click. Also, the quality and creative execution of too many Internet ads and other forms of branded content is poor, thus driving down CTRs. Fundamentally, though, most consumers are simply not interested in clicking on banners, flashing pop-ups, or floating ads that usually have little or no relevance to them. Such intrusions disrupt their enjoyment of the web experience. We'll address this issue in Chapter 3, where we discuss the second secret.

At best, CTR represents "potential interest" in learning more about the digital content. For example, many of us have clicked on an obtrusive ad that appears to be saying something that captures our immediate interest . . . wrinkle-defying cream, cheap medicine from Canada, an exotic travel offer, or even hair loss treatments. However, that interest does not usually result in a conversion to sales or a preference for the brand. CTRs can also be easily manipulated by click-fraud farms or by flashy or even provocative ads that can trigger the initial click but that don't represent qualified leads since they don't reflect inherent interest in the product.

In summary, we believe CTR is a valid diagnostic metric in that it gives an important view into the potential interest level in learning more about that specific digital content. It should not be used as an end objective, a common misuse of the CTR metric.

The Best Strategic Metrics

Our next set of metrics is strategic and addresses a current industry trend toward measuring the engagement, or magnetism of a digital asset (see Chapter 3 for more about Magnetic Content). Increasingly, we see marketers launching relevant, branded content designed to create unique and meaningful experiences for consumers. Although the new goal is to *magnetically pull in an audience and attract them to the brand*, the industry as a whole is still struggling with the question of how best to define and measure consumer engagement with a brand.

There is a tremendous need to define "engagement" and magnetism in the context of online advertising, given the interactive nature of the medium. Such an engagement metric will:

- Compare the ability of different digital assets to engage consumers in a consistent, repeatable fashion.
- Pinpoint content that is more/less magnetic and drive the redistribution of content based on the engagement metric.
- Segment consumers based on their engagement behavior, to then drive subsequent messages and even deeper engagement.

3. Use Engagement Score as a Diagnostic   We believe the right diagnostic metric for engagement is actually a series of metrics all bundled into one— something we call the *Engagement Score (ES)*. It represents the degree of magnetism of the branded content and is based on the following beliefs:

- What's important is what a visitor does with the branded content.
- Channels that efficiently deliver more engaged audiences are more valuable.
- The average number of pages per visit and the average time on a site are not important; what's important is whether the visitor obtains his or her desired outcome (and how that outcome aligns with the site's business objectives).

The ES works across all digital media, from videos and mobile apps to microsites and social community platforms. The methodology is based on ascribing value scores to the types of activities that are performed by the visitor. To capture these insights, the ES takes a visitor-centric perspective and not an average view.

The values of the ES vary based on the degree of engagement; for example, the mere viewing of content has a smaller value than does interacting with content. We recommend a hierarchy of seven levels of engagement with a recommended point value for each level in the engagement hierarchy. These levels are outlined in Figure 2.4.

As much as possible, the category levels should be kept consistent from brand to brand and across geographies so that the score can be used as a universal comparison of engagement effectiveness for a company or brand. The score assignments are developed through business judgment

Figure 2.4
Hierarchy of values for engagement

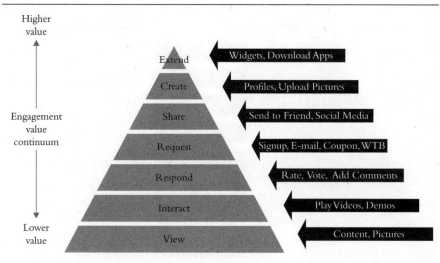

Source: Vipin Mayar.

and an assessment of your company's priorities. The point values range from 0 to 10. Figure 2.5 shows a sample set of scores you might see for a consumer package goods site. In this sample, once the values have been assigned, it is not difficult to compute the ES based on the average interaction of each visitor.

The ES defines engagement based on what each visitor does during a visit to the site or other content platform. It is based on actual behavior aligned to the objectives of the brand. It identifies the most engaging content and helps a brand optimize the content for its audience. Eventually, it becomes clearer to see how the audience is finding or searching for the desired content and reaching for it. It puts emphasis on producing high-quality Magnetic Content that draws the consumer in, as opposed to pushing out ads or promotions that disrupts the consumer's web experience.

In addition to being a solid measure for capturing engagement with digital assets, the ES is also a great metric you can use to optimize sources of traffic; that is, it can be used to identify which banner ads, search terms, videos, and sites where you are advertising are providing visitors that engage with your company site. This is done by using statistical analysis to determine the strength of the relationship between the ES and the different source channels (such as banners, search text-links, video site traffic) at the site/placement/

Figure 2.5
Determining Values within an engagement scorecard

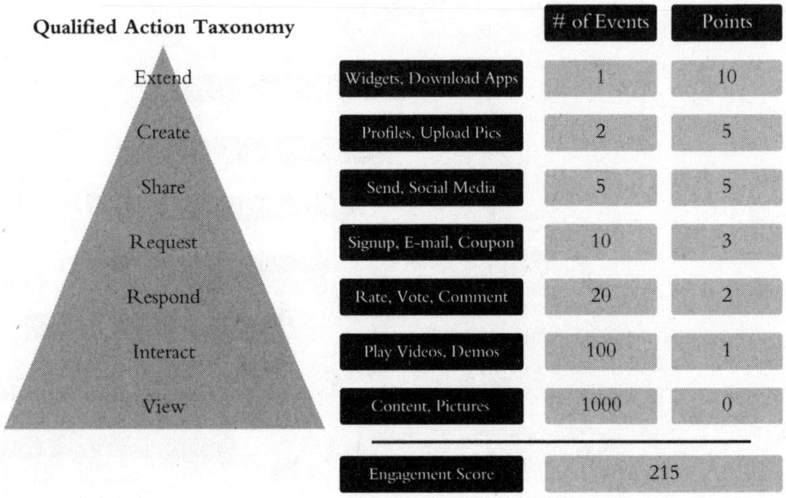

Qualified Action Taxonomy		# of Events	Points
Extend	Widgets, Download Apps	1	10
Create	Profiles, Upload Pics	2	5
Share	Send, Social Media	5	5
Request	Signup, E-mail, Coupon	10	3
Respond	Rate, Vote, Comment	20	2
Interact	Play Videos, Demos	100	1
View	Content, Pictures	1000	0
	Engagement Score	215	

Source: Vipin Mayar.

creative level. For search, this can be done at the search engine/keyword level, and for e-mails, links within the e-mail at the unique URL level. Thus, we can gain valuable, actionable insights and data-driven recommendations to optimize the design of a site, site section, or landing page and can also determine which landing pages are optimal, depending on the site driver.

It is vital to implement the Engagement Score metric to establish a common, consistent platform for comparing engagement across assets. We recommend the ES even in situations when a site or branded content initiative has a clear End Action (discussed next). The ES provides a rich metric for evaluating audience qualification, degree of content relevance, and expanded opportunity for immediate or future conversion.

4. End Action Rate Is an important Strategic Metric   The ES metrics apply naturally to all content-focused sites or initiatives, even if there is no obvious call to action such as a registration or conversion. An End Action, on the other hand, is any strategic outcome that results from the consumer interacting with the content. Another term for End Action is *Conversion*. End Action is more accurate because it describes an actual act, such as a coupon redemption, a trial, or a purchase. It is possible, of course, to have more than one End Action in mind for your web initiative. In these cases, we recommend counting the action that is closest to purchase. For instance, if you are looking at a trial offer download or an e-mail opt-in sign-up, we recommend the trial offer be used, because this is more likely to be predictive of purchase intent than a simple sign-up for a newsletter or coupon feed.

To calculate the End Action Rate, divide the total number of individuals who went on to perform the End Action by the total Qualified Reach or Qualified Visits. Simple and quick.

Despite its ease of measurement, End Action Rate is a vital performance metric and should be considered as part of every digital campaign. This is especially the case for small businesses that usually have a very clear End Action goal for their digital content. Typically, the goal is to drive purchase, trial of the product, or a download of information about the product or service. Let's look at a real-life example focusing on the End Action metric.

To retain market leadership, a pharmaceutical brand looked to digital channels as a means to efficiently connect with consumers and drive them toward brand trial and loyalty. The brand invested in a variety of digital platforms as part of this acquisition and CRM strategy. Key channels included display advertising, paid search, social media, and a branded website.

Two End Action metrics consistent with the two primary objectives of the entire campaign were developed: getting people to register for a trial offer and having them proceed to a paid prescription after the trail offer. The two specific End Action metrics in this instance were:

- Redemption rate—the share of registrants who redeemed the product trial offer
- Patient acquisition rate—the share of registrants who proceeded to a paid prescription after the trial offer

The marketing team kept a close eye on the exposure metrics and the end action metrics, making sure that as they were increasing or decreasing exposure, they did not affect End Action rates by getting traffic that was not qualified. The goal, which allowed for exposure adjustments, was to drive the highest End Action rates relative to an established benchmark, controlling for any variance in the quality of the traffic or visitors.

All of these actions indicate a degree of consumer interest or intent in the brand, which leads us to a very important strategic metric: brand perception lift.

5. Brand Perception Lift Is Your Key Brand Metric   Our next metric is lift in critical brand perceptions. Marketers have used these classic brand-lift metrics since before the Internet, mainly for understanding the effects of TV commercials. Online marketers can apply this metric to digital channels to measure the success of banner ads or videos and especially for social media content. Many in the marketing community have suggested that brand-lift metrics are undervalued by digital marketers, who are more accustomed to behavior-based data and often want the immediacy of metrics like time viewed or clicks. However, survey-based measurement of brand perceptions can offer brand marketers useful insights into how well their content is engaging with consumers and building the brand over the long-term.

Brand lift is calculated by determining the change in a brand perception before and after a group has interacted with digital content, compared with a controlled group that did not interact with digital content. This is the classic test of exposed versus control methodology, common to most brand-health studies. Typically, online brand metrics are gathered through audience panels or surveys—typically via pop-up windows that ask users if they would answer a few questions. Many companies provide these kinds of survey-based measurement capabilities, such as Dynamic Logic, comScore, InsightExpress, and Nielsen. The following are the most commonly used brand-lift metrics:

- Aided brand awareness
- Unaided brand awareness
- Brand attribute lift
- Brand consideration
- Brand favorability
- Purchase intent

The specific metric (or metrics) to be selected is based on the marketer's objectives. Several factors will influence the potential range of results from a campaign. These include:

- Advertiser's industry or product category
- Type of channel
- Quality of the creative or messaging
- Placement of the content
- Targeting of the campaign

Since brand-health measurements depend on audience survey data for their results, accurate ad targeting is essential for getting the most viable results. For example, a poorly targeted video ad might get significant lift for awareness—simply because the ad was entertaining—but purchase intent could be flat if the audience was not right. Imagine the brand-lift results for a female beauty product video ad on a male-oriented site, for example.

Now that we have identified the right set of strategic metrics, let's see how we bring in the financial metrics. This will answer the question, Are we being cost-effective and delivering value/ROI?

The Best Financial Metrics

These metrics are used for assessing the efficiency of the marketing spend and can be used across different marketing channels as an indicator of relative effectiveness. The two most important metrics for you to get under your belt are Return on Investment (ROI) plus an additional standardized method to measure efficiency of the marketing spend.

Efficiency metrics must exist on your metrics short list simply because financial resources are finite. As a marketer, you need to make sure that you are allocating monies to the channel or channels that result in the greatest efficiency, that is, those that provide the best cost per X.

If you do not currently have efficiency metrics on your roster, now is the time!

Efficiency Metrics of Cost/X Are Your Friend   Efficiency metrics are actually easy; they all work the same way and represent the cost to get a unit that is measurable. The unit can be any one of the following, including several we discussed earlier:

- Cost per Qualified Reach
- Cost per click
- Cost per order
- Cost per lead
- Cost per Engagement Score
- Cost per End Action (acquisition, download, trial, purchase, conversion)

The one we recommend using above all others is the *Cost Per End Action*. A financial efficiency metric that is based on your End Action not only complements the End Action rate metrics but also helps you estimate the volume of the End Actions you can expect from a level of investment. In other words, whether it is worth it to scale up or not.

In the case of the previous pharmaceutical brand example, the efficiency metric used was a cost per End Action, in this case, cost per acquisition of a trial offer redemption. This was calculated by dividing the total cost of the digital content investment by the number of individuals who went on to download the trial offer and then redeem it at their pharmacy. The marketer could also compare cost per End Actions for each of the various content platforms they had used, so they could see which platform was comparatively the most efficient when it came to getting prospective customers to download a coupon and bring it to their pharmacy for a product sample.

You can see how efficiency metrics can be extremely valuable to a marketer. But they're also relatively easy to measure once you figure out your key goals. Despite these benefits, efficiency metrics are surprisingly overlooked, especially when the focus is on volume or a branding goal.

In measurement conversations, efficiency metrics of cost per X are sometimes referred to as ROI based on the logic that "How many X do I get out of my invested dollars?" is synonymous with "How much return did I get out of my investment?" But that's not the case. A true ROI metric involves much more, as we will see in our discussion of the final and arguably most important metric.

7. The Right Approach to ROI Measurement Is Incremental Our final metric, ROI, is a primary financial metric. It is aligned with financial outcomes and drives improvement in profitability and margin. With more than \$1 trillion in projected marketing spending in the year 2011, it should be of vital importance to all marketers. The ROI metric has the power to significantly influence decision making for driving marketing effectiveness.

The ROI methodologies and concepts most valuable to marketers are built upon the principle of *incrementality*. This is a newer approach to the measurement of marketing spend, which we endorse. It posits that all marketing, whether it is offline or online, should result in an incremental improvement in *acquisition, retention, loyalty, key perception(s),* or *sales.* Note that traditional ROI for marketing accounting purposes is measured like this:

$$\text{ROI} = \frac{(\text{Net Revenues} - \text{Marketing Investment})}{\text{Marketing Investment}} \times 100\%$$

This is a standard operational formula. The end result is always expressed as a percentage because it's meant to be a way to easily compare the return on dollars from a variety of business investments, everything from the money spent on a banner or social media campaign to the purchase of a new delivery truck or the hiring of new customer service staff.

But when applied to marketing, especially online marketing, comparing the ROI on what you've spent for search marketing versus TV or magazine ads, or comparing e-mail to postal mail, isn't always helpful. Audiences may be different. Products may be different; for example, new products will have a different ROI than products that are mature in their markets.

A better way to measure ROI for marketing is to compare incremental lift as a percentage. This allows you to more effectively compare new platforms (social media, street teams) with traditional media, and it can also provide you with measures such as the relative success of a new product launch versus benchmarks of previous products.

To determine incremental lift, ROI is computed by a simple equation, as follows:

$$\text{ROI} = \frac{(\text{Incremental Profit} - \text{Total Cost})}{\text{Total Cost}} \times 100\%$$

With this equation, the only question in your estimation of ROI becomes, "How do I determine 'incrementality'?"

Two methods are used to determine incremental lift in marketing: modeling and testing.

The *modeling approach* to ROI is based on econometric models, also known as "marketing mix" models. These models assess the effectiveness of each of the marketing tactics within a multichannel campaign. The model equation computes the ROI of individual marketing channels, which enables you to measure the return on mass media and nontraditional media advertising, as well as assess their "halo" effect on direct response channels. We discuss ROI modeling in detail in Chapter 10.

The *testing approach* to ROI offers a relatively quick way to gauge ROI with minimum risks. It's also a good way to derive predictive ROI results if you're looking to fund a new initiative you haven't tried before. Tests provide knowledge of what works, what doesn't work, and what is the optimal combination of marketing tactics to maximize response, profit, customer satisfaction, and so forth. A marketing test can also determine the effect of marketing and/ or media variables on sales performance. It can further provide insights on the risk/reward associated with changing these variables.

Although most companies place a great deal of value on the importance of testing marketing campaigns—whether A/B testing, multivariate testing, or user testing—as a means of improving conversion rates, many other firms believe that introducing testing into the process is an unnecessary added step, an unwelcome delay to launching a campaign. Our belief, though, is that testing is still the most valuable method for getting the most out of your marketing spend. A survey by Econsultancy of more than 300 global online marketers found that simple A/B testing was still prized and valued (see Figure 2.6).

In the pharmaceutical brand example referred to earlier, the ROI testing methodology proved that the brand was able to efficiently reach, attract, engage, and educate consumers via the site and social media assets; motivate registration and trial; and deliver an ROI of 6:1. That is, for every dollar invested, there was six dollars of return.

Figure 2.6
Testing strategies can be as simple as A, B

Methods that Are Valuable for Improving Conversion Rates According to Companies* Worldwide**, July-August 2009
% of respondents

	Highly valuable	Quite valuable	Not valuable
A/B testing	53%	42%	5%
Customer journey analysis	49%	47%	4%
Multivariate testing	48%	45%	8%
User testing	47%	47%	6%
Cart abandonment analysis	46%	47%	7%
Segmentation	39%	54%	7%
Event-triggered/behavioral e-mail	35%	57%	8%
Online surveys/customer feedback	33%	61%	6%
Copy optimization	32%	63%	5%
Pinch-point analysis	26%	54%	19%
Expert usability reviews/consultancy	25%	61%	14%

Note: n=304; numbers may not add up to 100% due to rounding;
*client-side; **UK (72%), non-UK Europe (14%), North America (6%) and other (8%)
Source: Econsultancy, "Conversion Report" sponsored by RedEye, provided to eMarketer, October 2009

107784   www.eMarketer.com

Testing Tools and Methods for Performance Measurement

Test and control groups are the key components of testing and are used to compute incrementality and predictive ROI. The idea is to identify and segment those individuals within your target audience who were *exposed* to programs and content and then compare their purchase history or other outcomes with a *control* group of consumers who were *not* exposed to the program and content. The "lift" created within the exposed group is used to calculate ROI.

Test and control research can be done cost effectively using consumer panels. Several companies, including media solutions providers such as Nielsen and comScore, provide consumer panels for monitoring people's behavior in the digital environment. With approximately 2 million worldwide consumers under continuous measurement, comScore has the largest panel available to date.

In certain instances, it may make sense to set up your own panel. For example, you may want your own panel if you are focused on a highly affluent or specialized professional audience, who typically will not participate in a mass panel. Setting up your own panel requires some effort to find the audience, ensure that it is representative of the universe, enlist their participation, and establish reliable monitoring protocols and technology. But it can be very effective for companies that have the resources and are committed to tracking incrementality through testing.

How to Perform a Panel Test   Typically, a marketer should implement two waves of surveys for both the test and control groups, one conducted immediately after the exposure of the campaign or marketing program and a second one run about 30 days later, as follows:

Wave 1: Conducted immediately after exposure
Captures:
- Demographics
- Brand perceptions
- Intent to purchase or self-reported purchases

Wave 2: Conducted 30 days after exposure
Captures:
- Brand perceptions
- Intent to purchase or self-reported purchases

The second wave is done to determine the change in the metric (perceptions, intent to purchase, self-reported purchases) from Wave 1 for both the control and the test groups. The incremental lift is the difference in change between the test and control groups across the two waves. It can be translated into the ROI calculation as follows:

$$\text{ROI} = \frac{(\text{Incremental Lift in Purchase} - \text{Total Cost})}{\text{Total Cost}} \times 100\%$$

It is also necessary in this type of research to control for "noise," that is, outside factors that might affect the results, such as differences in ages or other demographic variables between the exposed and control groups. Often, the percentage of the potential audience exposed to a given program may be fairly low. Thus, you need to ensure that the sample size is large enough to net a sufficient number of "exposed" respondents for statistically projectable results.

If you have not done any market tests before, here is a simple checklist for how you should approach it:

- Set up comparable test and control groups (match them on the right characteristics).
- Ensure a statistically significant sample size (use sample size calculators you can find online).

Figure 2.7
Calculating ROI from testing

	Methodology
Business Goal	Acquire, retain, build loyalty, perception change or sales
Approach	Determination of incremental improvement in the appropriate above goal(s)
Incremental Lift	Lift determined from setting up test and control groups Sales lift obtained from panels or client data
Incremental Revenue	Calculation = Price × Incremental Sales Lift × Consumers Impacted
Incremental Profit	Calculation = Revenue × Profit Margin
Cost	Loaded costs, including media, creative, tech, etc.
ROI	ROI = Incremental Profit/Cost

Source: Vipin Mayar.

- Design the experiment with a clear understanding of different treatments.
- If testing for many factors, use advanced experimental design (fractional, factorial, multivariate, etc.).
- Take baseline readings before and after the experiment.

Figure 2.7 summarizes what we have just described. It shows how to determine ROI through testing by using the "incremental lift" approach and then dividing it by the entire cost basis for the campaign.

Conclusion

In this chapter we have presented a Performance Measurement framework built on two categories of metrics. The first category organizes metrics into three tiered buckets: (1) Exposure, (2) Strategic, and (3) Financial. The second category classifies metrics as Primary versus Diagnostic. We've also identified the seven most important metrics that every business should adopt to properly and efficiently measure their marketing programs. By following the disciplines, guidelines, and steps outlined in this chapter, you will be able to evaluate the performance of your marketing initiatives and compare results across programs and campaigns.

In subsequent chapters we deploy this framework and illustrate the performance metrics for the six critical digital channels—social, mobile, e-mail, video, display, and search. For each channel, we will show how to apply the appropriate sets from the top seven metrics. We will also introduce a few additional metrics that work specifically within each channel. If you focus on the top seven, you'll find you won't have to spend so much time or resources trying to evaluate and optimize your digital assets.

And if you do nothing else, try the one metric we believe is the most important—Qualified Reach; it will help you pinpoint an audience of both scale and quality. This will get you on the path toward continually improving Performance Measurement and help you reach your marketing goals.

Remember: measurement by itself cannot create marketing success. Creativity, which is one of the great strengths that marketers bring to their organizations, can also be advanced and its riches unlocked with the second key: Magnetic Content.

CHAPTER 3

Secret #2: Magnetic Content—Why Attraction Beats Distraction

"Advertising is no longer about blasting the most messages to the most people. Instead, it's about this: Ideas that spread, win."
— *Seth Godin, speaking at the IAB MIXX conference in New York, September 27, 2010*

Why is it that some multimillion dollar ad campaigns, launched by the brightest minds in advertising, fail to capture their audience? How can it be that some small companies, working with tiny shoestring budgets, can achieve outsized marketing results? In this chapter, we focus on the second secret to online marketing success, the power of creating Magnetic Content to attract customers and drive business results. In this chapter we will:

1. Discuss what Magnetic Content is and the consumer and marketing trends that require this new approach.
2. Describe how to establish a practical framework for creating Magnetic Content.
3. Discuss the seven proven strategies for making the most of your Magnetic Content.

We've learned that the first secret to online marketing success is all about Performance Measurement—specifically how to measure the effectiveness, or performance, of the marketing programs you run. The second secret—creating

Magnetic Content—is all about making marketing programs that work better in the first place. Be prepared to reset your thinking about your approach to advertising and marketing.

The unique property of magnets, of course, is that they attract. If you are—quite literally—trying to find a needle in a haystack, your best strategy might well be to hold a large magnet over the stack of hay. If the magnet is powerful enough, you'll zap that needle out in an instant. The needle will find the magnet, rather than you scrambling to find the needle.

For marketers, Magnetic Content is any kind of content they create on behalf of their brand—whether in the form of an advertisement, a YouTube video, an online game, a Facebook page, a Twitter promotion, or a mobile app—that has the effect of attracting consumers toward their brand and leads to increasingly higher levels of brand engagement.

Magnetic Content entertains, amuses, informs, serves a function, answers a need, or in some other way provides value to consumers such that they welcome it, ask for more, and want to share it with others. It complements the standard push ad model with a powerful pulling effect.

When adopting the Magnetic Content approach, you will think less about pushing ad messages out and more about pulling consumers in. You will focus less on interrupting or trying to borrow attention and more on *earning* that attention. You'll place less emphasis on directly selling product and more on providing something—and it could be just about anything— that adds genuine value to the consumer's life. Not only does the best Magnetic Content pull people in, it pulls in the right people—the kind of people who will most likely buy your product and want to tell others about it.

When it comes to advertising effectiveness, we know that not all ads are created equal. Furthermore, quantitative data supports the connection between creative excellence and advertising results. In one recent study, online researcher Dynamic Logic evaluated the ability of online display campaigns to move the needle on brand metrics like awareness, favorability and purchase intent (see Figure 3.1). By segmenting the campaigns into various levels of performance, including "top performers," "average performers," and "bottom performers," the firm discovered significant differences in performance, all based on the quality of the creative execution. Whereas top performers boosted brand metrics significantly, bottom performing campaigns actually weakened brand metrics and caused a significant decrease in purchase intent, specifically down on average by 4.1 percentage points.

In a world of infinite digital content, quality matters, which is why you need Magnetic Content to succeed online today.

Figure 3.1

Good creative boosts performance

Online Display Advertising's Effect on Brand Metrics in the US, by Ad Performance, Q3 2010
average delta* above control

	Top performers	Average	Bottom performers
Aided brand awareness	8.8	2.2	-2.6
Online ad awareness	13.8	4.4	-2.3
Message association	8.9	2.5	-2.0
Brand favorability	7.9	1.6	-3.9
Purchase intent	7.8	1.4	-4.1

Note: *delta defined as point difference in exposed vs. control groups
Source: Dynamic Logic, Feb 28, 2011

125338   www.**eMarketer**.com

The Magnetic Content Approach: A New "Best Practice"

The classic interruption/disruption model of advertising, where you seek to interrupt the consumer's enjoyment of content with advertising messages, is waning.

This traditional advertising model has been used by marketers for decades, and it's based on the following premise: in exchange for subsidizing desirable consumer content created by a third-party publisher, broadcaster, or some other form of content producer, the advertiser earns the right to interrupt the consumer's content experience with ads (for example, "This program brought to you by : . .").

Online, we too often see this model playing out in the form of irritating pop-up screens, pre-roll video ads with loud audio, and large home page "take-over" ads that spur viewers to frantically search for the "Skip this ad" link. Even in the realm of virtual worlds and online games, we see intrusive sponsorships where the marketer still triangulates between the consumer and the publisher of content. This interruption/disruption approach worked so well in the past largely because consumers didn't have much choice. They were willing to put up with the (mostly unwanted) ads because, well, what else were they going to do?

But despite the growing proliferation of ads, consumers find it easier than ever to zap them, click past them, or simply ignore them altogether—online and offline. They have gradually become more resistant to advertising messages and less trusting of the advertisers behind them. Yet we also know that some advertising is welcomed and even eagerly sought after by the consumer. In fashion magazines, for example, the glossy ads from major apparel and cosmetic brands can be as valuable to the reader as the editorial content. For many viewers of the Super Bowl, too, the amusing, over-the-top TV commercials can be as much a draw as the game itself. In the online world, most of us using search engines are not at all bothered by the sponsored links we get when typing in a query, particularly when we are researching products or brands; on the contrary, they are usually welcomed. In other words, some ads are so high quality, contextually relevant, or entertaining that they can be considered Magnetic Content.

The Magnetic Content approach becomes a best practice when it is applied consistently across digital channels and in ways that capture what's best about each online channel—for example, its immediacy, or the ability to reach a customer at early touch points for purchase consideration or purchase intent. When a fashion magazine is digitized for a tablet device, a visible link on a dress in a featured picture can send an interested consumer directly to the website of the retailer selling the dress. Great video spots created for web and TV enjoy a long life of their own when distributed virally and may continue to burnish a brand's reputation for years ahead.

Putting aside for the moment these tantalizing prospects, we maintain that, in general, consumers would prefer not to have to put up with advertising pitches which are usually irrelevant to their needs or wants.

To fully embrace this as a best practice, we believe marketers should acknowledge that just because they have "paid" for an audience, people will not necessarily pay attention or care. There are two cautionary notes here. First, don't fall into the ego trap of conceding that consumers generally dislike or ignore most advertising while silently thinking to yourself, "But that doesn't apply to *my* ads because they're so [relevant, clever, or whatever]." In a crowded content marketplace, your ads must be exceptional to stand out. A second caution is not to be misled into thinking that Magnetic Content can totally replace traditional "paid media" efforts. Magnetic Content improves the approach, but it is not a replacement.

If Content Is Everywhere, Where Is Yours?

In the old world order, things were simple and everyone had a defined role: publishers, broadcasters, and Hollywood produced all the content, consumers absorbed it, and marketers paid for it.

In the new world order, everyone is a content producer, including marketers and consumers. Companies of all sizes and across industries are creating entertaining videos for YouTube, producing information-oriented how-to microsites, designing utilitarian mobile applications, and developing a variety of other services that only conceptually relate to the brand—and are not designed to directly sell product. Marketers who embrace this new role include Beth Comstock, senior vice president and chief marketing officer at General Electric, who recently stated: "We are in the content business. More and more, we are needing to create content that our customers can use."

According to the Jack Myers Media Business Report, companies like Walmart, Whole Foods, Johnson & Johnson, and P&G are investing "significant organizational and financial resources in building media properties. These media assets are not intended only to deliver marketing value, but to generate enhanced economic value and enhance the companies' shareholder value." They also allow marketers to bypass the middleman (content publishers) to get closer, more direct contact with the audience they want to reach, as well as collect data for future marketing programs. Myers warns, "Dependence exclusively on traditional paid exposure for advertising that most consumers inherently don't want to see is counter-intuitive in the digital society."

We have entered the next stage of the digital marketing era, a time when brands strive to maintain a personal relationship with their consumers through direct, two-way dialogue, engaging experiences and shared context and content. This goes way beyond merely pitching products to the masses.

Publishers, meanwhile, have moved squarely into the marketing services business—creating soup-to-nuts advertising and marketing programs for marketers and bypassing the advertising agencies that usually serve that role. As but one example, Meredith Corporation has produced a robust series of consumer-oriented videos for its advertiser Kraft Foods, which the food marketer is using as a way to engage likely prospects. This is precisely the kind of marketing program traditionally created by an advertising agency or in-house marketing team.

Finally, consumers are no longer just consuming. They are creating their own content in the form of blogs, Facebook status updates, tweets on Twitter, YouTube videos, and photos posted to Flickr, to name a few examples. Consumers are also helping shape the marketing for brands: creating branded videos on YouTube, writing customer ratings and reviews, publicly declaring themselves "fans" of brands and discussing their product experiences—both bad and good—on social network sites. How often do we hear today, "Consumers now own your brand"?

With everyone in the media ecosystem creating content—consumers, marketers, and publishers—there is far more content available than consumers can digest. Consequently, only the best content will attract consumers and warrant their time and attention. Traditional, irrelevant ads stand little chance.

Understanding How Magnetic Content Works

Physical magnets exert a pulling force, selectively attracting only things made of iron (or other magnets). We use the term *magnet* in other, metaphorical ways, too, such as *magnet schools*. Magnet schools with specialized curricula draw students from across the normal boundaries of school districts in cities that may have hundreds of neighborhood schools. A magnet school barely has to advertise or promote itself—its reputation draws children (via their parents) from all over. What's more, they usually end up attracting the most proficient students.

Magnetism operates in the advertising world as well, and through a variety of forms. The funniest commercials on television, for example, demand viewer attention and get talked about at the water cooler and circulated on the Internet. Similarly, highly entertaining online video ads or other forms of branded digital content can go viral in an instant through their magnetic appeal.

Magnetic Content also represents a radical shift from how marketing has been implemented for decades. Instead of "targeting" consumer audiences, which almost sounds as if we are trying to hunt them down for a kill, we are seeking to attract them. Jaffer Ali, chief executive officer of Vidsense, put it this way on his blog at www.mediabizbloggers.com:

> The difference between attracting the right audience and targeting the right audience is profound. Isn't attraction the brand's real job? To entice, lure, persuade and dare I say it—charm the audience? What is the first principal of attracting the right audience? Content that engages them rather than repels them with advertising. To attract audiences in scale we simply must give them what they really want, engaging content! In an on-demand world, nobody demands more ads. Audiences vote by choosing videos that they want to see, by choosing articles that they want to read, by choosing music that they want to hear. Nobody chooses ads—not even the folks who produce them!

Think Fishing, Not Hunting   To extend the analogy, hunting is all about tracking and targeting your prey (the consumer) and then shooting them with your ammo (ad messaging). Fishing, on the other hand, involves an opposite strategy—attraction. When fishing, you find some good bait (Magnetic Content), attach it to your line, cast the line, and then wait as the fish (consumers) come directly to you—instead of you having to chase after the fish.

Marketing typically adopts the hunting/targeting approach. The emphasis is on finding better and better targeting techniques and fancier digital ammo, all in the interest of tracking down the elusive consumer. Of course, as we apply better filters in our efforts to refine our targeting, we end up shrinking our reach. If we take targeting to its natural, logical endpoint, we end up reaching only our existing customers! We propose, though, that you are better off fishing for consumers, rather than trying to hunt them down.

So, the Magnetic Content approach is all about fishing, where the key is to find the right bait—in the form of highly relevant, compelling, entertaining or engaging content that literally attracts the most likely prospects to your doorstep. The Magnetic Content approach allows you to more efficiently reach your most likely prospects while also avoiding wasting money on uninterested consumers. The powerful idea behind Magnetic Content is that you don't so much reach the audience, as they reach you.

Magnetizing Is a Process, Not a One-Off Event   The concept of magnetizing consumers is not a "hook 'em and leave 'em" single event. Rather, it is an iterative process that first hooks the consumer and then proceeds to lead them along an engagement path, enticing them with more and more engaging content that allows the consumer to further self-qualify themselves by exhibiting greater and greater levels of interest.

For example, your initial Magnetic Content hook might be a really funny video or entertaining webisode that you launch on YouTube. But to stimulate more engagement—from the most interested prospects—you could end the video with an invitation to a branded microsite, where they can view additional funny videos in the same vein and perhaps share them with friends. For the next, deeper level of engagement you could offer some sort of game or contest that plays off the theme in the videos. Eventually, you could lead interested consumers to your website, where they can download a coupon or sign up for a demo. In addition, you could also mix in a smattering of e-mail, search, specialty Facebook brand pages, and other digital engagements. The key is to adopt an iterative process where you initiate consumer interactions at increasingly deeper levels; the more consumers engage with your brand, the more they self-qualify themselves as possible customers down the road. Start with lighter interactions and then lead them down the path toward heavier engagements requiring a deeper commitment on their part.

This reflects classic opt-in marketing where you don't ask for the sale right off the bat, but rather entice the consumer along a progressive, mutually beneficial path of engagement.

Defining True Magnetic Content: A Five-Factor Framework

To consistently create and deliver Magnetic Content that captures consumers' attention and engagement, you need a framework, or a set of criteria, to direct your efforts. In our initial steps toward developing the framework, we looked at scores of examples of Magnetic Content and subjectively classified them into five broad rankings:

- Breakthrough
- Excellent
- Good job
- Me too
- Failure

Next, we examined each Magnetic Content example on many dimensions, including:

- How *well known* is the brand?
- How *new* is the idea?
- Is this content *fun*?
- How well is the idea *executed*?
- Is this content *unique*?
- Is this content *useful*?
- Does it have a large potential *user base*?
- Could you charge *money* for it?

We then constructed a regression model and found that five factors could predict or separate great Magnetic Content from poor ones. Here are the five critical factors that define Magnetic Content:

1. Is the content unique?
2. Is the content useful?
3. Is the content well executed?

4. Is the content fun?
5. Does the content make good use of the channel in which it appears?

Importantly, not all Magnetic Content needs to meet all five of the criteria, but obviously the more you can check off, the better chance you will have at engaging customers and prospects.

Let's explore each of the five factors in some detail.

1. Is the Content Unique?

Just as me-too products and copycat advertisements fail in the marketplace, Magnetic Content should offer something unique to consumers. Before you attempt to create Magnetic Content, look around and see what's already out there. Is there a need that is not being addressed, or is there a new, better way to meet that need? *Differentiation and being new or first is an important goal toward creating successful Magnetic Content.*

For example, Fiat created eco:Drive, which is a highly innovative computer application that helps consumers improve the efficiency of their driving by analyzing their current driving habits and then offering practical ways to reduce their fuel usage. It's a unique (and free) tool that provides a valuable service for eco-conscious consumers. It also underscores the brand's positioning as a highly fuel-efficient car (Figure 3.2).

Figure 3.2
Fiat eco: Drive computer app

Source: www.fiat.com/ecodrive.

2. Is the Content Useful?

Utility rules. Just as you seek to design your products and services to answer a genuine consumer need, you want to craft Magnetic Content that does the same. Even a simple advertisement that single-mindedly focuses on a product's core benefit can be useful to consumers—if it is relevant, clearly identifies an unmet need, and provides a clear solution.

Magnetic Content, when it's useful, transcends or complements the product you are selling, often in surprising and delightful ways. This entails altering your emphasis in marketing from "selling product" to identifying and solving a consumer need or want that goes beyond the physical product or service you offer. Your goal should be to create content that answers a practical question from the consumer that he or she would probably never even think of asking you: *Besides your product, what can you do for me?*

Your answer to that question will be Magnetic Content in the form of something useful that will add genuine, practical value to the consumer (while also subtly promoting your brand). To help you brainstorm Magnetic Content ideas that will be useful to the consumer, ask yourself what you can create for the consumer that will be:

- More convenient
- More timely
- Easier
- Quicker
- More accessible
- More sharable
- Less painful, simpler

Figure 3.3 shows an example of a stand-alone app that does not sell anything but is very useful for consumers, while being highly brand-positive for the company. The North Face, which makes and sells outdoor sports clothing and gear, created a cell phone app for skiers that collects and displays local snow forecasts. The app is well targeted because avid skiers are likely to purchase outdoor sports clothing, but it also serves a geographically relevant need to understand local weather conditions—and from the convenience of a mobile phone. Every time a user checks the weather conditions for skiing, he or she is reminded of The North Face brand and its relevance to the sport.

3. Is the Content Well Executed?

You can have the best idea in the world for Magnetic Content, but if it's executed poorly, it won't make a difference.

Figure 3.3
The North Face offers skiers a free app that shares
local snow forecasts

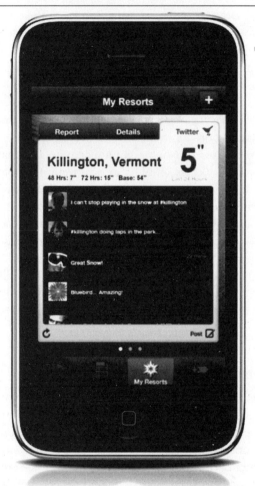

In the discipline of brand advertising, creative execution (the subjective quality of the ad) plays a huge role in the success or failure of a given campaign. Jon Gibs, a researcher at Nielsen Company and someone who has evaluated the effectiveness of many, many online and offline campaigns, estimates that creative accounts for upwards of 70 percent of the effectiveness of advertising. Quite frankly, if you're execution is crappy, you're not going to stimulate engagement—or sales. Period.

If creative execution is important for ads, it's doubly or quadruply (*sic*) important for Magnetic Content. Why? Because it has to go beyond simply being tolerated by consumers—it has to be welcomed by them. Make no mistake; if you buy into the idea of attracting consumers through Magnetic Content, then you are effectively raising the bar for creative execution in your marketing efforts. This is all the more true when you are talking about placing the content in owned and earned channels, such as social media environments, where the consumer has ultimate control.

Let's consider the 2010 Old Spice campaign, "The Man Your Man Could Smell Like," which became a viral success following a substantial TV campaign boosting awareness and driving traffic to a series of YouTube videos in a perfect circle of mass and one-on-one communications. But marketers racing to copycat the campaign's success should also not overlook another key element: the creative execution. The campaign worked so well largely because the creative, starring former NFL player Isaiah Mustafa, was funny, well acted, artfully shot, and therefore highly entertaining. That's not easy to achieve. Although most marketers would like to think of their TV commercials and other video assets as compelling and entertaining, that's clearly not the case. The fact is making videos, or other forms of content, that consumers actually want to watch (and indeed, choose to watch) is very, very difficult, and usually very expensive.

Consider hiring the best creative and production talents that you can afford.

4. Is the Content Fun?

Sometimes amateur-looking execution is the point, and it works if it's also fun. The famous Blendtec "Will It Blend?" web video series, distributed originally only on YouTube, showed how an unknown brand, from an independently owned blender company, can create a classic video viral hit—with the right Magnetic Content. Each video in the series features company founder Tom Dickson, who, donning a scientist's white lab coat and nerdy glasses, proceeds to blend just about everything imaginable, including a vuvuzela, a Barbie doll, and an iPhone. The videos are funny in a quirky sort of way, and anyone watching them wants to know what on earth he will blend next! One Blendtec video even parodied another video viral hit for a completely unrelated brand, namely the Old Spice "The Man Your Man Could Smell Like" campaign. The Blendtec results speak for themselves. The company claims home sales of its high-priced, high-tech blenders have jumped 700 percent since the video campaign began.

Magnetic Content doesn't have to solve the world's problems. It can simply offer a lighthearted diversion. For example, the lighter company BIC created a wildly popular mobile app that consumers could enjoy at rock concerts: a moving image of a BIC lighter with a flame. No risk of fire, just safe, pure fun.

Think of fun broadly. Ask yourself what you can create for the consumer that will be:

- entertaining
- amusing
- inspiring
- hilarious
- uplifting
- silly
- a welcomed distraction

5. Does the Content Make Good Use of the Channel in Which It Appears?

Each of the six digital channels covered later in this book has unique properties and possibilities for engaging with consumers through Magnetic Content, but the form and function that Magnetic Content takes will vary depending on the channel. The key is to design your Magnetic Content so as to take best advantage of the channel in which it is appearing. We've taken that into account the way we've structured this book. In each chapter covering a digital channel, we will explore the unique capabilities of that channel for delivering Magnetic Content and also of course show you how to apply Performance Measurement techniques to quantify your success.

Seven Steps for Developing Your Own Magnetic Content

Creating great Magnetic Content that attracts consumers and channels them through an engagement process linked closely to your brand does not happen without a great deal of planning, organizing, and thinking on your part. We've identified seven strategies that will help you get started with this new approach within your organization.

1. Educate and organize your teams around Magnetic Content.
2. Develop ideas based on prospective customer behaviors, attitudes, and lifestyles, not your products.
3. Define and own the value proposition.

4. Leverage your existing customer base to find and test ideas.
5. Build an Engagement Map.
6. Buy media to build reach (you'll need to draw attention to your Magnetic Content at scale).
7. Stay flexible: attract, engage, and measure.

Each of the above represents a strategic step you can take to develop and nurture your Magnetic Content program. You can do this using your existing marketing resources, and as you move along in further chapters, you will find many new ideas and strategies to fit your particular marketing needs. Let's discuss each of these seven strategies in detail.

1. Educate and Organize Your Teams around Magnetic Content

Unless you're running your own show, you'll need to educate and convince those at the highest levels in your organization that the creation and dissemination of Magnetic Content is essential in a world where the consumer is in control. All stakeholders need to understand that Magnetic Content is a vital complement to your traditional paid media efforts and is quickly becoming a core competency required for companies and organizations of all sizes and across industries.

To start, organize your in-house and/or advertising agency teams to combine media and creative in the planning stages for developing Magnetic Content, as well as the entire Engagement Map supporting it. The creation and distribution of Magnetic Content needs to be planned holistically.

As you assemble your teams, you should also look to balance them by pairing individuals with both left brain (logical, systematic, linear thinking) and right brain (creative, innovative, nonlinear thinking) orientations so they can jointly brainstorm ideas for Magnetic Content and how to get it seeded to the right people. Magnetic Content is as much art as it is science, and thus it requires a balance of logic and imagination. Think of the Walt Disney Company—it's well known as being highly creative but there is a tremendous amount of precision and planning involved to make the magic happen.

2. Develop Ideas Based on Customer Behaviors, Attitudes, and Lifestyles, Not Your Products

Plan to spend a great deal of time upfront researching consumer insights and behavior to better understand what kinds of Magnetic Content are most likely to resonate with your intended prospects, in what forms and channels that content should be delivered, and how it should be supported with traditional and online paid media. Only by thoroughly examining your target consumers' needs and wants—independent of your products' features and benefits—can you hope to create Magnetic Content that genuinely attracts people on a wide scale. You should also resist the temptation to jump on cool new technology ("Let's create a hot iPhone app!") just for cool new technology's sake. As with many things, form must follow function.

In addition, rather than focusing on pure demographics when contemplating your brand's potential Magnetic Content, think about how you can enhance some sort of lifestyle activity, situation, or experience your consumers are likely to find themselves in. Let's face it, all women ages 25 to 54 living in households with over $75,000 in income do not share the same values, needs, or activities. It's not so much about what demographic category your consumer happens to fall into; it's what their life is all about, and how you can help make it better, in whatever context. Think about ways you can enhance daily activities and situations, such as:

- Running to lose weight
- Running to improve race time
- Cooking at home
- Hanging out in a park
- Sitting in a movie theater
- Strolling in the mall
- Commuting from work
- Picking up children from school
- Killing time at the airport
- Folding laundry
- Fixing a flat tire
- Studying for a test
- Waiting for a friend at a restaurant

3. Define and Own the Value Proposition

Before you launch any Magnetic Content, attempt to validate the value proposition by asking two simple, but thought-provoking questions.

- "If I were the target consumer, would I use it?"
- "Would people pay for this (even if only a nominal amount)?"

If the answer to each question is, "yes," then you're likely providing value. If the answers come up, "no," then your "Magnetic Content" should be classified as merely advertising, or worse, a complete waste of time. Note that an affirmative answer to the second question does not mean you necessarily have to charge for your Magnetic Content, but you could. Remember that Kraft Foods is charging 99 cents for its handy iFood Assistant app. So many other marketers are doing the same, it's been said that "99 cents is the new free."

4. Leverage Your Existing Customer Base to Find and Test Ideas

As you create brilliant Magnetic Content to pull consumers in and plan for ways to keep those consumers engaged in deeper and deeper ways, don't forget to pay special attention to your existing customers. After all, the value of a current customer is far more than that of a prospect, and it's downright expensive to bring lapsed customers back to your brand.

So, what special things can you do for your current customers?

Naturally, when you create and launch new Magnetic Content out into the world, many of those being drawn in will be your existing customers. So why not offer them a first look? Assuming you have ways to directly and efficiently reach your existing customers—through opt-in e-mail, social network platforms, Twitter, and so on—you can increase brand loyalty by letting your current customers enjoy the Magnetic Content first. Not only will this reward them and thereby strengthen their attraction toward your brand, it is likely they will want to share the content (if it's good!) with their friends—a group of like-minded prospects for your business. In addition, if for whatever reason the Magnetic Content is off the mark or needs tweaking, your current customers can help you correct course before you fall on your face in front a larger, less forgiving audience. Let your current customers "beta test" your Magnetic Content and you'll make them feel special in the process.

Another strategy is to build Magnetic Content designed exclusively for the needs of existing customers. Domino's Pizza used this approach with their Pizza Tracker service that lets consumers who have just ordered a pizza for delivery track the progress of their order, from preparation and bake, to boxing and delivery (Figure 3.4). True, this idea is a spinoff of an earlier, global success story—FedEx's famed online tracking system, which became so popular that even the U.S. Postal Service had to add a similar service to stay competitive. According to Domino's, which has become the fourth-largest

Figure 3.4
Domino's Pizza Tracker

on-time retailer in America, 75 percent of people who order their pizzas spend at least a minute or two tracking its progress to their doorstep.

Another example of using Magnetic Content to assist existing customers comes from a joint marketing effort between ING bank and MasterCard. The duo created a downloadable application called ATM Hunter that enables their customers to find the nearest ATM machine. This app doubles as a service and an encouragement to transact at the bank. Simple, but effective.

5. Build an Engagement Map

Magnetic Content should not exist in a vacuum. Before you launch any Magnetic Content, no matter how exceptional, build an Engagement Map detailing what path or paths you want the consumer to take after the initial hook. Each subsequent milestone on the path represents a deeper level of engagement and self-qualification—and therefore identifies the consumer as being more interested, and more valuable to you. You've already learned how to do this—see the advice in Chapter 2 for a refresher on building the pyramid of conversions and then set up your goal levels for Qualified Reach and the rest of the important metric benchmarks.

Some Engagement Maps will be more complicated than others. The more choices you provide consumers, in terms of kinds of Magnetic Content, pathways to experience it, and opportunities for feedback, the more complex your map will be. Ideally, your Engagement Map for Magnetic Content should be integrated with your entire MARCOM plan to ensure the consumer has a seamless set of experiences (and so that you can properly measure engagement and return on investment!).

6. Buy Media to Build Reach

Don't throw out your traditional media buying plans just yet. The paid advertising model is by no means dead. It's just that you're going to use it differently—to alert as many consumers as possible that something useful/ entertaining is now available for their enjoyment (your Magnetic Content).

To build sufficient scale for your Magnetic Content, you will need to invest in offline and online paid media to get the word out. Even an exceptionally entertaining piece of noncommercial content on YouTube can sit languishing amidst the gazillions of videos there if it doesn't receive some kind of promotional boost, such as a pitch on broadcast television, a magazine promotion, a roadblock ad on Yahoo's home page, a carefully crafted paid search campaign, or some mix of all of these.

Remember back to the early 1990s, when marketers rushed to build websites and then sat back expectantly for the consumers to show up? The mantra was: *If we build it, they will come.* Were it only true. Similarly, when you're creating great Magnetic Content to attract consumers and invite them to engage with your brand, you will still need to draw attention to it using a balanced combination of paid media, including traditional and digital channels, paid search, organic search, optimization techniques, and good old-fashioned opt-in e-mails.

With Magnetic Content, your paid media efforts should be more effective, because you're not shilling a product but rather drawing attention to an experience or service that promises value. Magnetic Content acts as a no-cost, low-risk way for consumers to get involved in your brand. You're not asking them to part with their money; you're simply inviting engagement in some positive way. The only risk for them is wasting a fragment of time.

"But wait," you say. "Doesn't great content automatically go viral—without the help of paid media ad placements?" Actually, very few things, commercial or otherwise, go viral. And for those that do, they usually get a lot of help— including from traditional media, such as television, radio, magazines, newspapers, and public relations, as well as online banner ads, search, and e-mail campaigns. For a case in point, we look to a study done by Anita Elberse, a marketing professor at Harvard Business School. She analyzed the ranked popularity of commercial videos on YouTube, focusing on digital movie trailers and video games, based on the amount of media spending to support the videos. She found a very strong correlation between traditional media spending, particularly on TV, and the number of views on YouTube. Clearly, the videos that got watched the most were those that purchased their popularity. Elberse conceded that although it is possible for viral hits to happen out of the blue, they are the exception to the rule.

Social media boosters and other digital pundits often dismiss the role that traditional media can play in a so-called social media success story. For example, Procter & Gamble's now famous campaign for Old Spice cologne, "The Man Your Man Could Smell Like," topped the charts on YouTube during 2010.

Admittedly, the ads were a big viral hit and provided evidence of the power of social media, including YouTube, Facebook, and Twitter activity. What's more, the actor in the series, Isaiah Mustafa, shot no less than 186 personalized video clips to respond to influential bloggers and twitterers, many of whom were celebrities in their own right.

We've already mentioned the meticulous execution of this campaign. But overlooked in all of this social buzz was the fact that the ads got their introduction to the world through a very familiar traditional medium, namely network television. Moreover, these TV spots were run on the Winter Olympics, one of the most expensive slots on TV. In this instance, the television advertising catapulted the video spots into the mainstream and, later, the social media activity merely widened and sustained the viewership. As David Hallerman, senior analyst for eMarketer, said in *Advertising Age*:

> [The Old Spice Man campaign] effectively blended ingredients from the three marketing media types—TV commercials, supplemented by cinema ads (paid); then the campaign migrated to an interactive mix including a brand microsite with Facebook and Twitter pages (owned), and continued its momentum through consumer interaction and word-of-mouth on social sites and beyond (earned). Finally, the campaign got continued lift from additional online advertising—both banner and video ads—which drove traffic back to the brand's site and social media pages (more paid).

For an upscale example, look no further than Tiffany & Co. The brand with the signature blue box wanted to promote the release of its new iPhone app. The specialized app, called Engagement Ring Finder, allowed would-be-marriage-proposers to browse the company's ring catalog, determine their intended's correct ring size, and even book a one-on-one consultation via e-mail or phone, among other features. But rather than simply leave it to chance that the right kind of audience would discover it, Tiffany used its brand dollars to buy pricey ads in the online versions of the *Wall Street Journal* and the *New York Times*. Of course, the ads do double duty, because they not only link to a download for the mobile app, they also promote the venerable brand of Tiffany & Co. to a large, prestigious audience of potential lifetime customers.

7. Stay Flexible: Attract, Engage, and Measure

You know what they say about the best-laid plans. This applies to Magnetic Content as well.

Even if you adhere to the five-factor framework we've explained for ensuring your content is magnetic, and even if you then follow our seven guidelines for making the most of your Magnetic Content, things may not go as planned. Consumers, fickle beings that they are, do not always behave as you would expect, or would like. Be prepared to change plans, or modify your Magnetic Content midstream, multiple times.

This isn't as bad as it might seem. The creation of most Magnetic Content, along with its distribution and dissemination, is not usually that expensive, especially when you compare it with the relative production costs of, for example, a TV commercial. Besides, unlike most traditional forms of advertising, including print ads, TV commercials (typically costing \$350,000–\$500,000), and outdoor billboards, most Magnetic Content can be altered, modified, or even completely scrapped for relatively little expense, and often on-the-fly.

The low costs and risks associated with producing Magnetic Content should encourage you to emphasize experimentation over deliberation. Spend less time thinking and debating about what is going to work and more time creating stuff that goes out into the field—where consumers can be the judges. Adopt the attitude of "fail fast," or as best-selling author Mike Moran put it in his book, "Do It Wrong, Quickly." It's not that you're trying to get it wrong; it's that you have the humility to grasp that you can't really predict how a piece of Magnetic Content is going to fly in the real world. Embrace the power of feedback loops:

- *Attract*. Create and disseminate Magnetic Content into the marketplace
- *Engage*. Allow consumers to experience or interact with your Magnetic Content, or not
- *Measure*. Monitor results, based on the precepts reviewed in Chapter 2

By the time you get to step 3, measure, it will be time to start the process all over again—by either tweaking your Magnetic Content or the way it's promoted or by going back to the drawing board for a fresh approach. Repeat the process indefinitely, measuring all the way.

What's Old Is New Again

Other examples of Magnetic Content serving as marketing go back nearly a century. Remember the Michelin Guides? These were popularized first in Great Britain in the 1920s. The guides, which provided traveling consumers with handy ratings for the best restaurants and hotels, also served to burnish the tire company's image as a customer-focused brand. Later, in the 1950s, Guinness beer launched one of the most popular series of books of all times, the famous Guinness Book of World Records. While the book didn't sell beer directly, it was surely referred to in many a British pub. At the same time, in America, venerable packaged goods giant Procter & Gamble was attracting huge audiences of consumers through their steamy soap operas run on daytime television. Clearly, Magnetic Content is not a "new" concept, but it is taking on new life and urgency in the digitally enhanced social world we live in today.

Conclusion

The line between content and advertising has blurred incredibly in just the past few years. Recognize that you're dealing with groups of empowered consumers or business customers that have the ability to ignore your brand messages, recast them to suit their own needs or perceptions, and also the ability to "broadcast" them to other potential prospects and customers well ahead of your own attempts to do so.

Recognize also that the interruption model of advertising is on the wane. Today, consumer audiences have more choice and control in what they see, hear, and experience. Your messages have to have inherent value; they must be highly desirable, worthy of sharing, and able to stand alone as content in its own right. It doesn't matter if your Magnetic Content is serious, practical, influential, convenient, or merely entertaining—it just has to be something your target audience will welcome and choose to seek out.

The five-factor framework we've outlined provides a blueprint for creating great Magnetic Content. Just answer these five critical questions:

1. Is the content unique?
2. Is the content useful?
3. Is the content well executed?

4. Is the content fun?
5. Does the content make good use of the channel in which it appears?

These questions will get you started along the right path, but you also need a comprehensive set of strategies to help you maximize the value you get out of your Magnetic Content.

The seven strategies discussed will help you craft Magnetic Content within an integrated communications program that will support it, and help you attract the right customers, engage with them on a progressively deeper level, and spur them to share the experience with others. Remember that finding the most qualified audience now also means going beyond the limitations of targeting to cast a wider net and pull new consumers into your circle of influence. If you're planning to fish where the fish are, building Magnetic Content gives you not only the bait but the hook as well.

A Few Thoughts about Targeting

Let's think for a moment about how targeting works, or rather how it has worked for decades.

Unless you are selling happiness in a bottle, you likely want to reach only a select portion of the total population. Ultimately, you want to reach prospects—those people who are most likely to buy your product—and no one else.

The problem is, since you don't know who those prospects are within the vast universe, you resort to making guesses about them and what kinds of profiles they likely fall into, like demographics, psychographics, and other forms of market segmentation buckets. Of course, these buckets are just proxies for the real consumer you're trying to reach. There are two problems with this.

First, what if there are consumers in the universe who are highly likely, even destined, to buy your product and yet don't happen to fit into your preconceived ideas about who they are (for example, they don't fit the demographic profile)? They will not be reached by your campaign because they don't match the profile. You've missed an opportunity.

Second, what about the people who do fall into your proxy buckets and do see your campaign, but for whatever reason, have no intention of ever buying your product? You've just wasted your marketing dollars. This ties in with what we learned in the preceding chapter discussing the first secret: Performance Measurement. We are not really after *reach* so much as Qualified Reach, where we count only those who are not just exposed to our message but also demonstrate some level of interest and/or intent through their initial and ongoing engagement with the content and our brand.

PART II

CHAPTER 4

Search

"Your search strategy is your business strategy whether you realize it or not, because that's how potential customers are trying to find you."
—*Vanessa Fox, author of* Marketing in the Age of Google
(John Wiley & Sons, Inc., 2010)

A search strategy is essential; it is the online equivalent to your business's front door. Even if you are outsourcing search functions or have relegated them to agency or staff, it is important to understand what aspects will make your business thrive. Search is the number one engagement vehicle online, and it is still the most efficient way to magnetize new customers toward your brand. In one branding study, 39 percent of searchers perceived those in the highest page rank as the top brands in their fields!

In this chapter, we will:

1. Demystify search and provide an understanding of its role in marketing.
2. Teach how to use search marketing to draw your audience to your content, especially your website.
3. Provide guidance on the most important search metrics marketers need to follow.
4. Position you to take advantage of where search is headed.

Think back for a moment to when there was no search. Hard to imagine, isn't it? Yet it wasn't so long ago that we looked up telephone numbers in a telephone book or dialed a live operator. Homework assignments and term papers were researched in the library. Shopping was done on foot in the mall.

Comparison shopping, if you want to call it that, meant spreading out store flyers across the kitchen table and evaluating prices.

Today, more than half of all U.S. Internet users conduct an online search daily, according to the Pew Internet & American Life Project. According to estimates from J.P. Morgan, each Internet user will conduct, on average, 1,202 queries in 2011.

The Search Landscape Today

Google, the dominant search engine, is a noun, a verb, and an online marketing juggernaut. It's also a growing daily habit; Americans conduct *29 million searches per minute.* According to research firm Compete, nearly 7 in 10 of all searches in the United States are made through Google. Get it right for Google, one would surmise, and the rest will fall into place.

The other contender in domestic searches is Microsoft's Bing, which also powers the search function for Yahoo! Bing's rise to prominence owes much to replacing Google with Bing as the default search box for new editions of Internet Explorer bundled with millions of new netbooks and PCs sold since 2009. While "How to remove Bing as default search" calls up more than 100,000 responses on Google, Bing continues to seek ways to differentiate its search, and in June 2010, it introduced an Entertainment Search function to streamline the path to video and music on the web. These moves are not likely to displace Google's dominance soon, but they could alter how consumers view search over time.

IAC's Ask.com, which began life as Ask Jeeves, is a mere blip, followed by AOL. Baidu, Yandex, and AliBaba are in the top 10 globally, as tracked by comScore.

The explosion in social networks has also made an impact on search as Facebook and eBay rank in the top 10 search properties based on number of searches. People go to Google to get to Facebook, and from there they are searching the web. (See Figure 4.1.)

Search Data Is Critical to All Online Efforts

In one iProspect survey, nearly 4 in 10 Internet users (38 percent) eventually perform a search on the company, product, or service that is the focus of the online display ad to which they are exposed, and then they visit the website from the search results. These searchers become buyers. Two-thirds of those who are influenced to search buy at an extremely impressive 39 percent conversion rate.

Figure 4.1
Share of online search

Share of Online Searches in the US, by Search Engine, Oct & Nov 2010
% of total

	Oct 2010	Nov 2010
Google sites	64.3%	64.3%
Yahoo! sites	18.5%	19.3%
Microsoft sites	12.1%	11.3%
Ask.com	3.2%	3.3%
AOL	1.9%	1.8%

Note: home, work and university locations; includes partner searches, cross-channel searches and contextual searches for each property
Source: comScore qSearch as cited in press release, Dec 15, 2010

123005   www.e**Marketer**.com

From a marketer's perspective, search offers a way for learning *how* your customer is looking for the brands and products you offer. It's a real-time source of insight into what people want and need, and what are they looking for. Searchers represent the ultimate prequalified audience!

The abundance of free search data available through such tools as Google Insights (www.google.com/insights/search) gives marketers an unparalleled view into the way their customers think. This kind of market intelligence once required multiple focus groups to generate far less meaningful results. Searchers are telling you what they want and also provide a clear road map through the terms they use for the messaging and copy you should use to connect with them—they essentially are giving you the language—actual words—they want you to use when communicating to them. These are the words you can use when selecting keywords to lead the masses to your website.

This mother lode of data and intent unleashed by search is available not only for your own products, but also for those of your competitors. Want to know what your competitors are up to? Viewing the source code of their home page (available from the "View" drop-down menu of any web browser) will likely tell you pretty quickly what key words they are using, which you can compare with your own. Another tool, Google Insights, allows the Database of Intentions to be mined for searches compared by region and time period. Want to know what's trending in New Jersey? A deep dive into search activity in the state for the year-to-date 2010 showed the hot product (iPad) was the leading trend term. In overall search, Facebook and music lyrics ranked the highest. Searches defined by time frame and geographic region can create a more nuanced picture, for example a snapshot of holiday-related searches for the previous year.

SEO versus SEM

Search marketing involves both search engine optimization (SEO) and search engine marketing (SEM) tactics. Although often confused, the two are not synonymous. *SEM* was once used as a general term to describe online marketing activities through the channel of a search engine; today it pretty much means the purchase of paid keyword ads and sponsored links.

SEO generally (and for the purpose of this book) means organic or natural search, the art and science of getting your website to appear naturally on the first page of nonpaid search results. It's the process of improving the volume and quality of traffic to digital content from search engines via "natural" ("organic" or "algorithmic") search results.

According to Enquisite Performance Suite, 88 percent of online search dollars are spent on paid results, even though 85 percent of searchers click on organic results. The most cost-effective way to use search is to make SEO changes that will improve your web page rankings within the automated system of a specific search engine.

How much is your organization spending on search? Overall global search spending levels are expected to come in anywhere from $28 billion to $43 billion for 2011, according to various sources, with 18 percent of search spending going toward SEO services. When budgets are tight, investments in natural search are considered a better value for the long term.

How does SEO work? Search engines use a web crawler known as a spider to follow links to find pages on the web. What the engine "sees" is the text source code of the site, not the presentation it renders for the consumer. Crawled links come from external sites (those linking to you) as well as internal sites (the links within your own site).

You can help ensure your site is found by submitting a site map to today's most prominent search engines, at Google (www.google.com/support/webmasters/bin/answer.py?answer=35769) and at Bing (www.bing.com/webmaster/SubmitSitePage.aspx). This is basic stuff, but it allows these search engines to build a list of keywords and note where they were found. The engine builds an index based on its own system of weighting. This algorithm is constantly changing, to avoid manipulation of the index by astute programmers (aka "black hats"). After encoding and compressing the data to save space, the engine stores the data for users to access via the search results page.

A few important points: for acceptable speed, *when someone conducts a search, they are searching the index, not the actual Internet.* Where your page ranks within an index is a function of many different factors, including the relevance to a search query and the quality of your external links. Beating your competitors in the arena of search will rely on adjusting your SEM and SEO strategies to reflect the actual search behaviors of your target audience.

How Pages Are Read   Eye-tracking studies by Enquiro Research show that consumers typically read a search engine result page by scanning it in an F-shaped pattern starting at the upper left and moving down the left margin. Clearly, you will want to have your links positioned as closely as possible to this prime real estate. (See Figure 4.2.)

With the increasing frequency of universal results (for example, video, images, news, blogs, real-time updates, and social media results) making their way into the search landscape, new heat maps will be needed to understand how universal results affect user search and click behavior.

Figure 4.2
**Eye tracking shows that the upper left of a search results
page is the prime position**

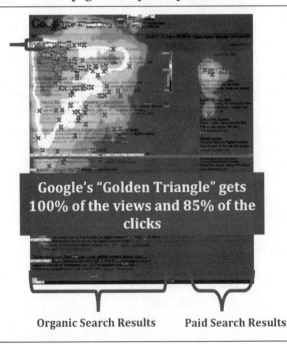

Google's "Golden Triangle" gets 100% of the views and 85% of the clicks

Organic Search Results   Paid Search Results

The brain's tendency to hold around seven chunks of information in its working memory means we tend to view three or four results at a time on a search page. *This is significant, because it suggests that ranking #1 in search results is not as important as people often think. If your headline and copy are the most compelling in a position on the first page, you might still get the clicks.* A Penn State University study indicated 60 percent of searchers rely primarily on the title of a result when deciding whether to click. So a strong title that ranks fourth might do the job. This also helps explain why the page title is the most influential on-page element to establish keyword relevancy with search engines. Thus, as a marketer you want to think of your title as Magnetic Content and use the same criteria found in Chapter 3 to draw a searcher in to click on your link.

Tribune's Brent D. Payne says he long ago stopped generating ranking reports for specific keywords that the newsroom optimizes for. What's key to track is results, in his case it is visits and page views.

Although being ranked number one may not matter, being on the first page is important because people are intrinsically lazy, with 68 percent of searchers typically clicking on only results found on the first page.

Where the eye goes, however, is starting to change with the advent of real-time search results and universal search, notes Adam Dince, Sr. Search Manager for MRM Worldwide.

How are marketers taking advantage of these trends? The online broker E*Trade, which runs the popular E*Trade Babies advertising campaign, does an excellent job of optimizing all its assets—including images and video—so they are readily accessible through search. As Figure 4.3 depicts, official E*Trade videos appear at the top of a search for "etrade babies." The official E*Trade story line ranks first in the organic listings. E*Trade official images appear above the fold, and a companion paid search campaign for the keyword offers a path to the official trading site for visitors who are ready to open an account.

Alison Mittelstadt, vice president of online marketing at the financial services firm, notes that the popularity of the E*Trade baby commercials, which routinely air on the Super Bowl, get widespread web dissection and news coverage before and after the big game. The E*Trade corporate communications group adds to the mix by cranking out company releases regularly. This helps keep positive coverage high in the rankings on search returns, and many portals take feeds from the official press sites. E*Trade also combs its server logs to find the terms searchers really use. For instance, they want to "trade stocks" not "trade equities."

For another example, consider search results for the search term "running shoes." In a recent review, Road Runner Sports and Zappos took the prime

Figure 4.3
E*Trade puts its assets forward

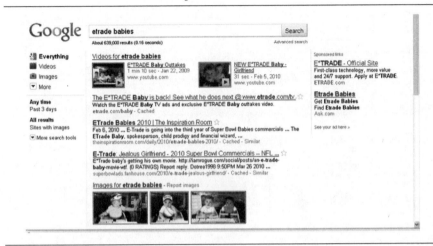

sponsored link positions at the top of the page. Nike dominated the paid column at the far right and inserts eye-catching product images. Google served up five brand names. *Then* come the organic listings, with RunningShoes.com, which has a domain name that precisely matches the search term, pulling top position. (See Figure 4.4.)

How to Excel in SEO—The Big Opportunity　　How do you win the footrace to the top of organic search results? Putting the user first is a good first step. Equate it to a customer's experience, says MRM's Adam Dince, whose clients include the U.S. Army. Dince's job involves making sure sites are constructed in a way that can be viewed properly by a search engine's automated crawlers.

"If a search engine has a bad experience, so will a user," Dince says. "If a user has a bad experience on a site, so will the search engine, which will ultimately affect the site's visibility."

Existing websites can be modified to improve the odds of their making it to the critical first page of sites returned. Results are gradual, with improved organic rankings taking up to six months to happen. But once a site has been optimized and a routine put in place for continued SEO efforts, the good news is these results do not vanish immediately. An optimized site rarely drops off the first results page even when marketing spending slows or stops, as it does with paid search.

Before starting the optimization process, it's important to step back and ask what goals you are trying to achieve. Is it brand awareness? Is it conversion?

Figure 4.4

A search for running shoes turns up a crowd of competitors

What action do you want consumers to take when they get to your site? As a marketer, you must always remember that SEO is not just the job of a specialist in a back room. It works best when integrated into the entire organizational structure, from the top down. It's also not just a concern for marketing—but also public relations, customer service, recruitment, and branding.

"The thing I learned early on is that I could not be the gatekeeper of all search. I had to make everyone a disciple or it wouldn't work. I couldn't be the chokepoint," says Marshall Simmonds, chief search strategist for The New York Times Company, recalling the earliest days of About.com, which launched in 1999 and built a network of 800 specialist guides. "Training in SEO is constant and never-ending," adds Simmonds, who is also chief executive officer of Define Search Strategies, the SEO division of the Times serving outside clients.

SEO tends to be less expensive than paid search. Small increases in SEO spending can yield outsize changes in marketing effectiveness relative to paid search. Behind that spending leverage is the recognition that, even though many people are willing to click on relevant paid search ads, they may prefer organic listings, if these are perceived as more trusted or impartial.

SEO and the Small Business Owner　One of the beauties of SEO is that it provides a level playing field for large and small businesses. In fact, the ability of small businesses to act more nimbly can even give them an advantage when it comes to search.

A special tip for businesses that want to rank highly in their local market is to focus on local search optimization (LSO); this means including the full city and state in each page title. In addition, put the address and phone number prominently on every page, because each page is a potential on-ramp to the site.

With the explosion of geo-targeting services and Google embedding businesses into "Google Places," it's even more important to optimize for local.

More Local SEO Tips

- Ensure your business is listed with the Internet Yellow Pages (IYP) and the directory services relevant to your geography. These include Zagat, Citysearch, Yelp, Yahoo! Local, chambers of commerce, and so on.
- Speak the way the locals do. In your copy, describe the neighborhoods you serve and any other distinguishing characteristics in local vernacular.
- Cultivate reviews and comments from your clientele on review sites to lift your searchable content quotient. For example, a Manhattan beauty salon offers a free shampoo and conditioning treatment (value $25) for customers who post a positive review on Citysearch.
- Add a detailed page describing in words how to find your business. Consider embedding a map link to a map service. A great example is Bank of America's branch locator: http://locators.bankofamerica.com/locator/locator/LocatorAction.do.

SEM: Using Pay-per-Click Models

Pay-per-click (PPC) is the identification and bidding for placement as one of the top terms selected in a search engine's sponsored text advertising. Note that when using Google AdWords, the marketer pays only when an ad is clicked. Text ads appear above and beside organic search results. Pricing uses an auction model that is based on cost-per-click. The position the ad appears in is determined by bid price, ad performance, and relevance of the landing page.

Paid search has an important role in the mix, particularly when you are selling products and services directly to consumers. As you spend more, you get more control, but it's easy to lose your shirt if you're not carefully watching your bids. So if your company lacks the commitment to monitor and track it constantly, we suggest you stay away from PPC search. Also, unlike organic SEO, once you stop spending, your PPC position vanishes immediately.

Bid management is critical. Do the math properly. Does it make sense for a publisher to pay $1 per click on a popular term if the revenue generated is only $15 per 1,000 page views?

Here's an example of the cost breakdown for a hypothetical Google AdWords campaign that attracts 450 prospects to your site at an average cost per click of $0.40. Let's say your landing page offers a 5 percent discount coupon in exchange for a valid e-mail address. You get 90 addresses and follow up with an e-mail offer that generates 10 sales totaling $600. Let's do the math. (See Table 4.1.)

Google rewards advertisers whose ads have superior click-through rates and relevancy. The reward comes in the form of a reduced bid price for the same keyword. The idea is that the ad is offering an optimal consumer experience. Time-of-day and day-of-week display will affect pricing. Running a campaign 24/7 requires a higher budget than one turned on and off. Google will also regulate the appearance of your ads based on your preset budget. The more goals and the more keywords used, typically the higher the budget.

Make Sure Your Landing Pages Are Relevant   Higher conversion rates lower the effective cost of your SEM ads. Do not automatically direct people to your home page unless it is so explicit that a visitor wouldn't think twice about the next move to make. You might instead want to link to a specific landing page that relates directly to their specific query. This sounds logical,

Table 4.1
Google AdWords Sample

Metric	Total Cost or Percentage
Total advertising cost	$180 (450 × $0.40)
Sales total	$600
Return on investment (ROI)	333% (600/180)
AdWords ad click–through rate	1.5% (450/30,000)
Landing-page lead conversion	20% (90/450)
E-mail sales conversion	11% (10/90)
Cost per visitor	$0.40
Average visitor value	$1.33 ($600/450)
Cost per lead	$2.40 ($180/75)
Average value of a lead	$8.00 ($600/75)
Cost per sale	$18 ($180/10)
Average value of sale	$60 ($600/10)

Source: Adapted from *Adwords for Dummies* by Howie Jacobson, 2007, John Wiley & Sons, Inc. Reprinted with permission.

but it's astounding the number of disconnects we see that still exist between search ads and landing pages.

The search engines provide conversion tracking codes for your landing pages. Launch your campaign, then analyze the results. Which keywords are generating the highest CTRs? Which are generating the highest rate of conversions? Generally, 20 percent of keywords will generate 80 percent of clicks.

Test and Optimize   Proper testing and optimization is a critical aspect of being good at PPC. Write at least two different ads that point to the same landing page. Google AdWords offers ad optimization so that the more effective ads are shown more frequently. Test alternative landing pages as well.

Use the findings of your paid campaign to optimize your site for organic search. Terms that generate the highest number of impressions and conversions should be integrated into your SEO efforts.

Should You Outsource Search?   Outsourcing your company's search practice can be a smart way to keep costs low and plan those costs out over time. With an in-house team, you must fund it constantly. With an outsourced team, you pay to play, and when the majority of the SEO work is completed, you can reduce your costs. Further, outsourcing provides access to competent and highly experienced search professionals with a proven record of success. This strategy should be considered for companies with smaller marketing budgets. On the other hand, if you are in the content business and search is a primary driver, build it internally. For example, if you are a local newspaper and are consistently creating new content and building out your site, it would make sense to bring in an in-house expert who will become an integral part of your organization.

SEO and SEM: Our Bottom Line   We recommend taking a holistic approach with both organic and paid together. It should be done in tandem so that you can eventually lower costs for paid search as your SEO improves. Consider the following as you measure and improve your search program:

"Buying" paid search is a common practice, but it's increasingly expensive. Bing's combined influence with Yahoo! is already reported to be driving up PPC pricing in some sectors.

Approximately 60 to 70 percent of clicks go to organic listings. A 2010 Performics survey of 500 users found that 79 percent of respondents "always" or "frequently" click on natural search results, whereas only 20 percent do so for paid search results.

An October 2009 study by search marketing firm iCrossing showed that when a brand appears in both organic and paid results, the searcher clicked on the brand 92 percent of the time, compared with 60 percent when it

Table 4.2
SEO and SEM Compared

PPC Strengths	PPC Weaknesses
Ads are trackable and cost-effective. They can be turned on and off as budget dictates.	Less credible. Research shows consumers believe organic results are more trustworthy.
Instant visibility. Depending on the keyword, your ad appears on the first page of search results.	More expensive over time. As competitors bid on words, your costs can rise if it's your only way of getting visibility.
Controllable messaging. Copy appears just as you write it and can be modified on the fly as the campaign unfolds.	Highly competitive and risky. It's easy to get wiped out in a minute.
Low creative costs. It's the cost of words.	No spend = No presence. You have to pay to appear.
Marketing-centric. Copy plays up the benefits and gives consumers a reason to act.	Volatile cost-per-click bids and volume. Issues include click fraud.
	Time-consuming and expensive to manage. You can't do it halfway. Expect to dedicate at least one full-time employee.
SEO Strengths	**SEO Weaknesses**
Provides consistent presence/traffic. Once your ranking is high, it won't disappear overnight	Results may be gradual and can take up to three months (depending on the site.)
Higher ROI than most online marketing	The process can be complex and seem like "black box" as it depends on ever-changing hidden ranking algorithms of search engines
Long-lasting effects. It takes time to erode rank.	Requires buy-in across the entire organization for most effectiveness.
Halo effects across accessibility. The tactics that make sites available to those with disabilities are the same used for SEO.	
More trusted, user-centric. Research shows searchers have more faith in organic listings than paid ones.	

Source: Vipin Mayar.

appeared in only one location. So, for those terms that rank high in organic, the additional cost of a paid listing can be justified. (See Table 4.2.)

Magnetic Content and Search: Five Best Practices

The most Magnetic Content you can dream up will be useless if your potential customer base can't find it. This is why we consider search as the first channel to get right: all your other efforts online will benefit if you have designed your search program to be magnetic on its own. You might review the following five best practices periodically for compliance, because it's the equivalent of "less work for mother" and pays off no matter what your campaign.

1. Optimize for natural search.
2. Develop fresh content around keywords that are relevant to your business goals and objectives; publish frequently.
3. Develop and organize keywords for all stages of your purchase funnel.
4. Make sure you have an organic link-building strategy that avoids utilizing paid links.
5. Use social media in conjunction with your SEO strategy.

The checklists that follow will assist you in both assessing and assigning your work in search.

1. Optimize for Natural Search

SEO is not an afterthought, so bring it to the table at the planning stage for your campaigns. Also prepare for success and server traffic increases. Get the navigation right: you'd be surprised how many major organizations fail at this. Make sure all internal landing pages have clear paths to the other key portions of your site. This includes ensuring that relevant and appropriate links are included within the main body content. People may arrive at your site straight to an internal page, and they should know where they are when they get there. Following is a checklist for the critical best practices your web design team should follow:

- Use best practices for site design for the handicapped and you will have created the text foundation that makes your site visible to a spider as well.
- Submit your XML *site maps* to the engines. This is a step that many smaller organizations skip, to their detriment. Google Webmaster Tools

and Bing Webmaster Central allow you to annotate the location of your site's XML site maps. An XML site map can be created so that it is dynamically updated each time a new page is added to the website. An XML site map can contain up to 50,000 links. Also, ensure that your robots.txt file points search engines to the location of your XML site map. (If you're not sure what we're talking about, ask your tech team.)

- Also link to the HTML site map of your site via a header or footer link. This will allow search engines to easily find your site map and more fully crawl the entire website.
- Eliminate technical barriers that can block a search engine from accessing your content: one big brand pharmaceutical marketer was instructing the spider to pass its home page because it had activated the robot.txt tag in the wrong place. The purpose of the robots.txt file is to instruct search engines as to which pages and folders to not store within its index. The robots.txt also allows you to direct search engines to the location of your XML site maps.
- Check that your page load time is not so slow that a crawler gives up.

2. Develop Fresh Content around Keywords and Publish Frequently

The more frequent and relevant your content, the more often your site will get crawled by the engines and ranked for words that appeal to your target audience. Here's another checklist for your SEO team:

- Identify through your site search logs and tools such as Google Analytics which keywords are bringing customers to your site. Then, if applicable, develop content specifically to meet the needs of those searchers or optimize existing content around those important terms identified within the logs and tools. If optimizing for a keyword like "cars with good safety ratings," you should have a landing page for that topic. Otherwise your relevance is low for both the searcher and the search engine crawling and indexing your site.
- Use tools like Google AdWords and Google Insights to find out additional keywords that searchers are using.
- Add optimized press releases to Business Wire or PR Newswire and/or blog postings (ideally two a week) to keep your content fresh. The more frequently you update, the more frequently your site will be crawled by the spider. This will ultimately boost your ranking by increasing your site's overall search authority. Get your blogs listed on sites such as

Technorati, an Internet search engine for blogs. Technorati looks at tags authors place on their sites and helps categorize the results and ranks them for influence. It now focuses solely on U.S. sites. The Bloglines website offers a similar function.

- Consider allowing areas on your site where customers and readers can write, providing a fresh source of user-generated content. But be sure it is available to be crawled and not walled off behind a password-protected gate. Because customers may not always be kind, user-generated content still needs to be monitored as you would any social media outlet. While it is important to develop content around relevant keywords, we strongly recommend against the use of content farming techniques. A content farm is a site or company that publishes a huge volume of content that lacks quality, but is able to generate a high ranking via search algorithms. Content farms are typically designed to maximize ranking without having high quality content, and many search engines now adjust their algorithms to penalize such pages and lower their rank.

Get Inside Your Customer's Head for Fresh Keyword Ideas   Step outside your office to find out how people really think, talk, and look for things. Consider how real people would find information. For example, sit at a dinner party and ask people to talk about their cars. People searching for a car might look for a brand: Honda, Mercedes, Ford, Chevrolet. They might search for a "family car" or might spell the brand name incorrectly. Keep in mind that it's very difficult to optimize for misspellings because including misspelled words within your on-page elements and content can create a poor user experience. Optimizing for misspelled keywords is much easier within paid search (SEM).

"The #1 thing is you have to think like a user does," says Marshall Simmonds of The New York Times Company. When doing keyword research, he taps the knowledge base of the writers, editors, and guides who have the deep audience expertise and a finger on the hot topics.

3. Organize Keywords for Your Purchase Funnel

People go through a series of stages before they make a purchase decision. Their search behavior reflects these. Consider each stage of the purchase funnel and identify the keywords and content that address each stage. A good exercise for this is to develop keywords that will lead each imaginary prospect to the appropriate landing page that addresses his or her need. For example, consider keywords that are important to the prospect during initial interest in the product (feature comparison) and those that are important during actual purchase (product location, price); even consider the last stages of loyalty (user community, service, and support).

The purchase funnel and different stages of consumer intent are equally important factors when doing PPC. Anticipating your consumer intent affects the keywords you choose to bid on. Also think specifically about long-tail terms with less competition. Look at multiple sources to generate your keywords and keyword phrases. How do people currently search your site? What keywords do competitors use? What words are people searching for most frequently? Google's keyword suggestion tool in AdWords (www.google.com/ads/adwords) can help.

"There is an 80/20 rule prevailing on our most valuable search terms," says Nicholas Utton, E*Trade's chief marketing officer. "It's interesting at the long tail where it becomes a science project. It becomes a matter of – what are we willing to pay? In a volatile (stock) marketplace, search increases dramatically and clicks can go through the roof."

4. Make Sure You Have a Link-Building Strategy

Link building is perhaps the most important consideration for ranking today. Links are more than a popularity contest. The more you have and the better the reputation of the sites linking in, the more important, authoritative, and popular the engines "think" your site is. Engines jump from page to page through links, so the more links, the more likely the engine will be to find you and attribute some of the "link juice" coming in from the authoritative third-party sites.

Links can come from directories, blogs, social bookmarks, and other sites. Find out who is already linking to you (and your competitors) through www .yourdomain.com or www.linkpopularity.com.

All links are not the same. Poor-quality links (so-called "link farms" where you pay for listing and do nothing but link to other pages) will do nothing for your site's ranking. Inappropriate links—links from sites that have questionable content—can hurt your brand's image with consumers. Reciprocal links that are not relevant in nature can prove to be useless. Also, avoid paying for links. All of these poor link-building techniques are labor intensive and may cost a significant amount of money to pursue, just to find out that all of the link value has been discounted.

How do you find good links? Marshall Simmonds of the *New York Times* says he tracks search referrals from the major news organizations and key social media sites such as Digg, Reddit, Facebook, and Twitter. He looks at month-to-month growth, as well as year-over-year trends, to make sure there is a sustained growth pattern. Dale Petruzzi, founder of Chromebattery.com, has one full-time staffer devoted to identifying quality content links, particularly in the areas of education, which score high with Google.

5. Use Social Media in Conjunction with Your SEO Strategy

YouTube is now the second largest search engine, and people go there looking for brands. For the first time in 2010, unique visits to Facebook exceeded those made to Google. People spend hours on social media. Content has become distributable. It's shared openly and easily. Facebook's Open Graph turned the web into one huge opportunity for friends to share their likes and dislikes. Now the company intends to introduce a web search of all sites deploying its "Like" buttons.

CNN's Topher Kohan monitors Twitter and Facebook in addition to Google Trends to see what terms and themes are trending during the day. Keywords optimized in the morning will change throughout the day based on the news cycle. Brent Payne, SEO director for the Tribune Company, actively engages with the social media team at the Tribune. He says Digg alone drives 6 to 7 million page views daily to Tribune sites.

Be aware of opportunities that arise when positive press affects your brand. One bra maker saw its clicks and conversions soar when it added to its paid search copy an on-air reference made by Oprah, whose endorsements help the products she touts.

Here's a short checklist of social search strategies for marketers to pursue:

- Make it easy to share your content via social media sites such as Digg, Reddit, StumbleUpon, and so on.
- Capitalize on Facebook Open Graph and embed as many "Like" buttons for your brand throughout your content as you can.
- Update your company's Facebook brand and community pages regularly and keep it open for searching by Google.
- Use free SEO-friendly blog platforms such as WordPress to easily add fresh content to your site, and encourage linking and conversation from other bloggers.
- Make your content available through RSS feeds, which also syndicate to search engines, raising traffic and visibility.
- Use Twitter when appropriate to lift your real-time search rankings, particularly when highly topical things are happening involving your brand.

(This is also a good strategy for reputation management to keep negative stories from spiraling out of control.) Keep in mind, it's important to tweet regularly with interesting "tweet bait" to keep your followers engaged and coming back for more.

- When participating in conversations on key blogs and online communities relating to your industry, include links to your site when relevant to enhance the discussion and generate traffic.
- Put your commercials on YouTube and optimize all videos with descriptive copy so they rank prominently in Google search results.

Deploying Performance Measurement in Search

Search marketers require actionable and timely intelligence to effectively manage their campaigns. The amount of data available can be overwhelming. It is important to have a framework and a set of tools for conducting the measurement. Let's apply the Performance Measurement framework, described in Chapter 2, to search. Starting with the three buckets we outlined, you will select metrics for the following:

1. *Exposure*—metrics that typically relate to the short-term aspects of the campaign, such as the reach/frequency and engagement of digital marketing.
2. *Strategic*—metrics that capture strategic marketing objectives of customer and brand growth.
3. *Financial*—metrics that quantify the return on investment (ROI), or financial outcomes, of the marketing activity.

You'll need to select metrics from each part of the framework. For measuring search, we recommend using the following five metrics.

Exposure Metrics for Search

Exposure metrics for search typically relate to the short-term aspects of a campaign, such as reach and frequency or engagement level.

1. Qualified Reach, or Qualified Visits　One of the key objectives of search is to increase the volume of traffic to your content using both SEO and PPC. Increase in search traffic is an effective metric to measure the performance of your search. Here is where the Qualified Reach metric comes into play, as an indicator of valid traffic from search. It is defined as *the number of consumers who clicked on a keyword resulting in a visit to your website or to other places where your brand's Magnetic Content is present.*

To determine the increase in traffic, decide on a set of keywords to track rankings. Then compare the Qualified Visit numbers you gathered at the beginning to reports down the line to see if there is any net increase or decrease in traffic from those keywords.

Other metrics also need to be considered to optimize search, especially with SEO. Let's look at these next.

2. Rank   Although not part of our seven key metrics outlined in Chapter 2, keyword and page rank are critical metrics when it comes to SEO and PPC for search. As discussed earlier in the chapter, it is important for the keywords to be either ranked high enough to show up in the "golden triangle" (see Figure 4.2) or on the first page. For SEO, page rank is also important; it is a ranking of the page by the search engine and is based on a variety of technical factors described in the section on optimization for natural search.

With SEO, focus on getting your keywords right and don't worry so much about page rank. Page rank will come as you follow the best practices tips. It's more important that you get the right traffic from the right keywords.

3. Click-Through Rate (CTR)   We discussed the value of clicks or CTR in detail in Chapter 2. It is an important metric for search and is calculated by dividing the number of users who clicked on an ad or a link by the number of times the ad or link was delivered (that is, impressions). We believe CTR is a valid diagnostic metric, particularly for search, because it gives an important view into the interest level in learning more about that specific digital content.

Ad groups or keywords with a high CTR often do not result in conversions. This can happen because the ad text can be made provocative or eye catching but may not be representative of the website content. Or the problem may be that the site/landing page is not optimized. However, the opposite can often be true: keywords with a low CTR can result in a high conversion rate. Thus, it is important to look at the next metric: End Action, or conversion.

Strategic Metrics for Search

Strategic metrics are those that capture the strategic marketing objectives of your search campaigns that are related to customer and brand growth.

4. End Action Rate   End Actions represent the action taken by a user, also often called a conversion activity. An End Action can be a sale, a lead generated, a download, a video view, a form completion, and so on. It is the end goal of the content and it is important to identify the right end outcome to measure before the start of the optimization of search.

Conversion is especially critical to look at for determining the cost effectiveness of pay-per-click campaigns. It is the combination of the CTR and the efficiency of your conversion that will really determine whether or not the campaign is working. For example, a keyword with a low CTR but a high conversion rate leads to a low cost per conversion, which results in a higher ROI. Let's look at a metric that addresses the ROI issue next.

Financial Metrics for Search

Financial metrics quantify the return on your investment, or other financial outcomes associated with your spending on search.

5. Cost per Click or Cost per End Action   Cost per conversion is an important metric for PPC campaigns and represents the potential ROI. Your PPC efforts will generate a return for you only if the revenue associated with each conversion is greater than the cost. Search advertisers can use tools (discussed next) to compare the cost per End Action with the revenue and determine exactly how much revenue their PPC efforts are driving; they will then be able to manage their keyword bids using these ROI results.

Critical Tools for Search

Tools are a vital part of search. No matter how confident you feel about your understanding of your business and your ability to guess what is important to your customers, you *really need* these tools to provide insights for optimizing search. We have organized the tools discussion into four areas, including a look at key benefits.

1. Keyword research and traffic analysis
2. Rank and coverage analysis + bid management
3. Link analysis
4. SEO site auditing and optimization

We promise what follows will not be the eye-glazing technical material that many marketing executives take pains to avoid. It is important for a marketer to understand these common tools to get the most from the resources (staff and dollars) you invest each year.

1. *Keyword research and traffic analysis* are the foundation for any search strategy and execution. You simply cannot ignore them—no matter how well you believe you understand your customer's search patterns! In our experience, keyword research is the most commonly skipped step, and yet it is the most vital one. If your business is providing vacation rentals in New York, should you choose "family vacation," "summer vacation," "beach vacation," "hiking and biking vacation," and so on, as your keywords? There can often be 2 to 10 times the difference in the frequency such terms are searched. Tools in this area will answer key questions such as:
   - What are the most important keywords to my target audience?
   - What keywords are driving traffic to the website?
   - How can I expand my keyword lists?
   - What sites are referring visitors to our site?
   - Roughly how many users are visiting the site across a specified time period?

   Some features of these tools will also help identify your competitors for certain keywords and phrases. You may also discover gaps in competitors' SEO and SEM strategies and deep insights on your consumers. For example:
   - What percentage of traffic is from paid versus natural search?
   - What are the demographics (gender, age, income level) of my site visitors?
   - How do people get to my site, and where do they go when they leave?

   There are many tools in this space. Two important resources are Compete (www.compete.com) and comScore (www.comscore.com).

2. *Rank and coverage analysis + bid management* is the vital measurement during search campaigns to continuously examine rank and coverage and then decide on the right bid for the keywords. These tools will help answer questions such as:
   - What is my rank, coverage, and even share of voice?
   - How have these metrics changed over time?
   - What are my competitors' traffic and bid on keywords?
   - What is the synergy between paid search and natural search?
   - What is the cost/conversion for each keyword?
   - What is the incremental ROI of PPC performance at various positions (page rank)?

   Some key tools in this space are SearchIgnite or AdGooroo (www .adgooroo.com).

3. *Link analysis* is critical for measuring and continuously evaluating the effectiveness of links. These tools help answer key questions such as:
   - Who is linking to the site, and what keywords are they using?
   - Who are competitors receiving links from?
   - Are any of the links broken on the site?

   This tool also enables us to see who is linking to competitors' sites. It keeps track of all links, making sure they are always active. It helps improve a website's link popularity by searching for link partners within the links that are related to a site's targeted keywords. One of our favorites in this space is Advanced Link Manager, which allows you to select from a list of a large number of search engines.

4. *SEO site auditing and optimization* is a means to achieve fast-cycle optimization of SEO. Some concerns that can be addressed are:
   - Are all of the on-page elements incorporating keywords properly?
   - Do URLs include parameters and/or session IDs?
   - Is the site navigation crawlable?
   - Are there quality inbound links pointing to the site?

   Features available include actionable reports and remediation recommendations, automated site and page-specific SEO audits, at-a-glance views of overall organic search ratings, and standardized and centralized SEO metrics and reporting worldwide. It is always used in conjunction with manual review for duplicate content, domain strategies, and other non-HTML SEO elements. The leading automated tool in this space is Covario (www.covario.com). Covario uses a proprietary knowledge base of information about the search engines, their algorithms, and SEO best practices. We believe it reliably provides a global view of organic search ratings for websites.

Small Business and SEO: The Story of Batteries.com

Ask Dale Petruzzi the secret to his small business success, and his response is simple: SEO.

Petruzzi co-founded Batteries.com in 1998, back when few people spent time on the Internet or engaged in e-commerce. The site was designed as a one-stop source for any type of battery. It took five years before he came to understand the full interplay between SEO and sales.

In 2003, Petruzzi decided to change the look and structure of the site and renamed the URLs. Once relaunched, the site seemed to fall off the map, a steady stream of national traffic dried up, and he couldn't figure out why.

"No one knew that if you changed a character in your URL, Google thought you were a new company," he recalls, after losing the coveted first-page organic positioning on many search terms. "When you're a new company, you're starting from scratch. You've got to earn it."

The company was already investing $120,000 per month for PPC ads. One of its top keywords, "laptop batteries," gets a half-million searches at $2 per click. It took some time, but eventually Batteries.com figured out what had happened and worked its way back to the front page organically.

Petruzzi really got SEO religion when he noticed that the organic search links were converting at a much higher level than the paid links. He hired two national search firms, which did a full SEO audit and implementation, and Petruzzi shadowed every move they made.

By 2006, the $120,000-per-month PPC budget had dropped to $18,000 per-month and site traffic was tripled. Some 1,400 keywords were appearing as natural search results on the first page of Google results; think "RCA battery," "Sony battery," and so forth.

"When you can drop a million dollars a year in paid search costs," Petruzzi says, "I'll take that million dollars and go on vacation."

It cost $160,000 for the services of the two firms (iProspect and iCrossing), and Petruzzi figures that work would now go for between $200,000 and $250,000.

Petruzzi estimates he spent many thousands more in his own search education at conferences around the country because of his passionate interest in the topic, which was clearly a business driver. He also met the "rock 'n roll stars" who "sleep with Google" and therefore were on top of the 400-odd algorithmic changes made any given year.

"Natural search is all about being relevant," he says. "If someone types in 'blue shirt' they want to see a blue shirt. Google was reading my website three times a day. Most sites are crawled once a month. The bigger you get, the more you're out there, the more you're trusted."

Batteries.com was putting up a lot of information on the site every day and making sure to use best practices (meaning not putting the keyword term 10 times into the first paragraph just to try to pull a rank.)

"It's a lot of work. It's not easy. But it's worth it." And it was done by just two people.

Petruzzi believes pure-play smaller companies are the best to follow at organic search because, lacking the brand name awareness of a Best Buy or Radio Shack, they need it to survive.

(continued)

Eventually, Batteries.com was able to write programs that would make a massive title word change on all 71,000 pages at once.

The executive's passion for SEO prompted him to turn right around after selling Batteries.com for $21 million in November 2007 and start his own agency, SpinShark. The intention was to help smaller companies, but he wound up attracting national brands like Brookstone and Bloomingdale's. SpinShark was sold to PMD Digital in September 2009. The serial entrepreneur got right back into the game, launching a new battery site, chromebattery.com, containing more than 2 million pages and built from the ground-up to be optimized by SEO. It launched in November 2010.

Chromebattery.com was built with the intention of 100 percent natural search, although Petruzzi believes a certain amount of paid participation is necessary for Google to rank you as the lead organically.

There are 2 million potential on-ramps to the website. Pages exist for every potential model and model number for products that run on battery power. Each page has a video, as well, involving battery safety, disposal methods, and so forth.

Petruzzi has a full-time employee devoted to obtaining quality links. Educational sites get more respect from Google, so links to sites like Purdue University, which does a lot of scientific investigation of batteries, are helpful. The new e-commerce site has a companion site for kids, Battery Kids, with Disney-like content about building a science project and school projects involving batteries. This content is designed to get the coveted links from educational sites and also serves as a marketing platform through things like contests where kids can enter to win $1,000 toward education for their schools.

"I don't think there's a lot of people out there just shooting the breeze about their batteries," quips Petruzzi, so social media is less of an emphasis. What goes on Twitter is more about products that could use batteries and the Battery Kids efforts.

Everything Chromebattery.com is doing is optimized for mobile as well. "I think mobile will be it in a few years. I think computers will be mobile."

Unlike the $300,000 to $500,000 he says it cost to build Batteries.com, Petruzzi bought an off-the-shelf package, Magento (www.magentocommerce .com), for about $100, and built Chromebattery.com for $20,000. It fills the basic needs for the product and a checkout. In the category, cross-merchandising of related products is not relevant. The other relevant search strategy Petruzzi employs is sending a product feed to Amazon.com, which is another important source of sales.

The business goal is to do $1 million in sales for each employee. Every time he goes up another million, he'll bring on another employee.

The Future of Search—Planning Ahead

Where are things going? We see five big trends driving the future of search. If you're not already planning for them, start today.

Local Search Local is the fastest-growing vertical out there. According to The Kelsey Group, at least one in every four searches is local, going back as far as 2004. With the explosion in mobile computing devices and smart phones, the importance of local is only growing.

Local is not just mom-and-pop. The emergence of Google Places and inclusion of businesses in Google Maps means national establishments want to ensure it's possible to find their individual locations. One way to stay competitive with larger rivals is to focus on language that locals use. Brent Payne of the Tribune Company says part of what he does is focus on the key phrases the natives use, compared with what's common nationally. What words, for example, do Chicagoans or Angelenos use for their foods, their sports teams, and their neighborhoods?

Payne also employs a page rank "sculpting" methodology where the SEO level dial is set differently depending on the nature of the news day. On a day with many different news stories occurring, none having any particular prominence, the dial might be set at five, allowing all to be ranked. But on a day with a significant story such as a Presidential inauguration, it will be set at one so that all traffic to a page is credited to that story, resulting in a higher ranking on the Google search results page.

Social Search / Real-Time Search In 2009, Google integrated real-time Twitter feeds into universal search. Twitter Search alone drew 2.7 million unique visitors in April 2010, according to Compete. A strategy that marries social and search adds to the likelihood your brand will get highly ranked by Google. Blogs and Facebook's Open Graph make what happens outside your own site as important as what's within it.

SEO was all about architecture and external links. With the rise of social, it will be important to use a keyword strategy to get key influencers to talk about your brand. These conversations will also feed real-time results and add to the likelihood of a higher page rank on Google. SEO is increasingly social and sits at the intersection of multiple business functions such as public relations, customer service, recruitment, and branding.

"Social media gives you nearly infinite opportunity to show up for any number of queries that use language you may not even realize your customers are using," notes author and SEO consultant Vanessa Fox. Blogs, content-sharing sites, social networking sites, Twitter feeds, review sites, and discussion forums are all areas to exploit the explosion of social search.

Mobile Search   According to M:Metrics, 60 percent of iPhone users and 37 percent of all smart phone users visited a search engine. This is truly search whenever and wherever you want it. By the year 2015, any demarcation between mobile and computer platforms may be gone. It already is in Europe and Asia. To prepare for this, be sure your site is readable on a mobile device browser, and then consider the mind-set of someone on the move when selecting keywords. For example, a transient searcher in a hurry to find the nearest pizzeria or drugstore is less likely to type long search queries and even less willing to wade through layers of content.

One of the big unknowns heading into this decade is the role apps will play in displacing traditional search, as the iPhone, iPad, and Android platforms and other smart phones take on more apps that allow customers to hone right in on specific information needs. Search visionary John Battelle, former CEO of Federated Media, predicts apps will get into the search business to fill the need for a way to navigate the proliferation of apps that are being developed just for the iPhone/iPad platforms.

"If marketers are going to find value in AppWorld, they're going to need a proxy for engagement, a trail of breadcrumbs, some signal(s) that show where consumers are, what they are doing, and ideally, predicts what they might do next," Battelle explains. "Don't tell me a Google-like metadata play isn't going to evolve inside such an ecosystem. After all, search did all those things for the web. But so far, we don't have a similar signal for AppWorld. But we will."

Vertical Search   Specialized search engines crawl specific databases that pertain to their area of interest or industry sector. They can be organized by topic (industrial metals, real estate, software), audience (parents, kids, art collectors), or even type of content (photos, audio, menus). You want to be sure your business is located on these engines because they offer built-in guidance on a consumer's mind-set. Someone searching for "MP3" on a shopping site is most likely looking to buy. Someone searching for "China Garden" on a restaurant site is looking for a place to eat, not an actual garden.

Listings in directories help categorize your business if there is any possibility of misinterpretation. Search engines like directories because they are typically organized in neat, systematic hierarchies. So if you get your site into the proper vertical directories, you're more likely to show up correctly in vertical searches.

Personalization Search engines take into account your personal searching patterns over time in an attempt to deliver the results best matching your search intentions. When Google officially introduced personalized search in December 2009, it sent SEO specialists like Danny Sullivan into a tizzy, declaring that "normal search" was gone for good.

The way it's playing out so far does not seem to have impacted results in quite so major a way. Google executives say at most, two of the results on the first page of returns are personalized, and it doesn't occur on every search. What this does is render ranking reports increasingly meaningless and ramp up the importance of relevance. As social profiles feed more information into the system, the ability to customize searches will only become easier.

Conclusion

To be seen, you must be found. SEO and SEM make that happen. Best practices drive your audience to your content using SEO. Some of these practices, such as having the right site architecture and removing technical barriers, are just basic requirements to get in the game.

We believe *thinking like a searcher* is the most impactful thing you can do to create Magnetic Content for search, succeed in search, and ultimately, achieve and surpass your business objectives. That extends to everything you do—from keyword research, to relevant landing pages for different phases of the purchase funnel, to fresh quality content. *Provide value and relevance to the consumer, and Google will reward you, too.*

On the paid search side of the equation, it is important to remember this is a highly competitive business where keywords are bid up rapidly. Success in PPC is all about proper bid management and ROI monitoring. If you are unwilling or unable to commit the time to proper management, don't do it; just stick with organic search. *Ultimately, we believe a holistic approach combining SEO and PPC yields the best business return.*

As you move forward, keep this in mind: we see search and social media coming closer and closer together. Content is no longer about a destination; it is about distribution. It is mobile, shared, and driven by the consumer. Search is about making it possible for people to find the content they want from where they are. Content will be absorbed in new ways and through what others are saying about the content.

CHAPTER 5

Online Display Ads

"If I don't have a display campaign to support my paid
search campaign, I'm basically giving the traffic
away to my competitors."
—*Robert Murray, CEO, iProspect, May 2009*

Are you planning to skip this chapter because you read the title and have already lost interest? Perhaps you've come to the conclusion that display ad banners of any shape and size simply don't work. After all, isn't the average click-through rate at about 0.09 percent these days?

Pity the conventional banner ad, the workhorse of web advertising. It does not dazzle with rich media or video, nor does it impress marketers with its obvious and immediate return on investment like search does. Some research even suggests a good portion of banner ads are ignored.

We believe, however, that the demise of display ads has been greatly exaggerated. Banner ads, when used correctly, provide an essential overlay to any digital campaign, often working subliminally, behind the scenes, over time. They can play an important role in driving consumers to conduct a branded search or even make a purchase. Display ads can also drive site traffic and boost your efforts in social media marketing; and, they are becoming a viable new strategy for mobile marketing as well. Despite these benefits, marketers tend to misuse, undervalue, and incorrectly measure their contribution, particularly as it relates to branding efforts.

In this chapter, we will:

1. Explore why display ads are growing in use and spending, and remain relevant and important for marketers.

2. Discuss important changes in the way display ads are purchased (real-time bidding, demand-side platforms, and self-service platforms).
3. Learn effective ways to magnetize and measure display ads to drive business results.

Notwithstanding their bad rap in online marketing circles, banners are destined for growth. In 2010, U.S. marketers spent a combined total of $6.4 billion on display advertising, including banner ads ($5.9 billion) and sponsorships ($0.5 billion), accounting for just under one-quarter (24.7 percent) of total online advertising spending for that year, according to eMarketer. The $6.4 billion figure represents an 18 percent increase over the recessionary year of 2009. Furthermore, growth is continuing in 2011, with spending on banner and sponsorship ads climbing to $7.15 billion, up 12 percent versus 2010. Note that these figures do not include two other even faster growing forms of branding oriented ads, namely rich media and online video, which accounted for a combined $3.0 billion in 2010 (and gets its own chapter later in this book).

eMarketer projects that by 2014—that is, in just a few short years—banner and sponsorship ads combined will grow to just under $10 billion in spending, accounting for 23.3 percent of total online ad spending. Clearly, despite a slight dip in share (from 24.7 percent in 2010), display ads will continue to be a key component of online ad spending plans for the foreseeable future.

Remarkably, online ad spending for *total* display advertising, including rich media and video, will rise faster than search over the next several years, according to eMarketer calculations (Figure 5.1).

What accounts for this surprising growth, for what has been regarded as a beleaguered channel? Several factors contribute to the continued viability and use of banner ads:

- Marketers are getting smarter about metrics and how to measure the impact of banners within their campaigns.
- Growing evidence suggests that banners work subtly and over time to pump up business results, as measured by increased search activity, higher site traffic, improved brand metrics, and, importantly, boosted online and offline sales.
- Social networks such as Facebook are creating new markets for banner advertising as they look to monetize their rapidly growing base of users.
- New developments in the buying and distribution of banners ads, such as real-time bidding (RTB) and demand-side platforms (DSPs), are making them both more efficient and effective.

Figure 5.1

Online ad spending by format

US Online Ad Spending, by Format, 2009-2014 billions						
	2009	**2010**	**2011**	**2012**	**2013**	**2014**
Search	$10.70	$12.37	$13.59	$15.43	$17.00	$18.84
Banner ads	$5.06	$5.88	$6.56	$7.40	$7.92	$8.63
Classifieds	$2.25	$2.53	$2.74	$2.93	$3.10	$3.30
Rich media	$1.51	$1.57	$1.60	$1.63	$1.62	$1.58
Video	$1.02	$1.42	$1.97	$3.03	$4.07	$5.71
Lead generation	$1.45	$1.29	$1.23	$1.24	$1.28	$1.34
Sponsorships	$0.38	$0.50	$0.59	$0.68	$0.76	$0.83
Email	$0.29	$0.24	$0.24	$0.25	$0.26	$0.27
Total	**$22.66**	**$25.80**	**$28.50**	**$32.60**	**$36.00**	**$40.50**
Source: eMarketer, Nov 2010						
122076					www.**eMarketer**.com	

- New self-serve platforms created by firms such as Google, AOL, Yahoo!, Facebook, and others are making it easier for small and medium-sized businesses (SMBs) to join the banner bandwagon, which is expanding the universe of banner buyers.
- New platforms are increasingly commoditizing banner ads, which drive down the cost of banner ad rates (as measured in CPMs—cost per thousand impressions) and makes them more attractive for buyers, particularly smaller businesses.

Over the next few years, the total volume of banner ads, as measured in sheer billions of impressions will rise much faster than CPM prices. This downward CPM trend creates opportunity for marketers, because they can buy display ads at a relatively cheap price.

According to a September 2010 study by ITZ Belden and American Press Institute, 53 percent of small and medium-sized businesses use display banner ads in their online marketing efforts. And they allocate the same percentage of their online advertising budget to display ads as they do to their own websites (both receive 22 percent).

Online Display Ads Play Multiple Roles Today

You might be surprised at what the lowly banner ad can accomplish.

A January 2009 study commissioned by iProspect and conducted by Forrester Consulting showed that when Internet users were exposed to a promotional display ad, less than one-third (31 percent) of them clicked on the ad itself; however, most respondents did take some other form of action:

- Twenty-seven percent searched for the product, brand, or company using a search engine.
- Twenty-one percent typed the web address directly into the browser and navigated to the advertiser's site.
- Nine percent investigated the product, brand, or company through social media.

Overall, the iProspect study concluded that Internet users were more likely to engage with or make a purchase from brands with which they were already familiar, and online display ads are one way to get there.

Display Ads Improve Branding Metrics

For brand marketers, often the goal is less about driving immediate sales, but rather focused on cementing the brand name in the consumer's mind—such that when they are eventually looking to make a purchase, the advertised brand is top-of-mind, considered, or preferred.

Aggregated data from online researcher Dynamic Logic, based on 2,512 campaigns and 3.8 million respondents, showed that those respondents exposed to online display advertising registered slightly higher increases in key brand metrics, on average, than those who were not exposed (that is, the control group). The delta lift (expressed as a point difference) for exposure to display ads was 2.1 for aided brand awareness and 2.3 for message association. Other data from comScore substantiates the brand lift effect from display ads (Figure 5.2).

Display Ads Stimulate Search

Often, consumers get the idea to conduct a brand or category search after being exposed to display ads. The display ads push the message out, whereas search pulls the consumer in to find out more. Yahoo! ran an experiment

Figure 5.2
Online display ad effects on brand metrics

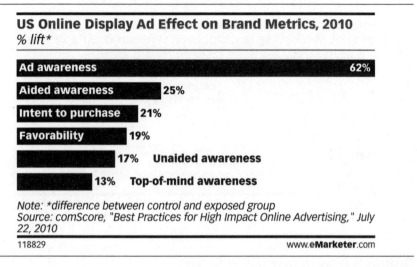

US Online Display Ad Effect on Brand Metrics, 2010
% lift*

Ad awareness	62%
Aided awareness	25%
Intent to purchase	21%
Favorability	19%
	17% **Unaided awareness**
	13% **Top-of-mind awareness**

Note: *difference between control and exposed group
Source: comScore, "Best Practices for High Impact Online Advertising," July 22, 2010

118829   www.**eMarketer**.com

with 60 advertiser clients in eight verticals and found that display ads drove a 155 percent lift in search activity, according to David Zinman, vice president and general manager for display advertising at Yahoo!. The tests further revealed that display ads affect search activity for both brand and generic terms.

Similarly, an iCrossing study found that when display ads are combined with search marketing, there is a significant boost in search visits and unique visitors (Figure 5.3).

Online Banners Help Drive Site Traffic

Many advertisers have the goal of driving qualified traffic to their corporate or brand websites. Numerous studies support the fact that banner ads can effectively get this job done. In 2008, comScore evaluated and aggregated 139 separate studies linking display ads to site visitation levels and found that the average lift in the number of visitors to the advertiser's site—comparing visitation levels of exposed and nonexposed groups—was 65 percent during the first week following the first exposure to an ad. Additional, although somewhat muted, lifts were seen in the following three weeks. These results were confirmed in a more recent set of comScore studies conducted in 2009 in Europe, where even higher lifts in site visitation levels were seen due to exposure to display ads.

Figure 5.3
The effects of display media on search traffic

**Effect on Search Visits and Unique Visitors When
Search Marketing Is Combined with an Online Display
Ad Campaign, January 2008-February 2009**
% change

	Change in search visits	Change in unique visitors
Period 2 vs. period 1	13.7%	2.5%
Period 3 vs. period 2	-30.8%	-15.0%
Period 4 vs. period 3	22.1%	0.5%

Source: iCrossing, "The Effects of Display Media on Search Traffic," August 27, 2009

106477   www.**eMarketer**.com

Online Banners Influence Sales

Since we have established that banner ads are effective at driving search as well as traffic to your website, logically that suggests they can also help influence sales, whether they occur online or offline. For most product categories, eMarketer estimates that between 70 and 80 percent of Internet users shop or browse online when they are considering a purchase—and much of that surfing behavior happens on branded or product websites. Given this proclivity, marketers have an obvious opportunity to influence the awareness, preferences, or even behaviors of these online shoppers—at the precise time when they are in exploration or consideration mode. In the 90 days leading up to a sale, consumers see an average of 18 ads for a product, according to Microsoft's Atlas Institute.

Of course, the tendency to shop on the web varies by category. A world-wide survey from Universal McCann indicates that relatively high-priced/high-consideration categories, such as holidays and destinations, consumer electronics, and travel, are the most-shopped categories online. However, less expensive products are increasingly researched online as well. Consumers today access the Internet to look up even relatively low-interest products such as shampoo to check out prices, ingredients, or the product's ecological impact on the environment. Display/branding ads can also influence consumers to the point of purchasing products online, although rarely is the impact in the form of an immediate click.

As a rule, the impact of online research/shopping behavior is greater on in-store sales than web-based sales. According to comScore, for retailers with online and offline sales channels, approximately 68 percent of the impact of display ads was found in the offline channel (brick-and-mortar stores). This knowledge is useful not just for devising online banner campaigns but also when searching for budget dollars to fund an initiative.

New Challenges and Opportunities in the Online Ad Marketplace

If you look at the modern online ad marketplace today, you'll see that it functions more like the financial stock market—with display ads being bought and sold through a real-time market exchange, much the way stocks are traded.

For the past few years, much of the news and developments taking place in online display advertising has concerned ad networks. These organizations, large and small, aggregate ad inventory by connecting up websites that are looking to sell ads (publishers, portals, blog sites, and even social media sites such as Facebook) with advertisers who want to deliver their ads to select target audiences. An ad network typically amalgamates thousands of web properties ranging from small, niche websites to larger, premium sites, all with ad inventory to sell.

An advertiser can come to an ad network to buy ads armed with a preferred audience profile, as well as pricing ranges for placing the display ads. The ad network, in turn, purchases the ads from a variety of publishers and other sites, and sometimes even from other ad networks. Through this process, an ad network can reach audiences comparable in size to those at the larger websites, but at a lower cost. Some of the big ad networks are Backpage.com, Advertising.com, and 24/7 Real Media.

However, there are two major drawbacks with ad networks. First, they have yet to deliver on the promise of truly cost-effective scale. Second, advertisers usually have no clue about where their ads are getting placed. Brand advertisers are particularly sensitive about the kinds of contexts in which their ads appear, so they are increasingly demanding greater transparency.

These two issues have led to some significant transformations in the online ad market place, both driven by technology created for real-time bidding (RTB) and demand-side platforms (DSPs). Traditional ad networks are being replaced by these more cost-effective, transparent systems that provide the advertiser with greater buying control. What we are talking about here is an auction-based, media-buying platform in an RTB environment. There is no middleman—no ad network that takes a percentage cut to administer the inventory. As a result, prices for display ads are being significantly reduced as they slip down to true, market-driven equilibrium.

Ultimately, this real-time bidding approach shifts the advertiser's focus from purchasing website pages to buying actual audiences—wherever they are—based on detailed audience profiles. This leads to far greater buying efficiencies, and often better business results.

Almost all large ad agencies and their respective holding companies have started to create in-house display ad trading desks that use these exchanges and demand-side auction platforms to access online ad inventory directly and buy ad space for advertisers. The market leaders in this space are MediaMath, Invite Media, x+1, Triggit, Turn, and eXelate.

If you are a sizeable marketer, you need to ensure that your agency is using these platforms and employing real-time bidding and demand-side auction platforms for placing your display ads. Otherwise, you are paying significantly more than you should for your media.

Another development in the display ad marketplace is the emergence of self-service platforms that enable even relatively small businesses to easily purchase inventory for banner campaigns. Such services, being offered by leading Internet players such as Google, Facebook, AOL, and Yahoo!, reduce the amount of time it takes to buy online ads as well as the associated costs. They also increase the universe of display ad buyers.

Six Best Practices for Magnetizing Customers through Display Ads

We've now established that display advertising has an important role, particularly for brand advertisers. But what are the secrets to achieving success? The following six guidelines will direct your path:

1. Creative counts.
2. Size matters.
3. Pay attention to context.
4. Behavioral targeting is a must.
5. Integrate search and display for maximum synergy.
6. Use display ads to drive consumers to your Magnetic Content.

What we've said before about Magnetic Content applies to banner ads as well; they must strive to be unique, useful, well executed, fun, and make good use of the channel. Banner ads fun? Yes, even a lowly banner has the capacity to spark a little fun or stir up some amusement that can serve to draw the viewer in and get them engaged with your brand. In addition, banner ads can be used as a promotional tool to redirect consumers to the content you really want them to see—your Magnetic Content. The real-time bidding option and ad exchanges make this kind of precise targeting more viable.

1. Creative Counts

It pays to invest in good creative execution! According to Jon Gibs, vice president of Media Analytics at Nielsen Company, "Creative is about 70% to 80% of the effectiveness of advertising." Sharing this opinion is Ken Mallon, senior vice president of Custom Solutions & Ad Effectiveness Consulting at Dynamic Logic, a company that has evaluated the brand impact of thousands of online campaigns. Mr. Mallon says: "By far the biggest driver of brand impact success is the creative. The best ads that we see in terms of performance online tend to be ones that almost have a magazine feel. They look nice; people think about things like having the right human form in there, the right product shot."

If there is a really compelling piece of content—that just happens to be an advertiser's brand message in the form of a display ad—consumers will gravitate to it and respond. A strong image can pack a lot of punch. Even in campaigns for text-heavy websites—such as publishing websites, print book retailers, financial services, and health care products—it's been shown time and again that strong images with limited text provide the emotional pull to draw audiences in (see Figure 5.4). There's also considerable credence to the idea that a static banner ad with a strong, emotional image can be as effective as a busily animated display ad.

As proof that creative execution really matters with display ads, Dynamic Logic evaluated results from 2,512 online campaigns and found significant differences in brand metrics from those campaigns deemed "best," versus "average" and "worst" campaigns (Figure 5.5).

Another creative approach with banners is to focus on giving consumers what they want. In a 2010 study by Cone (Figure 5.6), whereas only 21 percent of online consumers said they wanted marketers to "market to me," 77 percent said they would like marketers to offer them incentives, such as free products, coupons, and discounts. Furthermore, a healthy 46 percent said they would like marketers to "solve my problems/provide product or service information," and 39 percent wanted marketers to solicit their feedback on products and services. Thus, even banner ads can serve as Magnetic Content—if they are useful, offer help, entertain, or inform consumers.

Figure 5.4

Strong, simpler images for Harlequin's fantasy fiction boosted online e-book sales by 400 percent compared with traditional "book cover" banners for the same series

Source: DynamicsOnline.

Figure 5.5

Not all display ads are created equal

Online Advertising's Effect on Brand Metrics in the US, by Level of Campaign Performance*, Q1 2010**
% of respondents impacted

	Aided brand awareness	Online ad awareness	Message association	Brand favorability	Purchase intent
Best	8.1%	13.1%	8.4%	7.4%	7.2%
Average	2.1%	4.3%	2.3%	1.3%	1.1%
Worst	-2.3%	-2.1%	-2.1%	-4.0%	-4.2%

Note: n=2,512 campaigns and 3,768,482 respondents; *best performers are the average of the top 20% of campaigns per metric and worst performers are the bottom 20% of campaigns; **includes three years through Q1 2010
Source: Dynamic Logic, provided to eMarketer, July 27, 2010

118050   www.eMarketer.com

Figure 5.6

What consumers want from their interactions from
companies and brands online

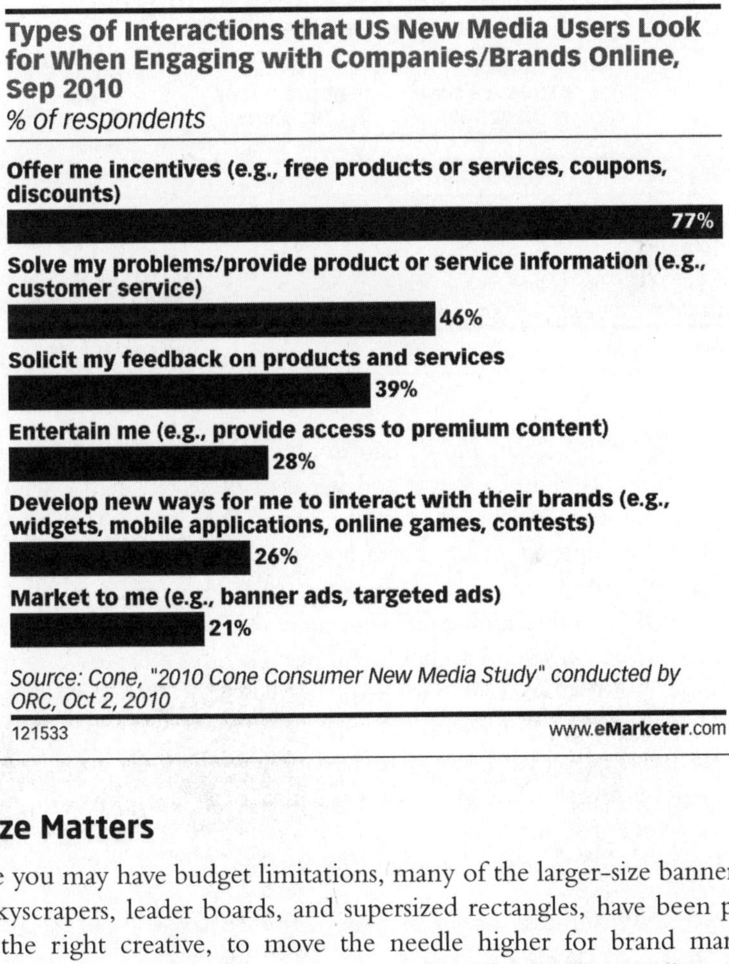

**Types of Interactions that US New Media Users Look
for When Engaging with Companies/Brands Online,
Sep 2010**
% of respondents

**Offer me incentives (e.g., free products or services, coupons,
discounts)**

77%

**Solve my problems/provide product or service information (e.g.,
customer service)**

46%

Solicit my feedback on products and services

39%

Entertain me (e.g., provide access to premium content)

28%

**Develop new ways for me to interact with their brands (e.g.,
widgets, mobile applications, online games, contests)**

26%

Market to me (e.g., banner ads, targeted ads)

21%

*Source: Cone, "2010 Cone Consumer New Media Study" conducted by
ORC, Oct 2, 2010*

121533   www.**eMarketer**.com

---

2. Size Matters

While you may have budget limitations, many of the larger-size banner units, like skyscrapers, leader boards, and supersized rectangles, have been proven, with the right creative, to move the needle higher for brand marketers. Larger, more impactful ads consistently perform better than smaller ones, on average. Numerous Dynamic Logic, InsightExpress, and MediaMind studies have proved this correlation.

The size and shape of display banner ads can also affect engagement results, at least as measured by time spent. According to a time–exposure study conducted by Lotame Solutions (Figure 5.7), the large 300×250 rectangle caused Internet users to spend significantly more time with this unit versus more narrow (and creatively limiting) ads, specifically 728×90 and 160×600 banner ads. Consumers spent more than 13 seconds with

Figure 5.7

Effects of display ad size and shape

Time Spent with Banner Ads Among US Internet Users, by Ad Size, January-February 2009

	Total exposure time (seconds)	Total impressions (millions)	Average time per impression (seconds)
300x250	867,700,956	66,466,701	13.05
728x90	161,590,364	29,925,805	5.40
160x600	97,539,062	51,938,746	1.88

Source: Lotame Solutions, Inc., "Time Exposure by Banner Size," provided to eMarketer, April 8, 2009

103793   www.eMarketer.com

---

the rectangle (300 × 250), more than double the next-best-performing ad unit, the 728 × 90. The large size and shape of these rectangles, which end up smack in the middle of valued content, means they are difficult to ignore.

If you really want to make a splash with display advertising, consider running a home page takeover or an interstitial on a major portal such as Yahoo! or AOL, or other high-reach sites such as CNN, ESPN, the *New York Times, USA Today,* or even Facebook. All of these sites offer the opportunity to surround editorial content with sequenced banners or roadblocks or to offer exclusive use of home pages.

On the other hand, be aware that the larger your ad size unit, the more likely it will be perceived by consumers as intrusive. This is why you need to refer back to the first guideline—creative counts. If your message is compelling and/or relevant enough, consumers won't mind if it takes up more space.

3. Pay Attention to Context

Marketers also need to pay attention to the context in which their display ads appear. For example, it's a given that branded, premium websites create a sort of halo effect that extends to the brands that advertise on their web pages. According to a study by the Online Publishers Association (OPA) and Dynamic Logic, display ads within branded content sites (for example, NewYorkTimes.com, Weather.com) do a better job of boosting brand metrics than when those same ads are placed within more generic environments.

Furthermore, numerous other studies from Dynamic Logic, InsightExpress, and MediaMind show that brand messages that are in sync with—and therefore, relevant to—the surrounding editorial content tend to be more effective for highly targeted categories, such as autos, pet care, and baby and pharmaceutical products. In general, you also want to select sites with more focused content as opposed to those with more general content aimed at a diverse audience. Many other studies support the ability of contextual placements to boost online display ad results through the power of relevancy.

4. Behavioral Targeting Is a Must

Context provides one form of relevancy, but behavioral targeting offers another. With behavioral targeting, made possible by cookie technology, online ads are served up to Internet users based on their past surfing and searching behavior. A consumer who has visited multiple travel-related sites in the past month, for example, might be served ads from advertisers that promote vacation packages. Importantly, these behavior-based ads can be displayed even when the consumer is accessing web content unrelated to travel. Conceptually, this means that advertisers are buying audiences, not web pages or impressions.

Behavioral targeting is good for the advertiser, because it makes for a more efficient media buy. It's also good for the publishers involved, because they can sell advertising space that might have gone unsold. And finally, it is potentially good even for consumers, because they are more likely to see ads that are relevant to their interests.

Poor use of targeting has been identified as a culprit in many a failed ad campaign. Too often, even on the Internet, we see ads for products and services that will *never* be appropriate for us. Because behavioral targeting has the potential to efficiently get the "right" ads in front of presumed interested parties, much like search ads, marketers are taking a greater interest in the tactic. Forrester Research currently estimates that nearly one-quarter (24 percent) of online campaigns rely on some form of behavioral targeting data. In addition, Datran Media surveyed marketers and found that 65 percent either already used or planned to use behavioral targeting in the future.

Another related strategy is to retarget Internet users with multiple exposures. Consumers are more likely to click on ads that they have already seen, but most end up seeing a campaign only once.

On the other hand, a couple of serious issues are associated with behavioral targeting that could limit its usage in the future. Both issues relate to cookie technology, which allows marketers to track web behavior of consumers, potentially invading their privacy.

- Between 30 and 50 percent of Internet users regularly delete their cookies, rendering behavioral targeting virtually useless for these consumers.
- Mounting privacy concerns are drawing the attention of politicians and various consumer privacy groups, which could end up derailing the use of behavioral targeting, or at least seriously limiting its impact.

5. Integrate Search and Display for Maximum Synergy

The combination of display ads with search creates a powerful, one-two punch for marketers. In a November 2010 iProspect study, it was found that online display advertising is effective at producing lifts in brand metrics, but it makes its strongest contribution when used in conjunction with search engine results (including paid and organic). (See Figure 5.8.)

Combining display and search can also boost online purchasing behavior. In several studies, comScore evaluated the combined influences of search and display ads on consumer online buying behavior. Search, given its obvious indication of purchase intent (that is, those who take the time to search for a product are usually in-market), has a stronger influence on consumer buying behavior than display ads alone. But when both search and display ads are combined, the overall impact is significantly greater than that of either search or display ads individually.

For example, whereas display ads alone provided a 42 percent lift (test versus control) on the percentage of consumers making a retail purchase online, and search generated a 121 percent lift, the combination of search and display ads together produced a 173 percent lift. Furthermore, the one-two punch of search and display resulted in significantly higher dollar spending per thousand consumers exposed.

Similarly, the search/display ad combination works on offline sales as well. The comScore study found that by using search and display ads in tandem, marketers can significantly boost the dollar value of their offline retail sales versus using either search or display only (Figure 5.9).

The challenge for marketers is to fully integrate the display and search functions. This entails making sure that your in-house or outsourced search experts understand the basics of buying display; it also means having your media buying professionals know the basics of search. You need to manage the free flow of dollars between the two to achieve maximum impact and efficiency.

Figure 5.8
Pulling the right digital levers to boost unaided brand recall

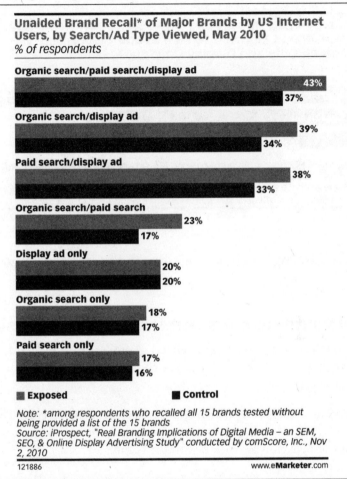

Unaided Brand Recall* of Major Brands by US Internet Users, by Search/Ad Type Viewed, May 2010
% of respondents

Organic search/paid search/display ad
- Exposed: 43%
- Control: 37%

Organic search/display ad
- Exposed: 39%
- Control: 34%

Paid search/display ad
- Exposed: 38%
- Control: 33%

Organic search/paid search
- Exposed: 23%
- Control: 17%

Display ad only
- Exposed: 20%
- Control: 20%

Organic search only
- Exposed: 18%
- Control: 17%

Paid search only
- Exposed: 17%
- Control: 16%

■ Exposed   ■ Control

Note: *among respondents who recalled all 15 brands tested without being provided a list of the 15 brands
Source: iProspect, "Real Branding Implications of Digital Media – an SEM, SEO, & Online Display Advertising Study" conducted by comScore, Inc., Nov 2, 2010

121886   www.eMarketer.com

6. Use Display Ads to Drive Consumers to Your Magnetic Content

This can be a great use of display ads—as promotional hooks to redirect consumers to your Magnetic Content. Rather than trying to impart your entire brand message within the confines of a small banner ad, why not use this limited real estate to lure consumers into engaging with your Magnetic Content? Display ads can be used to entice consumers to do simple activities like check out a video you've placed on YouTube, participate in a contest

Figure 5.9

Incremental impact of online ads on offline sales

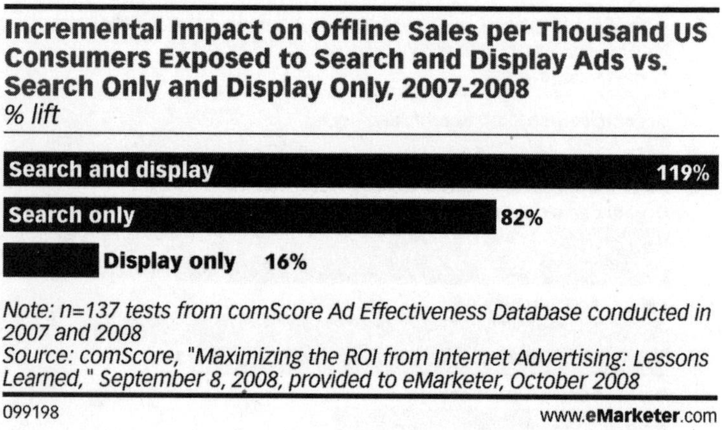

Incremental Impact on Offline Sales per Thousand US Consumers Exposed to Search and Display Ads vs. Search Only and Display Only, 2007-2008
% lift

Search and display	**119%**
Search only	**82%**
Display only	**16%**

Note: n=137 tests from comScore Ad Effectiveness Database conducted in 2007 and 2008
Source: comScore, "Maximizing the ROI from Internet Advertising: Lessons Learned," September 8, 2008, provided to eMarketer, October 2008

099198   www.**eMarketer**.com

---

you've set up on your Facebook page, or sign up for weekly promotions you announce via Twitter.

Performance Measurement for Display Advertising

Anyone attempting to quantify the effects of online branding efforts needs to separate out the two basic measurement components of a successful branding campaign:

- How successfully and efficiently did I *reach* my intended target consumer?
- Did my advertising campaign *influence* the consumer's attitudes, perceptions or behaviors associated with the brand?

The first question is all about the currency that is bought and sold in media-buying circles; the second question gets at the issue of ad effectiveness. These are two different metrics, and they must be measured separately. You can create an advertising message or campaign that strongly engages a very small group of people but fails to achieve the reach necessary to drive mass sales. Alternatively you can reach millions with your media plan, but if your ad creative is lackluster or your message not relevant, it will similarly fail to move the dial on your business.

Before you launch display advertising, take the time to nail down your objectives and make sure you take into account the difference between *reaching* your intended audience and *influencing* them.

The Display Ad Measurement Challenge

Online banner ads have gotten a bad rap in marketing circles, and much of the fault lies with poor measurement. Specifically, the ubiquitous click-through rate (CTR), which has become the default standard for measuring the effectiveness of online advertisements, has been both misused and overused. Today, large sums of money are exchanged between advertisers and publishers based on the CTR for an ad unit. Conceptually, it represents the number of consumers who clicked on a specific ad unit after being exposed to it. By far, click-through rate is the most commonly used metric among digital marketers.

But how accurate can CTR be when used in branding campaigns? When digital campaign solutions provider MediaMind analyzed more than 100 million conversions through thousands of online campaigns worldwide, the results found that only 20.4 percent resulted from clicks, whereas 79.6 percent were the result of viewing the banner without clicking.

Because marketers have relentlessly and exclusively focused on clicks, they have been ignoring most of the potential value of their display ad campaigns. This is particularly true for branding marketers. The click-through rate will not tell you whether your ads created awareness in the mind of the consumer, or if it served as a reminder to buy the product at a later time. Clicks also can't measure whether the ad created a more favorable impression of the brand or reinforced customer loyalty. These subtle, longer-term attitudinal shifts—so important to the life of a brand—simply do not occur in the instant of a click.

For display, the click-through rate works better as a direct response metric, because it measures immediate response to an offer or promotion. For brand marketers, we advocate that while the CTR can also be used as one metric—from among a group of metrics—to measure branding campaigns, it should not be used exclusively. To do so, is to set your self up for failure. The CTR should always be combined with other metrics such as those that can capture ad or product awareness, consumer attitudes, purchase intent, social media participation levels, and so on.

Once you've gotten over any remaining obsession with clicks, the next step is to rethink and create a more useful framework for identifying, managing, and organizing display ad metrics. The measurement framework and the seven metrics from Chapter 2 once again provide a quick way to select the right performance measurement for display ads that tell the entire story.

Starting with the three categories we outlined, you will select metrics for the following:

1. *Exposure*—metrics that measure immediate impact of a campaign (such as click-through rate).

2. *Strategic*—metrics that capture strategic marketing objectives of customer and brand growth.

3. *Financial*—metrics that quantify the return on investment for display ad spending.

For measuring display ads, we recommend using the following five metrics.

Exposure Metrics for Display Ads

There are several metrics for display ads, and you are probably familiar with most. Following are the best.

1. Qualified Reach   A typical goal for display ads is to reach a large number of people and make them aware of and interested in your brand, product, or service. Our definition of Qualified Reach from Chapter 2, as applied to display advertising, is *the number of visitors who may have actually seen an advertisement and have either immediately clicked on it, or later choose to have some other form of further engagement with your brand's content such as on a website or video.* This metric offers quantity (number of individuals who have seen the ad) and quality (they have performed a desired interaction, which in turn suggests a degree of intention on the part of the consumer).

2. Click-Through Rates—Use Judiciously!   The CTR is easily measurable by web analytics software and also provides quick insights into who is clicking the ads, what they do when they visit your website, and ultimately, if they complete an End Action or convert. According to MediaMind, the average annual CTR reached a plateau of 0.09 percent in July 2010.

As we mentioned, the big problem when counting clicks for display ads is that brand advertising doesn't work this way. In traditional media campaigns, on television or with print ads, we don't expect consumers to view a single ad and go rushing off to the store to buy the product. We realize that it takes time—and frequency—for a message to sink its way in to a consumer's head and subtly, slowly change preferences. We sit back patiently and wait for the campaign to work its magic over time—weeks, months, or even years. Yet somehow we forget this logic with interactive campaigns. The knee-jerk reaction is to tabulate the number of clicks—simply because they're so easily measured. And given the various ways that banner ad clicks can be undercounted, wrongly counted, or fraudulently counted, it would seem foolhardy to rely on these statistics by themselves.

However, the CTR can provide a kind of crude measure for the general interest level in the ad message or branded content. *In summary, we do believe CTR remains a valid metric for display ads because it provides an important view into the consumer's potential interest level in learning more about the specific digital content encountered. However, it should not be used as an end objective, a common misuse of the CTR metric.*

Strategic Metrics for Display Ads

This is the second area of our measurement framework: the metrics that capture your campaign's strategic marketing objectives of customer and brand growth.

3. End Action Rate or Conversion Rate   Conversion rate with display ads refers to the number of people who click on the ad and then go on to download an application, sign up for an offer, or engage in some other desirable action after seeing a display ad. This metric applies *only* to those display ads where there is an end action, outcome, or direct response being sought from the ad unit or campaign. It does not apply to online ads that have a branding objective. If you are single-mindedly focused on branding goals, you can skip this metric and move to the next one.

On the other hand, if direct response is the goal, pay careful attention here. Conversion rate is an important metric, but it's tricky to calculate accurately. The challenge is how you attribute the click with the conversion event. For example, a consumer may click on one of your display ads and then visit your site but decide to take no action. A week later, however, that same consumer might come to your site by way of a search engine and then go on to make a purchase. If you adopt the commonly used "last click" method, your ad will receive no credit for the sale, while your search program garners full credit. Obviously, that's not a fair representation of the respective contributions, and you will be undervaluing your display advertising.

We will explore the proper approach to attribution models in Chapter 10. That is a must-read for anyone who wants to get the conversion attribution correct between display and search initiatives.

If you do not have the time, expertise, or resources required for attribution models, use the next best approach, which relies on tracking tags. First, make sure that each of your display ad partners has a unique measurement coding tag. This identification is passed to your site (or to a third-party partner) each time a visitor comes to your site after clicking an ad. This allows you to associate each ad placement with the subsequent activity.

Given the importance of the End Action, you should conduct the appropriate analytics to understand what strategies drive the highest conversion. For example:

- Are there certain ads and placements that drive the highest conversion?
- Does a specific time of day result in higher conversion rates?
- Which target segments and audiences provide the best conversion rate?
- Does positioning on a page affect conversion?

4. Brand Perception Lift   One of the desired outcomes for display ads is to get your brand top-of-mind with consumers and/or improve their perceptions of your brand. This represents the next Strategic metric for display ads—measuring the improvement in critical brand perceptions. Brand lift, as we have explained in other chapters, is calculated by determining the change in a brand perception before and after interacting with display ads, as compared with a controlled group that did not interact with display ads. For example, a control group might be a group within an ISP or market area not served by the ad platform used for the test.

The most commonly useful brand–lift metrics are:

- Brand awareness
- Brand attribute lift
- Brand favorability
- Purchase intent

It is important to serve the test and control surveys immediately after consumers in the test group are exposed to the ads. Many companies can provide the survey capabilities for test and control measurement of display ad campaigns. Some of the major players are Dynamic Logic, comScore, InsightExpress, and Nielsen.

Financial Metrics for Display Ads

Let's examine the third area of the measurement framework. These metrics quantify the efficiency and return on investment, or financial outcomes, of your spending on display. These apply whether you are conducting a branding campaign or creating one designed for direct response.

5. Efficiency Metrics of Cost per Click (CPC) or Cost per End Action   With display ads, the metric most often used is the cost per click (CPC), which measures what you pay for a click. It is literally the cost of getting one click to your end destination from any given ad source. However, cost per End Action or cost per conversion is a better efficiency metric. Getting clicks is not the end game of display ads. Realizing an end action/conversion resulting in revenue is the right goal. Your display ad efforts will generate a return for you only if the revenue associated with each conversion from these ads is greater than the cost.

Conclusion

Display ads can act as a powerful underlying force behind your digital marketing efforts. With the emergence of new demand-side platforms and targeting technologies, there is a mini-resurgence of display ads. It is now a great channel to target consumers, engage them, and deliver very targeted messages to them cost effectively—especially if you follow the recipe of Magnetic Content to create ads that are unique, entertain, and add value.

But it is critical that you establish a clear delineation between brand objectives/metrics and direct response objectives/metrics. Otherwise, there will always be a tendency to mash up the two, creating confusion and likely putting too much emphasis or attribution on the direct response component. Resist the temptation to measure everything with a click!

Your branding measurement efforts need to go beyond the click and encompass the more subtle, longer-term magnetizing effects that reflect the consumer's awareness, perception, and engagement with your brand. Don't overlook, too, the opportunity to use display ads as promotional signage to flag consumers down and direct them to your Magnetic Content.

CHAPTER 6

E-mail Marketing

"If you receive an email in eight of the next 12 months,
do you spend more than the person that didn't receive emails?
Analytics are key. People are kind of shortsighted in that area."
—*Jeanniey Mullen, CMO, Zinio*

E-mail marketing was the original social media, and today it may seem dowdy when compared with its flashier contemporaries. But the surge of activity on Facebook, Twitter, and other social sites has given e-mail an even more important role in the overall digital marketing mix. In this chapter, we will:

1. Address how to execute e-mail using best practices for segmentation and relevance.
2. Examine how to apply Magnetic Content for e-mail.
3. Discuss the right measurement tools to drive performance and improve conversions for your e-mail campaigns.

E-mail remains popular for a reason: it's inexpensive, and when well done, it works. Traditionally, e-mail is used to establish and then to cement a relationship, but the ability of e-mail to improve brand magnetism is often neglected in favor of a numbers game.

eMarketer forecasts U.S. e-mail ad spending at $240 million in 2011. According to a June 2010 research study by ExactTarget, e-mail is a leading way people *like* to find out about deals and discounts, with 62 percent of all e-mail users signing up for e-mail promotions from a brand's website. It's estimated that one-quarter of all e-mail flowing into the inbox is permission-based commercial messaging. The remainder is personal messages, transactional messages, and spam. As for audience, U.S. e-mail use will reach 194 million people in 2011. Penetration is nearly 100 percent, with 92 percent of all Internet users (65 percent of the total U.S. population) using e-mail, according to eMarketer.

As for perceived value by the marketer, U.S. chief marketing officers surveyed by service provider Epsilon ranked e-mail well above any other form of online marketing as the tactic they would cut last. E-mail and social topped the list of marketing tactics included in the 2010 plans of U.S. media planners surveyed by the Center for Media Research. Combining the two has proven to be a winning combination.

Despite its continuing popularity, all is not rosy. E-mail marketers face challenges. Cluttered inboxes and the increased use of mobile devices make segmentation and personalization of experience ever more important. Open rates are on the decline in part because of the growing habit of turning off e-mail images (Figure 6.1).

The rise in mobile and social media are having a transformative effect on e-mail. SMS texting is increasingly popular for personal communications. Another trend worth noting is that because of the unlimited storage capacity

Figure 6.1
E-mail open rates are dropping fast

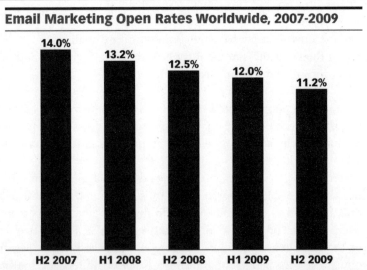

Source: MailerMailer LLC, "Email Marketing Metrics Report: Top Ten Words Used in Email Subject Lines," Jul 19, 2010

afforded by most Internet service providers (ISPs), people now look at e-mail as a personal archiving system.

In business communications, e-mail continues to dominate in part because of its perceived security. The e-mail address is becoming the universal identifier and the e-mail inbox is the storage cabinet. People will continue to use e-mail for business purposes because it remains the most secure means to communicate.

The Devil in the Details: Best Practices for E-mail

The constant challenge for marketers is to create e-mails that customers feel compelled to open. For both consumer and business-to-business (B2B) communications, the effects of e-mail can be supercharged—with social e-mail components, as well as with Magnetic Content. Where to start? As we've discussed, one of the five factors for Magnetic Content is how well your idea is executed (factor 3). E-mail is so easy that it's also easy to get sloppy. If your open rates are declining or you are launching a significant new initiative, check first to see that industry best practices are being used.

The List: Before anything else, the most critical measure for your campaign is sheer deliverability. If your e-mail doesn't make it past the filtering of either your recipient or of their Internet Service Provider (ISP), it has no chance of being opened, clicked, or acted upon.

Having accurate, opted-in addresses is a key to deliverability. This is why it's critical to maintain your lists and give your customers an easy way to unsubscribe to your e-mails. If you're not doing this already, set up a schedule (at least once a month) to remove from your e-mail database any names that bounce back as undeliverable. If too many names are undeliverable, an ISP may label you a spammer. It takes even fewer spam complaints to an ISP to put you on a "block" list. As an industry benchmark, you need less than 1 percent of your list complaining to their ISP to avoid cancellation.

Subject Line: These are the words first seen in the "inbox" and the first thing seen by the customer. Subject lines should be clear and compelling, and they should drive a desired action. Apply the criteria of Magnetic Content—this is your opportunity to be unique, or useful, or fun, or all of these.

(continued)

One of the fastest ways to get e-mail recipients to open and click on messages is to send notices of abandoned shopping carts within the subject line. As Sara Ezrin, senior director of strategic services at Experian CheetahMail, explained to eMarketer, recipients of such messages are already thinking about the items in their cart, and because they are, or were, in the market for those products, it will spur them toward quick response. Such messages are personal (unique to the user) and directly reference a product already considered as useful by the customer. (Figure 6.2.)

Put *benefits* into your subject line rather than overhyping a sales message. Don't be afraid to have some fun. Although subject lines should fall within the 35- to 45-character length, feel free to go shorter. Here are a few examples of successful subject lines:

Sports Authority—Take The "Fat" Out of Fat Tuesday - Check Out Our Fitness Deals

PETCO—PETCO Celebrates Mardi Gras With 72-Hours of Sitewide Savings!

Barnes & Noble—This Week—Coupons, Save up to 30% on Oscar Winning DVDs, J.D. Robb, More

Dell—Act Fast! Dell's 4-Hour Sale Starts Today

L.L. Bean—Top Values—Pima Shirts at 1992 Prices

Crutchfield—DIY value: Save with FREE installation gear & instructions

Ann Taylor—30% Off Pants (Your legs will thank you.)

Tiffany & Co.—New Designs from Frank Gehry

Neiman Marcus—The Rock Goddess from DIANE VON FURSTENBERG + Free online shipping

Saks Fifth Avenue—Runway Trends Are Here Now

Ralph Lauren—New Arrivals: Polo Club Makes The Ultimate Iconic Statement

JC Whitney—Drive Safe - Talk Hands-Free Plus $40 Off!

Just as you may use Google's AdWords tool to hone in on the right keywords for search optimization, you can research terms that are trending on Twitter and the search engines when crafting e-mail subject lines. There is a wide variety of applications online and on smart phones that can help you identify and graph out recent Twitter trends. Just do a search on the "applications" for Twitter trends and

Figure 6.2

Open rates by subject line content

Open Rate for US Email Marketing Campaigns, by Subject Line Content, Mar 2010

	1 day	3 days	7 days
Abandon cart	84%	95%	99%
Welcomes	76%	91%	97%
Offer	79%	92%	98%
Time-limited offer	79%	93%	98%
Free shipment	81%	93%	98%
Coupon	76%	91%	98%

Note: response based on 1, 3 and 7 days from when email was sent
Source: Experian CheetahMail, provided to eMarketer, Jun 21, 2010

117397   www.**eMarketer**.com

you will see a variety of them. It is fairly straightforward for you to select the right one based on three characteristics—simplicity/ease of use, real time, and visualization.

"From" Field: Be recognizable. It's best to use your company's name so the e-mail has credibility to the customer. This also helps you maintain your e-mail reputation as an online business.

Everyone in the e-mail marketing (and message security) ecosystem has a different view of what a good reputation actually means. You are less likely to need to worry about the context of your e-mails, and enjoy an 80 percent clearance rate, if you have:

1. *A good public reputation* (not on blocklists and have not upset any ISPs). You can get on a blocklist by mailing indiscriminately to names that have opted-in to receive e-mail from you or others. If recipients complain or e-mails bounce back as undeliverable, it can increase the likelihood an ISP will label you a spammer. Then even your good customers won't receive your e-mails.

2. *Good legislative adherence* (for example, CAN-SPAM compliance). The law prescribes what you can and cannot do as an e-mailer. Get familiar with the law, or you will get blacklisted by firms whose main purpose is to find e-mailers not in compliance.

(continued)

3. *Good infrastructure* (for example, DNS, MX records). You need to make sure there are valid MX records for all outbound e-mail servers. MX records identify IP addresses that accept inbound e-mail for a particular domain name. To get mail to, say, linux .com, a mail server picks an MX record and attempts to deliver the mail to that IP address. If the delivery fails because a server is out of action, the delivering server may work through the domain's MX records until it finds a server that can accept the mail. Without at least one MX record, mail cannot be delivered to a domain.

4. *Good identity* (for example, you have a correctly configured SenderID record). Make sure the contact information for your domain is valid and up to date.

5. *Best practices* (such as list scrubbing, opt-in). ISPs set up so-called honey-pot addresses designed specifically to catch spammers, in the same way direct-mail list vendors seed names to ensure a list is not being overused. They also keep track of servers they suspect of sending spam and will block these, so it matters which e-mail provider you choose. If you get names from a new source, test those names first in a separate mailing to ensure they are deliverable.

Add to Address Book: Once your e-mail gets opened, ask—right at the top—for recipients to put your "from" address in their safe senders list/address book. This is your best protection against ISP e-mail filters and helps make the use of this channel more efficient for you.

If too many of your e-mails bounce or get flagged as spam by the recipient, the ISP may put you on their blacklist. This means those messages will never make it to their intended recipients' mailboxes. Getting off the blacklist involves negotiating with each individual ISP. It is not fun. If you are a high-volume e-mail marketer, this is a good reason to use a high-volume e-mail provider who is on top of the latest rules regarding deliverability.

Dear First Name: You know your corporate culture. If it makes sense to include first name personalization in your e-mails, do it! If the e-mail address came from a social media site, such as Facebook or LinkedIn, the name you use should reflect the formality/informality the customer is using on that site. Check a few e-mails periodically to see if the level of formality you're using is off-putting or right on target.

How personal can you get? Marketing Sherpa tracked significantly higher open rates for e-mails that include an additional level of personalization:

- If both the subject line and message are personalized: 28.0 percent
- If only the subject line is personalized: 24.3 percent
- If only the message is personalized: 22.2 percent

Body Message: Keep it focused and concise and *always* include a clear call to action.

Kraft North America, for example, has attracted more than 4 million subscribers to its weekly e-mail program (available in English and Spanish). Yes, it's all about food, but e-mails aren't coupon-driven, explains Kelley Woodland, senior director of consumer relationship marketing. They contain thought-starting solutions and are informational. "One of the things that we're finding is that consumers need help in managing their pantry," Woodland told eMarketer. "We might share the items they can stock that are extremely versatile and are considered staples. One item might have 10 uses."

Fun is a key ingredient in the recipe for many of Kraft's e-mails. During football season, for instance, mailings carry a lot of football game–watching recipes. Other seasonal themes include holidays and back-to-school. According to Woodland, it's up to the individual brand managers if they want to include a coupon offer. Kraft e-mailings are also targeted: as part of the registration, all enrollees complete a questionnaire indicating their interests and preferences. This information determines which products the customer is most likely to engage with.

Another program, Kraft First Taste, gives enrollees a chance to try new products before anyone else does. Participants receive coupons they can share with friends and family by e-mail, extending the reach for new product introductions.

Forward to a Friend, Join us on Twitter, Join us on Facebook: These social-sharing prompts can improve exposure for your message and help build your database.

(*continued*)

Footer Components: These are especially critical for business e-mails and are recommended for consumer marketing as well. Currently, CAN-SPAM legislation requires that all e-mails contain an accurate physical address. The footer is a good place to put this. Other appropriate footer elements are:

- "How was I added?" link (to remind subscribers when and where they opted in to your database)
- "Date added" reminder
- "Update your profile" (a link to your survey page)
- E-mail address the message was sent to
- Privacy policy link
- Customer service phone number/e-mail address, when relevant
- Feedback link (but *only* if you have resources to manage feedback)
- Copyright information
- Unsubscribe link

If you want to learn more, the E-mail Experience Council (www.e-mailexperience.org) has a treasure trove of examples and concrete pointers.

Common E-mail Marketing Missteps

1. *Sending out sloppy copy.*
   Run your text through spell check. Click on all the links to make sure they do in fact go where you want them to. Also make sure the URLs won't be changing. If there are phone numbers in the copy, dial them first.
2. *Inadvertently spamming.*
   One of the best reasons to work with an e-mail service provider is to protect yourself from violating the federal CAN-SPAM Act. More than one e-mail newbie has loaded e-mail addresses into the To: field, thereby exposing names to the entire customer base and creating an instant CAN-SPAM violation.
3. *Crossing gender lines.*
   If your message is gender-specific, make sure your list is segmented by gender.

4. *Being invisible.*
   Every e-mail client by default does not display images. If your e-mail is one big image, it won't be seen.
5. *Being irrelevant—or worse yet, boring.*

That said, if you *do* make a mistake, be prepared to apologize. According to the e-mail experience council, apology e-mails have higher open rates than even welcome e-mails!

Creating Magnetic Content for E-mail Marketing

The reasons why people do or don't open their e-mail are hardly a mystery. It is a lot easier to engage a potential customer who has already expressed an interest in getting communications from you. The more customers are engaged with your web activities, the higher your open rates can be. Following are nine different approaches for incorporating more Magnetic Content in your e-mails.

1. Motivate People to Give You Their Name, Permission, and Preferences

E-mail marketing begins with a name in the form of an e-mail address. Lists can be rented, but the best results always come from people who choose to do business with you. Best practice is for the customer to "opt in" to receiving your e-mail and for you to verify that choice with a validation e-mail before sending anything. Offer opportunities to "opt in" from every page of your website. The best way to motivate someone to give you an e-mail address is by promising something of value. U.S. Internet users surveyed by e-mail provider ExactTarget said they give an address mainly for the promise of discounts and freebies, yet other motivations can't be ignored (Figure 6.3).

For the recipient, e-mails are free. But would you be able to charge money for the information you're sending out? If so, you're well on your way to creating e-mails with magnetic appeal.

2. Welcome New Customers with Open Arms

When someone gives you their e-mail address, they've expressed an interest in starting a relationship. A quick welcome message from you helps cement this relationship while it's still in the honeymoon phase. This is also the perfect time to qualify, or requalify, an e-mail prospect, by prompting an additional action.

Figure 6.3
Reasons for opting in to e-mail lists

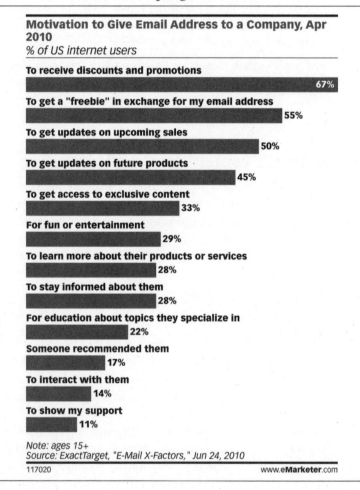

Motivation to Give Email Address to a Company, Apr 2010
% of US internet users

To receive discounts and promotions
67%

To get a "freebie" in exchange for my email address
55%

To get updates on upcoming sales
50%

To get updates on future products
45%

To get access to exclusive content
33%

For fun or entertainment
29%

To learn more about their products or services
28%

To stay informed about them
28%

For education about topics they specialize in
22%

Someone recommended them
17%

To interact with them
14%

To show my support
11%

Note: ages 15+
Source: ExactTarget, "E-Mail X-Factors," Jun 24, 2010

117020   www.**eMarketer**.com

The conversion desired doesn't have to be a sale at this point, but it should advance the prospect by deepening their level of engagement. This is not hard! A welcome message should offer links back into your website and specifically:

- Thank a subscriber for signing up.
- Briefly explain the benefits of the e-mail relationship.
- Include a call to action.
- Offer an incentive for the recipient to take an additional, desired action, such as redeeming a store coupon, visiting the website to take

a survey, encouraging friends or colleagues to join, or downloading something of value.

3. Have a Personality

Despite its ubiquity, e-mail remains a personal form of communication. Giving your brand a distinctive voice and personality can pay off in spades. One example is the success story of journalist-turned-entrepreneur Dana Levy, who used e-mail with a distinct personality to grow her business, Daily Candy.

When Levy started Daily Candy in 1999, her business model was simple: every morning, feed subscribers a list of hip sample sales and boutique and restaurant openings in the New York area. In an interview with *Inc.* magazine, Levy described the concept as "something that would weed through all the schlock . . . short, entertaining, intelligent, and had service at its core."

In a move that was unusual for the era, Levy decided to make the e-mail look like nice stationery. Knowing that the Forward button is a built-in marketing tool, Levy sent e-mails to all her journalists and nonjournalist friends asking them to forward it to their friends with the promise of being first in the know. Before launch, she had 700 subscribers. (See Figure 6.4.)

Figure 6.4
A Daily Candy e-mail

Media mogul Bob Pittman bought the newsletter in 2003 for $3.5 million and earned a 36× return on his investment by selling it for $125 million to Comcast in 2008. Daily Candy now has a national footprint in every major metropolitan area. And it continues to grow. In August 2010, Daily Candy launched an app for the New York market sending mobile editorial content alerts to Android users whenever they are geo-located near a designer sale, spa deal, or underground concert it recommends. Throughout, the e-mails retain their femininity, combining a sense of breathless excitement in the text with playful, high-style graphics that are consistent across the brand.

4. Be Timely

When Silverpop surveyed business-to-consumer (B2C) and B2B marketers, more than half said identifying the right time to send the message ranked as the most important tactic for overall campaign performance. What time is the best time? The best way to find out is to A/B test various date-and-time scenarios. Examine your open rates by day of the week or "daypart" as well. Another useful gauge is to look at your website traffic by existing customers, by day or daypart, to see when they are most primed to spend. For example, one small retailer catering to women found that Friday evening was the most active sales period online, so began sending promotional e-mails on Thursday evenings or by Friday morning.

Remember that your customers are operating on their time, not yours.

5. Be Relevant

All people are not alike. The most common and costly mistake an e-mail marketer can make is to blast all the names on its list with the same generic offer. A new customer is not the same as one who has been a customer for two years. Depending on your product or service, men and women should not receive the same mailing. Someone who has already purchased the product you are featuring in an e-mail is likely to be turned off to receive an offer for the very same item.

Marketers such as Amazon.com use previous purchase behavior to send e-mail alerts for new products—say, books by the same author, line extensions of a clothing or fashion accessory, or promotions on products related to something you've already purchased. And even Amazon gets it wrong sometimes—we've seen a one-time purchase of a nursery item (for a gift) translate into four straight months of e-mails pushing baby-related products.

More than any other factor, *relevance* will most influence the open rate and action taken on your e-mail marketing message. The rules applying to traditional direct marketing and CRM all apply to e-mail marketing as well: *Don't send people e-mails they don't want to receive.* Best practices companies send relevant e-mails based on a consumer's behavior. Often referred to as trigger e-mails, these e-mails typically have open and click rates two or three times the usual e-mails.

Coupons especially can be a very relevant driver of e-mail response. There are strategies to pursue to increase the impact of a coupon in e-mail while maintaining price controls. Instead of offering coupons to everyone, apply selectively to drive reengagement where you see the most need.

For example, coupons can drive a "discount ladder" where you present the most aggressive offer to those who have been least responsive or have longer inactivity.

- Higher markdowns to those least likely to respond
- Lower markdowns to those most likely to respond
- Reduce markdown even more for those likely to spend anyway

How do you make sure your e-mails are relevant? Segmentation and continued attention to customer behavior and profiles is the key.

6. Control and Manage Frequency

The more successful your e-mail marketing, the more leads, customers, and prospects you will attract. These contacts deserve consistent, valuable communication from you. Consistent communication is the foundation to any relationship. But don't overdo it. Sending too many messages is as lethal as sending irrelevant ones.

Among the types of information you can send to customers on a regular basis are:

- News of upcoming events, such as sales, seminars, and sponsored promotional events
- Weekly tips and tricks for your industry or product
- News of requested products or preferred products
- Weekly or monthly newsletters
- Daily digests of industry news or updates relating to a consumer niche

If you say you're going to deliver something on a specific schedule, stick to it so your customers come to anticipate your e-mails. For higher frequencies, be sure the customer had opted-in to receive multiple e-mails per week before you deluge them with offers or newsletters.

7. Make It a Multimedia Effort

The ubiquity of e-mail marketing has taken away some of the personal connection. People know it's easy to send and it can feel machine-like. Adding multimedia elements to your e-mail gives your customers a feeling they're worth spending time on. Customers are coming to appreciate embedded video clips, interactive polls, and the like.

An important design note: Watch your imaging! If your entire e-mail is made up of one large image, you're much less likely to reach recipients who have image-blocking turned on. Aim to separate text from images so your offer and call to action are visible even if the images are not displayed.

8. Make Sure It's Mobile-Friendly

The proliferation of mobile devices means your e-mail is likely to be read on a smaller screen. Optimize your e-mails so that they can be read on a handheld or portable device such as a tablet. If you are a retail marketer, put yourself in the mind-set of a consumer who is on the go when you create your messaging and offer. Cradled in the hand, receiving a mobile e-mail can be a richer, more engaging experience. Yet compared to mobile text messaging, it is actually less expensive for both the sender and the recipient because it doesn't fall into the SMS text fee system, which can cost 3 to 15 cents per message on both ends.

Mobile e-mails demand clarity of message. There are also size limitations. A good rule of thumb is to keep the weight of your e-mail below 20 kb for mobile.

Remember that each device will display your e-mail differently. Find out what mobile devices your customers are using and design templates optimized for these devices. Tools such as Unica's NetInsight web analytics and Pivotal Veracity Mailbox IQ can provide marketers with this level of insight.

Apple's iPhone and operating systems like Google's Android give e-mail marketers new opportunities to reach consumers on the go in compelling ways. Even if you're a smaller organization, have a variety of handheld devices or mobile phones available to you so that you can periodically check to see how your design specs look on different screens.

Take this responsibility personally; don't expect your information technology (IT) team or e-mail agency to tell you it's time to tweak e-mail specs. Stay updated to new device trends, which are moving faster and faster. This is really the only way to keep up with your customers today. Currently, about 30 percent of all U.S. mobile users regularly access e-mail on their handheld devices, whereas almost 90 percent of those with smart phones do so.

A study by ExactTarget found that 52 percent of mobile owners use the same e-mail account across devices. Sometimes they may see your e-mail from a desktop or laptop. At other times, it may be opened on a smart phone. So it's important to ask directly about mobile e-mail preferences and provide an easy way to change this preference. Knowing where your customers are reading e-mail can drive more relevant messaging based on whether the recipient is deskbound or on the go.

9. Make the Creative Compelling and Clear

Don't make your customer guess what they're supposed to do. Use buttons in the e-mail's design to make it easy to take action quickly, to make a purchase, or to forward your message.

Strategies for Maximizing E-mail with Social Media

Obtaining an e-mail address through social media outreach can be the beginning of a beautiful relationship with your prospect (and their connected peers) if you keep firmly in mind that the medium must continue to be social to succeed. Although we tend to see e-mail as a one-to-one communications vehicle, try to view it anew, through the social media lens. Anticipate your messages to be viewed by not just the recipient but by others in their shared networks and continually extend the invitation to share on diverse platforms.

Consumers are spending more time in social networks, but they are not abandoning e-mail. In fact, there's a natural link between the two in the consumer's mind. An e-mail address is required to register for a social network, and social updates are frequently announced via e-mail.

1. Link E-mail and Social Media Messaging to Multiply the Sharing Opportunities   Place calls to action in your e-mail messages allowing people to sign up for your Facebook page or become a Twitter follower. Create prominent ways to share the e-mail message with friends. Analyze who comes to your company via a forwarded e-mail, who comes via social media, and where overlaps occur. Market to each of these segments accordingly, but keep your imaging consistent.

Men's clothier Perry Ellis demonstrates a good example of a marketer that extends the look and feel of its web brand onto its Facebook brand page. What looks like a web page (Figure 6.5) is actually an e-mail that shares visuals with the current campaign.

2. Encourage Your Best Customer Brand Advocates to Share with Friends through Social Media
- Identify your best e-mail marketing customers.
- Target them with incentives or discounts to encourage new-customer referrals or brand advocacy.
- Offer multiple ways to interact with your company, handing control to the consumer. Phone numbers and website links should always be there, along with the tools or buttons to forward, comment on, or unsubscribe to the e-mail. Your customer may prefer ordering online, their grandmother may prefer telephone ordering, and their business colleague might prefer to go to a brick-and-mortar store.
- Use e-mail to communicate your message, but encourage two-way communication and listening through a social environment.

3. Evaluate Your E-mail Communications for Their Hard-Sell versus Engagement Appeal   People use social media platforms to engage in conversation

Figure 6.5
**Look and feel should be consistent between
social media and e-mail outreach**

and generally resist a hard sell. A direct sale conversion should not be your immediate goal with e-mail subscribers who have opted in through a social media platform. Keep the content of these e-mails brand-focused, but keep it light. Offer shareable opportunities and take better advantage of social media's potential for brand building. E-mail by its nature is more direct response— and conversion-oriented, but the conversions you seek from e-mail lists built off social networks might first be those that either qualify the prospect, supply more profile information about the prospect, or encourage a deeper level of engagement with the brand.

Social Media and E-mail Tactics for B2B and Small Business   Permission-based e-mail marketing has been used very effectively by small-business owners. For example, Nick Unsworth, based in Hartford, Connecticut, built a six-figure social media consulting practice in 12 months using e-mail as a primary communications vehicle to promote a series of webinars and videos on his blog.

His e-mail list has grown to 5,000+, and he sends weekly e-mails that are a combination of tips and personality. Unsworth has determined that it's the value of the message, not flashy style, that engages his audience. Some of his tips for using e-mail and social media together follow:

- Identify the "What's in it for me" (the benefit) and get it in the subject line. "How are you, Nick?" "You're invited to attend [event name goes here]."
- Don't be a perfectionist. Get your ideas out, measure and then modify based on how many people took action.
- Did you send them to your blog? If so, did your traffic increase?
- Did you invite them to a webinar? If so, how many people registered?
- Did you pitch a product? If so, how many sales resulted?

Unsworth keeps his e-mails short and sweet, a maximum of 250 words. As for content, he follows the unofficial social rules of 90 percent give and 10 percent ask. His messages clearly make a call to action and tell people what to do, even if it's a click to a link to get more information.

Other techniques are also in play here. Be engaging. Ask questions. Ask for input. When people respond to e-mails, it's another indicator you did a good job. Share something new that's happening in your business and your life. Unsworth always links to his social networking presence on Facebook, LinkedIn, and Twitter. He also *asks* for referrals.

Unsworth runs and manages the entire operation using Infusionsoft .com, which handles his e-mail marketing, shopping cart, affiliate program, accounting, and contact management for a mere $200 per month. He estimates it automates about $30,000 worth of work that would otherwise require an assistant. (GetResponse.com is another package he recommends, which allows free mailing up to 500 addresses and $18 per month for up to 2,000.)

Unsworth keeps his eye on key conversions and results. How does your e-mail operation measure success?

Driving Impact through Performance Measurement

How do marketers measure the success of their e-mail programs? Click-through and open rates are still the leading ways e-mail marketers are measuring success, according to Forrester Research, although other metrics are also considered (Figure 6.6).

Figure 6.6
How do marketers measure e-mail success?

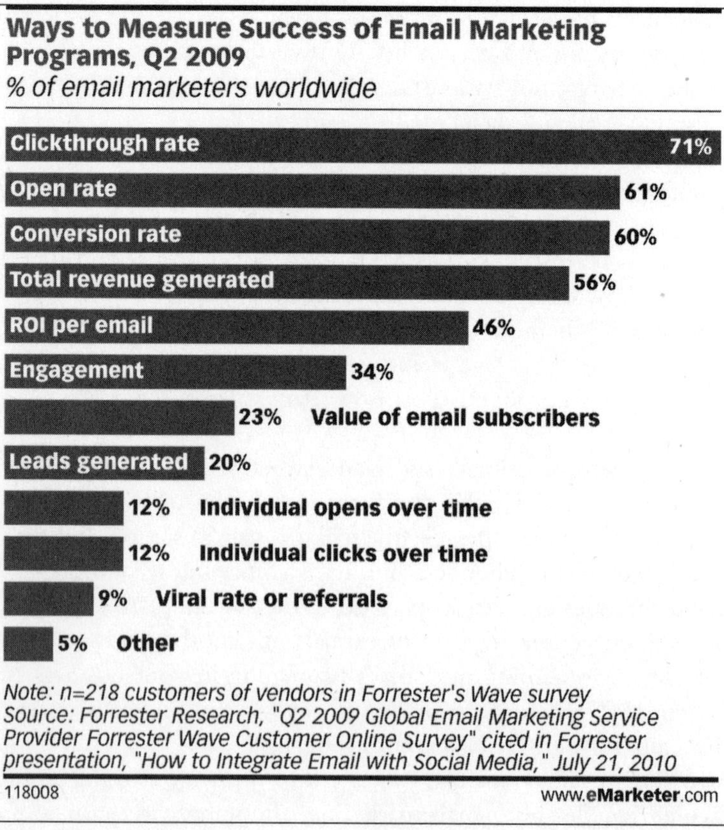

Ways to Measure Success of Email Marketing Programs, Q2 2009
% of email marketers worldwide

Clickthrough rate 71%
Open rate 61%
Conversion rate 60%
Total revenue generated 56%
ROI per email 46%
Engagement 34%
23% Value of email subscribers
Leads generated 20%
12% Individual opens over time
12% Individual clicks over time
9% Viral rate or referrals
5% Other

Note: n=218 customers of vendors in Forrester's Wave survey
Source: Forrester Research, "Q2 2009 Global Email Marketing Service Provider Forrester Wave Customer Online Survey" cited in Forrester presentation, "How to Integrate Email with Social Media," July 21, 2010
118008 www.eMarketer.com

Let's build out the Performance Measurement framework described in Chapter 2 for e-mail. You'll need to select metrics from each part of the framework to have the right balance of short- and long-term metrics.

For measuring e-mail, we recommend using the following five metrics. Let's delve into these a bit now.

Exposure Metrics for E-mail

While somewhat similar to other channels, the exposure metrics for e-mail are often easier to measure; most marketers are familiar with such statistics.

1. Qualified Reach This primary metric for e-mail is defined as *the number of consumers who may have received an e-mail and opened it.* A key aspect of understanding this metric is looking at how many people had bounce backs where the e-mail could not be delivered. As stated earlier, having proper e-mail addresses is critical; undeliverable e-mails will affect this metric significantly. A second factor affecting Qualified Reach is the open rate, one of the most commonly used metrics for evaluating e-mails.

2. Open Rates Relevance and a compelling subject line are the two factors that have the greatest effect on your open rate. An e-mail open rate is a comparative measure of how many people on an e-mail list open (or view) a particular e-mail campaign. The open rate is normally expressed as a percentage:

$$\text{Open rate} = \frac{\text{E-mails Opened}}{\text{E-mails Sent} - \text{E-mails bounced}}$$

. . . So a 30 percent open rate would mean that of every 10 e-mails delivered to the inbox, 3 were actually opened.

It's tempting to use e-mail "open rates" as a benchmark for success, but be careful. Benchmark figures for industries may be based on many different types of audiences and different offers. A financial e-mail open rate might combine results from banks, stockbrokers, small consultancies, corporations, and advisers. The types of e-mails they send may range from hourly stock alerts to monthly newsletters. These do not make for apples-to-apples comparisons and may have absolutely nothing to do with your business.

A recent study provided by Campaign Monitor looked at activity sectors and found that open rates tend to be highest (40 percent) among subscribers who have opted in to noncommercial lists, for example, those who subscribe to e-mails as part of their affinity to a religious group or to keep updated on

Figure 6.7
Some industry benchmarks for open rates

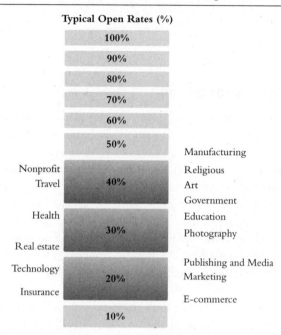

Figure 6.7
Some industry benchmarks for open rates

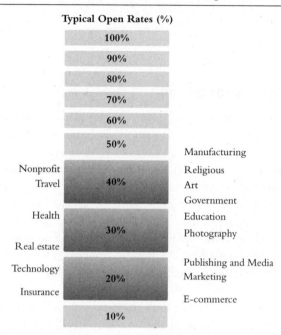

their local government (Figure 6.7). The same figure is expected for e-mails from travel or nonprofit entitles, which are again likely to be more informational than sales-oriented.

What open rate benchmarks do provide are trends. Shop for an open rate list that best matches your audience and type of e-mail marketing. Some rules of thumb:

- Larger e-mail lists tend to have lower open rates because they are inherently less segmented.
- Busy audiences tend to have lower open rates.
- Enthusiast audiences and niche topics tend to have higher open rates.

Each e-mail sent out typically contains a piece of code that when opened is downloaded to record the "open." But e-mail users have accumulated a battery of spam-protective techniques that may skew the recording of the code. For example, a text-only link or an e-mail viewed with the images turned off will not record this open. E-mail that is only read in "preview" panes will not be counted as an open either. That preview pane might be displaying your e-mail automatically (and therefore downloading the images) without the reader ever having to click on it or read it.

3. Click Rates—Getting Them to Click   Here again, relevance trumps all other factors in encouraging a customer to click once the e-mail has been opened, although timing is also a consideration.

According to MailerMailer, the vast majority of actions will take place in the first 72 hours after sending a message, including about 90 percent of opens. Experian CheetahMail reported in March 2010 that 92 percent of opens and 93 percent of clicks came within the first three days. A full 98 percent of these actions occurred within a week of sending the e-mail.

The more explicit your call to action is, the more likelihood it has of getting a click.

Strategic Metrics for E-Mail

Again, Strategic metrics are those that capture strategic marketing objectives related to customer and brand growth.

4. End Action Rate   End Actions typically associated with e-mail include redemption rates for couponing, or in some cases, the conversion goal may be passalongs of information or a link. The End Action rate for e-mail is often referred to as the conversion event because it represents the conversion or any desired final outcome for the e-mail program.

Given the importance of the End Action, you should conduct the appropriate analytics to understand what drives the highest conversion. Remember to test, test, test. Testing will help you identify the elements of the e-mail that drives the best response/conversion, for example, the subject line, day of week, time of day, creative format, content, and offer.

As we outlined in Chapter 2, test and control groups are the basic components of testing. The idea is to have similar groups within your target audience who receive an-e-mail versus those who do not and compare their open rates, click rates, and purchases to determine which group does better. When testing:

- Set up comparable test groups (match them on the right characteristics).
- Ensure a statistically significant sample size (use sample size calculators).
- Design the experiment with a clear understanding of different treatments.
- If testing for many factors, use advanced design (fractional, factorial, multivariate, etc.).

- Ensure there is enough variation across the different groups.
- Take baseline readings before and after the experiment.

Financial Metrics for E-mail

Financial metrics for e-mail are usually the easiest for a marketer to obtain and understand.

5. ROI for E-mail   Let's start with some givens. Research by Marketing Sherpa and ad:tech, among others, demonstrates that e-mails to house lists far outperform e-mails sent to third-party rented lists. Some 44 percent of marketers reported that house list e-mails had great ROI, and 16 percent said it was poor. However, only 12 percent of these marketers said third-party lists had great ROI, whereas 49 percent reported poor ROI for third-party lists.

Long-term analysis can be of great value, even if e-mail remains cheap. You should be able to track your e-mail metrics by using different types of e-mail streams and programs that allow you to allocate resources to the highest ROI and revenue-generating programs.

Segmentation Will Improve Your ROI   Effective e-mail marketers know everything about their contacts: name, gender, e-mail address, location, marital status, and occupation, as well as:

- Interests, particularly as they relate to your products and/or services
- When and what they last purchased
- Whether they open and click on e-mails
- Their behaviors (Have they visited your website?)

It's not strange to realize that some customers who opt in to an e-mail relationship with you may view this as similar to relationships they have with their other correspondents. In a survey of U.S. and U.K. e-mail recipients by e-Dialog's Center for Digital Marketing Excellence, a solid 64 percent *expected* mailers to know what types of products and services they liked. And 61 percent expected them to send preferred types of offers.

The more you know about your customer, the more you can build a magnetizing relationship. Use custom fields to pull database information or dynamic content that is unique to a specific subscriber (offers based on past purchases, birth dates, expiration dates, etc.).

Segmentation also allows you to predict or forecast future sales. There are several important behavioral indicators of future performance. Figure 6.8

Figure 6.8
Tools for segmenting

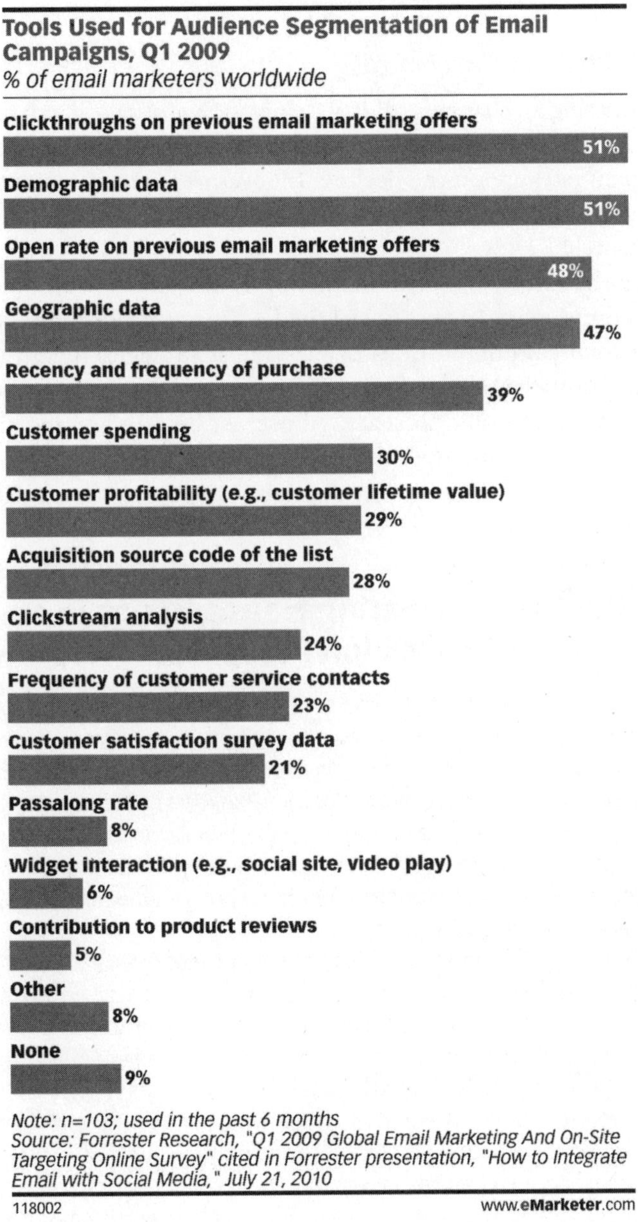

Tools Used for Audience Segmentation of Email Campaigns, Q1 2009
% of email marketers worldwide

Clickthroughs on previous email marketing offers
51%

Demographic data
51%

Open rate on previous email marketing offers
48%

Geographic data
47%

Recency and frequency of purchase
39%

Customer spending
30%

Customer profitability (e.g., customer lifetime value)
29%

Acquisition source code of the list
28%

Clickstream analysis
24%

Frequency of customer service contacts
23%

Customer satisfaction survey data
21%

Passalong rate
8%

Widget interaction (e.g., social site, video play)
6%

Contribution to product reviews
5%

Other
8%

None
9%

Note: n=103; used in the past 6 months
Source: Forrester Research, "Q1 2009 Global Email Marketing And On-Site Targeting Online Survey" cited in Forrester presentation, "How to Integrate Email with Social Media," July 21, 2010

118002   www.**eMarketer**.com

shows how e-mail marketers use past behavior to drive timely future segmented e-mail streams.

Conclusion

E-mail marketing is changing, but it is not going away. Stand-alone e-mail marketers face challenges with cluttered inboxes and increased use of mobile devices. Open rates are on the decline. Innovators will be those who improve their segmentation, make connections with social media, and pay attention to mobile e-mail trends.

We'd say the future of e-mail marketing is inseparable from the evolution of mobile communication and social media. It is critical to look at e-mail as part of the total communications plan. Align it strategically and in the look and feel of your social media efforts.

Make it easy for people to share. Above all, be relevant and timely. And continuously measure and optimize for open rates and click rates.

Publishers Clearing House Hones in on 10 Million Prospects

Publishers Clearing House (PCH) has an e-mail database of roughly 10 million people and uses it to deliver targeted offers. Some programs focus on converting new prospects and new visitors to first-time buyers, says Alex Betancur, vice president and general manager of the Publishers Clearing House Online Network. Other programs are targeted e-mail promotions based on purchase history in affinity categories such as coins, jewelry, horticulture, food items, and collectibles. It also has programs for offline buyers who have engaged with the company online but have yet to purchase.

Betancur primarily looks at click rates and engagement rates. In PCH business culture, engagement is not just order response. Entry rates into a contest or actions taken to engage with a program, lotto game, or quiz are considered valuable conversions toward developing engagement and figure into subsequent segmentation. With little hard sell at the outset, PCH e-mails have an open rate of 25 to 30 percent, which he attributes to the fact people have opted in to the programs and are looking for the sweepstakes entry opportunities and sweepstakes information.

"One important best practice is segmentation," Betancur says. "Make sure you understand your audience and that you're sending what your audience wants. We do a lot of creative variation and testing and we try to offer a compelling call to action. In our subject line, you see "another opportunity to win."

"In our e-mail programs we are looking at the full customer profile across our online and offline engagements to determine past purchase history, as well as products they may have looked at in the past to target product offerings to them," says Betancur. If PCH finds that a customer engages more with one type of content, like a lotto-type game instead of a standard contest promotion, it helps determine the upfront communication. On the back end, past purchase history may determine which products to feature. PCH also actively cleans its list faster than most, removing people if there is no action after a certain number of days, offering easy opt-out and authentication.

CHAPTER 7

Social Media: Connections That Count

"We spend the majority of our time engaging with people on these networks, not advertising on them."
— *Scott Monty, head of Social Media, Ford Motor Company, in an interview with eMarketer*

"If you do not listen carefully, you are a fool—not because the crowd is a threat (although, of course, it is) but because it is your greatest resource. What if its wisdom were harnessed and its power unleashed . . . ? Here's what: payday."
— *Bob Garfield, former ad critic, Advertising Age*

Facebook, Twitter, Ning, Stumble-Upon, Loopt, foursquare, Gowalla, and new social media sites popping up like dandelions every day—it's enough to make a marketer's head spin.

Ever since the early days of MySpace, before Facebook or Twitter came on the scene, social media has dazzled marketers with the allure of connecting brands with consumers on a deeper, more nuanced level. But while dreams of adoring brand evangelists, exploding viral pass-alongs, and Twitter-induced purchases dance in marketers' heads, the reality is that most brands don't have a firm grasp on their strategy for social media, nor do they have a clue about how to measure success in this channel.

In this chapter, we will seek to answer these three vital questions:

1. Why, as a marketer, should I care about social media?
2. What are the best ways to use Magnetic Content in social media to engage customers and prospects?

3. How can I measure my social media efforts and achieve a return on investment (ROI)?

In this chapter, we'll examine the key trends and special market dynamics of social media and describe how many marketers and small businesses are taking advantage of the channel today. We'll also reveal how to achieve marketing impact with social media, based on seven best practices for engagement, including adding value through specialized forms of Magnetic Content. And finally, we'll provide a framework for measuring social media and, ultimately, how to reach a quantifiable return on investment.

The Social Media Landscape

The web is not just about surfing, searching, and shopping anymore.

Online, consumers have gravitated to a new kind of digital hangout, one where they find themselves poking, friending, "liking," checking in, and tweeting—typically participating multiple times each day with online communities they find and often create themselves.

The consumer usage statistics for social media are eye opening. According to eMarketer, more than 140 million Americans visit social sites regularly; that represents a majority—more than 60 percent—of all Internet users (Figure 7.1). Social sites also account for a growing share of web pages consumed and time spent online—more than 25 percent of total time spent online, according to some sources. Based on findings from a global research study conducted by TNS in September 2010, the average time spent with social media in a given week, at 4.6 hours, beats all other activities online, including e-mail, at 4.4 hours.

The 60 percent overall penetration figure for social media usage doesn't even tell the whole story, because many key demographic groups are far more active in the social sphere. Whereas those at the polar extremes of age—namely older baby boomers, seniors 65 and older, and young children—are somewhat underrepresented on social networks, affluent households, online moms, teens, and young adults are significantly overrepresented. In fact, for those 25 and younger, social sites are a daily part of life, often sucking up more time than TV, homework, jobs, or, in some cases, sleep.

Facebook alone has already accumulated a stunning 600 million-plus users worldwide within just six years of its existence. If Facebook were a country, it would be the third largest in the world, after China and India. Moreover, some pundits predict Facebook's global population will top 1 billion by 2015, or earlier.

Figure 7.1
Social networks continue to grow

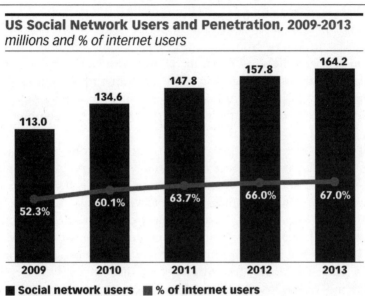

US Social Network Users and Penetration, 2009-2013
millions and % of internet users

■ Social network users   ■ % of internet users

Note: internet users who use social networks via any device at least once per month
Source: eMarketer, Feb 2011

124527   www.**eMarketer**.com

Marketers who want to reach online consumers today need to follow them (and friend them!) on social sites. Not surprisingly, it turns out they already are.

Your Competition Is There. Are You?

Just as with consumers, a majority of U.S. companies claim they are active in social media today. In fact, according to eMarketer, four out of five (80 percent) U.S. companies with 100 employees or more are using social media tools for marketing purposes. Among small businesses, the usage factor is closer to 40 percent, or at about half the rate of larger ones, according to four independent surveys conducted in 2010: the America Press Institute (40 percent), American Express (39 percent), Zoomerang (37 percent), and the University of Maryland (24 percent). The penetration for social media usage among business-to-business (B2B) marketers is lower, at 24 percent, according to Forrester Research.

Even the CEOs of big companies are getting social media religion. Brian Dunn, the chief executive officer of big box retailer Best Buy, involves himself personally on Facebook and Twitter and had this advice for marketers in a December 12, 2010, article in *Fortune,* "We're past the tipping point. You have to be where people are."

Marketer interest in social media shows no signs of waning. In survey after survey, marketers, from both large and small companies, claim that they plan to spend more on social marketing in the near future. Although the surveys aren't always clear as to what forms that marketing might take, between 40 and 80 percent of marketers and small businesses polled claim they are planning to boost their social spending in the coming months (Figure 7.2).

By this point in time, marketers have transitioned from cautious engagement to full deployment on social media platforms. It is no longer considered an add-on or afterthought. At PepsiCo Americas Beverages division, for example, social media is now an integral part of every brand's marketing efforts. Similarly, in 2011, carmaker GM will be moving social media marketing into every one of its brand groups. As summed up in a December 2010 eMarketer report, "Marketers that have spent the past few years ramping up their internal social media marketing infrastructure—and their presence on sites such as Facebook and Twitter—will take social media to new heights in 2011."

Figure 7.2
Changes in strategy and measurement priorities

Change* in Online Marketing/Measurement Priorities in 2010 According to US Companies
% of respondents

	More priority	Same priority	Less priority/ not applicable
Social media	73.5%	23.0%	3.5%
Web analytics	60.5%	36.5%	2.0%
User experience	59.5%	33.5%	7.0%
Rich media	49.5%	38.5%	12.0%
Personalization	42.7%	41.2%	16.1%
Mobile	41.6%	30.7%	27.7%
Content management	40.8%	46.7%	12.5%
Intranet	29.5%	39.0%	31.5%
Multivariate testing	24.6%	38.7%	36.7%

Note: numbers may not add up to 100% due to rounding; *vs. 2009
Source: ISITE Design, "2010 Web Strategy Report," January 30, 2010

Despite the widespread and deepening involvement, however, the actual dollars marketers spend on social media have been relatively small. In 2010, for most marketers, social media spending represented only a fraction of their total media expenditures. But social spending will be much bigger in 2011 and beyond. In aggregate, eMarketer sees social media ad spending in the United States growing from $2 billion in 2010 to $3.1 billion in 2011, accounting for 11 percent of total online ad spending. Worldwide, social media spending will top $4 billion. The spending action in B2B is slower. Social media spending by B2B companies was only $11 million in 2009—an experimental 1 percent of most budgets—but is expected to rise to a still low $54 million by 2014.*

Why isn't social media spending bigger, given all the hype? There are four reasons why marketers are still somewhat cautious when it comes to investing in social media, despite their obvious interest level and involvement.

First, marketers are concerned about their ads being placed adjacent to content that is not appropriate, or even potentially detrimental, for their brands. Second, research data strongly suggests that social network users, who primarily visit such sites to communicate and keep up with friends and family, tend to ignore advertisements in social environments. Third, when it comes to the measurement of social media programs, especially the determination of some kind of ROI, most marketers are left scratching their heads.

But the fourth and most important reason why social media dollars lag marketer interest is simply this: most companies realize that social media success is less about placing ads on third-party websites such as Facebook, MySpace, and CafeMom, and more about finding appropriate ways to listen in and join the conversations taking place all over the social web. Traditional advertising placements play second fiddle to more genuine, personal forms of consumer engagement. You've heard it before, and you'll hear it again: social media is less about *paying* for media and more about how you can *earn* and *own* it. This is why offering Magnetic Content is so important in this channel.

Does Your Firm Suffer from Social Schizophrenia? Marketers' attitudes toward social media can best be described as bipolar. On one hand, they intuitively grasp the importance of social media to drive business results. They are exhilarated by the seemingly unlimited potential to engage with consumers in ways they never could before. They also love the notion of "free

---

*Sources: Goldstein Group, Nov. 2009; Forrester Research, March 2010.

research" as they "listen in" on conversations, follow along with tweets, and read blog posts. On the other hand, the prospect of directly engaging with consumers in a Wild West–like environment, where there are no communication scripts or rules, is profoundly unnerving to marketers, who have yet to fully trust the channel. Although 68 percent of marketers in an Alterian survey rated social media as "critical" or "important" to their business, a separate study by AdMedia Partners found that an almost equal number (63 percent) believe that social media is "overrated." Both surveys were conducted in December 2009.

The fear factor with social media is palpable. Here's what's being said in the office corridors:

"Whoa! Did you see what they said about our brand on the blogs?"

"What if someone spoofs our TV commercial with a YouTube video and the whole thing goes viral?!"

"How should we respond to this Twitter stream that is spreading a false rumor about our employees?"

"What on earth will our CEO say when he hears about this?!"

These familiar emotional pain points notwithstanding, there is a lot in social media to commend itself to marketers.

What Makes Social Media So Attractive? (There are plenty of positive aspects to social media that any marketer would love to capitalize on—beyond the fact that the audience is vast and growing. Three big ones come to mind:

1. Peer-to-peer networks facilitate trust.
2. The possibility exists for messages to spread virally.
3. It can be dirt cheap.

Consumers are emotionally connected to brands through the carefully nurtured bonds of trust. High levels of trust signal a strong relationship; low levels warn of a poor or deteriorating relationship. This is particularly crucial in the digital age, where consumers can instantly verify the claims of a marketer through a Google search or discover unflattering aspects of a product on blogs or Twitter. Marketers who are not completely honest and forthright in their dealings with consumers will be found out and labeled accordingly.

But marketers also see exciting opportunities to boost their trust quotient through online engagements, particularly via social networks. Specifically, they are looking to piggyback on the inherent trust and influence consumers share with one another. After all, when it comes to making a decision about a product or service, consumers are far more likely to rely on the opinions and experiences of fellow consumers—as a source of trusted, unbiased information—than they are a marketer's advertising claims or marketing pitches. It is one thing if a brand of laundry detergent claims in its advertising that it gets clothes whiter. It is quite another thing if real consumers tell their friends and family about the brand's benefits.

A battery of surveys and studies document this fact.

As but one example among literally dozens, research company Nielsen Online conducted a massive global study in 2009 of more than 25,000 consumers in 50 countries (Figure 7.3). The consumers were asked to rate various media formats, including traditional and digital channels, in terms of their trust in the content as a source for decision making about products and brands. The results were conclusive: trumping every other media source by a huge margin was "recommendations from people known," with 90 percent of consumers placing their trust in these interactions.

Trust is important to marketers, but so is having their messages go viral. Marketers can get giddy thinking about how their ads or other forms of branded digital content, such as videos, mobile apps, or consumer endorsements, have the potential to spread virally over social networks. (Of course, the bad stuff can also go viral, too.)

Finally, companies appreciate the notion that social media can be an incredibly inexpensive way to connect with customers and prospects—since consumers often end up promulgating the marketers' messages free of charge. As we've seen, marketers are increasingly looking to "earn" social media, as opposed to buying it outright.

The Company Size Factor   Social media isn't just for the corporate giants. Companies of all sizes can enjoy the benefits of social media tools and platforms, such as blogs, Facebook, LinkedIn, and Twitter. While a handful of multinational brands such as Starbucks, Coca-Cola, and Oreo enjoy followers in the millions, and other national brand-name companies such as Dunkin' Donuts and Staples have followers numbering in the hundreds of thousands, there are scores of smaller, local businesses that are seeing impacts from their social media efforts with only thousands or even hundreds of followers. Take La Boulange, a French bakery operating in 11 locations in the San

Figure 7.3
The Nielsen Trust Study

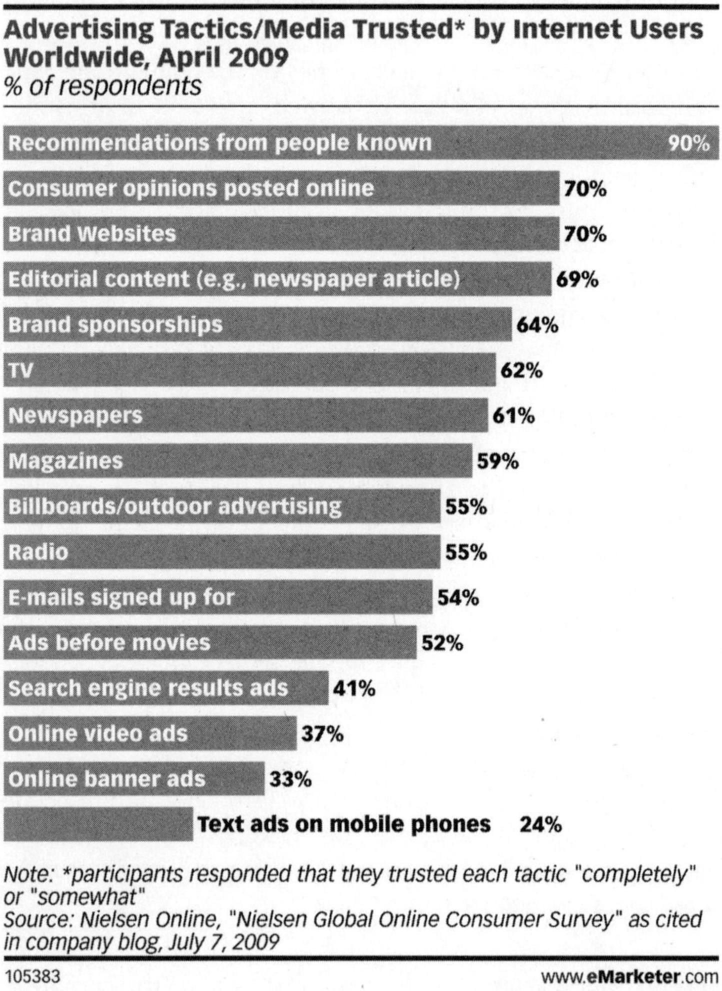

Advertising Tactics/Media Trusted* by Internet Users Worldwide, April 2009
% of respondents

Tactic/Media	%
Recommendations from people known	90%
Consumer opinions posted online	70%
Brand Websites	70%
Editorial content (e.g., newspaper article)	69%
Brand sponsorships	64%
TV	62%
Newspapers	61%
Magazines	59%
Billboards/outdoor advertising	55%
Radio	55%
E-mails signed up for	54%
Ads before movies	52%
Search engine results ads	41%
Online video ads	37%
Online banner ads	33%
Text ads on mobile phones	24%

Note: *participants responded that they trusted each tactic "completely" or "somewhat"
Source: Nielsen Online, "Nielsen Global Online Consumer Survey" as cited in company blog, July 7, 2009

105383   www.**eMarketer**.com

Francisco area, as an example. Although La Boulange has only 1,000 followers on its Twitter account, the bakery sees great value in being able to inexpensively communicate with those geographically proximate fans on a regular and often timely basis.

While numerous surveys confirm that small and medium-sized businesses see social media as a way to increase brand/company awareness and customer loyalty, they also identify a third important objective: using it as a means to attract new customers. According to a March 2010 survey by office services firm Regus, 44 percent of small businesses worldwide that are using social media say they had acquired customers through social sites; similarly, in the United States, a September 2010 study conducted among small and medium-sized businesses by the University of Maryland Robert H. Smith School of Business put this figure at 53 percent.

Small firms with limited marketing budgets may benefit even more from using social media. For them, it can end up being the most inexpensive way to boost exposure for their business, and it can help them efficiently attract site traffic and new customers/clients. For example, promotions on platforms like Twitter don't generally cost a dime (unless you're paying a celebrity to "tweet" for you). An IDC "Top 10 Predictions 2011" report predicts that many small and medium-sized businesses will turn to social networks in 2011 to "establish a free online presence that improves their ability to acquire, engage and retain customers—without the hassle and cost of setting up a traditional website."

Social Media Demands the Magnetic Content Approach

If there is one digital channel that demands that marketers rely on the Magnetic Content approach—as opposed to running traditional ad campaigns with interruptive banners—social media is it. As we've seen, people hang out on social platforms to communicate and share experiences, information, and entertainment with others. Marketers who choose to play in this environment need to contribute accordingly—finding ways to add genuine value, aka Magnetic Content, to social media conversations.

In the social media realm, Magnetic Content can take on many different forms and functions:

- Advertising sponsorships placed on Facebook's home page.
- Twitter updates as a delivery mechanism for targeted promotions.
- A fun video experience shared via the brand's profile page on Facebook.
- A series of posts on MySpace inviting young adults to participate in a branded online game.
- "Like" or "friend" options for your brand.
- A brand representative on Twitter available to assist a customer with a service problem.
- An opportunity for customers to rank or rate products on your e-commerce site.

All of these tactics, and more, can be forms of Magnetic Content within social media—as long as they engage the consumer and are not perceived as unwelcome intrusions.

Remember how in Chapter 3 we explained that the concept of magnetizing consumers is not a hook 'em and leave 'em one-time event, but rather an iterative, gradual process of engagement? That's particularly true in the social media channel where relationships need to be carefully nurtured over time. No single Magnetic Content interaction is likely to make a big impact on your brand or business. Rather, social media lends itself to a patient, graduated approach where dozens, hundreds, or thousands of small engagements cumulatively lead to an outsized impact, in terms of improving brand trust, connecting you on a deeper level with customers, and encouraging them to share your brand story with others. As such, Magnetic Content within social media should be thought as more of a constant flow of engagements than a one-off program, campaign, or promotion.

We can also apply our five factor criteria for Magnetic Content to social media efforts:

1. *Is it unique?* If you stay true to your brand values and engage with social media denizens in a genuine, personalized way, then your brand personality will keep you unique, and you will likely meet this criteria.
2. *Is it useful?* It is vitally important in the context of social media to be adding value to the conversation. As we'll see in the next section, there are many ways to deliver meaningful, practical contributions within the social media space.
3. *Is it well executed?* Often in social media environments, "well executed" can simply be a matter of "fitting in"—speaking in a natural voice, being honest, and using a tone that is appropriate for the situation.
4. *Is it fun?* Social networks, blogs, and community forums frequently lend themselves to fun, amusement, and entertainment. This should inform the kind of Magnetic Content you create for these platforms. Are there "fun" aspects to your brand?
5. *Does the content make good use of the channel in which it appears?* In the next section, we share a specific set of guidelines for deploying Magnetic Content on social media platforms. In fact, we identify seven best practices and explain in detail how to execute them.

That's an overview. Now let's get down to brass tacks.

Seven Best Practices for Magnetizing Customers through Social Media

The following seven guidelines were carefully culled from a wealth of published articles, white papers, analyst reports, consultant opinions, social media pundits, and, of course, the collective wisdom of this book's authors.

1. Don't think social media; think social marketing in the broadest possible sense.
2. Leverage the secret ingredient: trust.
3. Listening comes first.
4. Don't just barge into a conversation; add value.
5. Be authentic, transparent, and humble.
6. Recruit from your core: the brand enthusiasts who already love you.
7. Target the coveted influentials.

Perhaps more so than in any other digital channel, social media requires that marketers rely heavily on the use of Magnetic Content, versus standard advertising formats, to communicate their brand messages. This reflects the fact that consumers in social media environments are far more interested in communicating, sharing, and being entertained and therefore much less interested in receiving advertisements. Marketers seem to be on board. A June 2010 survey by King Fish Media found that marketers using social media were significantly more likely to use branded content (73 percent), expert content (72 percent), video (51 percent), and other forms of compelling content to attract consumers. Notably, only 35 percent said they were using advertising for social media efforts.

1. Don't Think Social Media; Think Social Marketing in the Broadest Possible Sense

Paid media advertising on social sites represents a relatively limited opportunity for most companies. Rather, marketers should recognize that social interactions can—and should—be linked to nearly every facet of their organization— not just marketing, but also employee communications, customer relationship management (CRM), product design and packaging, public relations, and even research and development (R&D).

Successful social marketing will require organizing, training, and empowering select staff members—across multiple departments—to engage with consumers on social platforms. The aim is to build a corporate social presence that goes way beyond paid media placements.

2. Leverage the Secret Ingredient: Trust

As we've seen, a big part of the attraction toward social media is the opportunity to transfer some of the trust and influence consumers share with each other onto your own brand. In fact, social media–influenced trust can be one of the strongest magnetizing forces at your disposal. Consumers flock to trusted brands.

Following are some simple, tactical ways you can use social platforms and connections as a means to leverage consumer trust and magnetize audiences around your brand:

Let Your Fans Come to Your Rescue   By monitoring social networks and blogs, you may discover that someone is inappropriately trashing your brand or spreading false rumors. Try to resist the temptation to immediately step in and set them straight. It's far better if one of your loyal brand fans comes to your rescue and speaks up on your behalf. Consumers expect corporations to defend themselves, but they are far more likely to believe customers like themselves.

Consider the experience of retailer 1-800-FLOWERS. The company was faced with an out-of-control customer who was using Facebook to lodge a barrage of over-the-top complaints with negative phrases like, "terrible service," "negligent," and "deficient." The company initially responded with a full refund, and then later apologized a second time in an attempt to resolve the issue privately. But what finally quelled the fire was a brand fan who stepped in and wrote, "It's obvious thousands of customers use 1800flowers .com and are satisfied customers . . . accept the apology like an adult."

Allow for Customer Ratings and Reviews   Although it may seem scary at first, because people might say negative things, providing customers with the opportunity to rate or review your products or service on your site can serve to not only boost your trust quotient, it can actually drive more business. Many retailers have seen conversions improve dramatically when they implemented the capability for ratings and reviews. The magic equation here is:

$$\text{Transparency} = \text{Trust}$$

The fact is, by allowing some negative comments to bubble up, consumers will feel a greater sense of trust that the favorable comments are indeed genuine. A little of the bad stuff makes the good stuff all the more believable! What's more, if you promote the highest-rated products on your home page, you can expect to see even greater returns.

· ***Let Consumers Share the Love***   Identify your brand enthusiasts (see also best practice #6) and provide them with the tools, platforms, and apps that will enable them to easily share their passion for your brand with others. Giving them a chance to "like" your brand on Facebook, for example, is a simple way to encourage fans to spread their influence. A survey by Morpace found that 68 percent of Facebook users say they would be more likely to buy a product or visit a retailer after seeing a positive Facebook friend referral (Figure 7.4). What other ways can you leverage trust to multiply referrals?

Mine for Mentions   Monitor the relevant blogs and social sites to look for positive mentions of your product or brand. If appropriate, consider reaching out to these enthusiastic individuals to request permission to use their quotes as a testimonial or endorsement. Such positive, trustworthy statements can be used on your website, in e-mail campaigns, and, of course, in traditional broadcast and print media.   .

Figure 7.4
Social media and trust

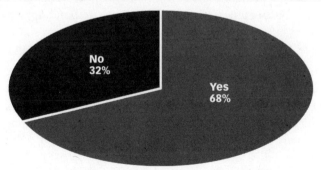

US Facebook Users Who Are More Likely to Buy a Product or Visit a Retailer Based on a Positive Facebook Friend Referral, March 2010
% of respondents

No
32%

Yes
68%

Source: Morpace, "Facebook's Impact on Retailers," provided to eMarketer, April 1, 2010

113959   www.**eMarketer**.com

Build Your Own Forum   If you want to create a really powerful magnet for consumers, design a social platform or virtual community to engage with consumers on a particular topic, theme, or set of passions. Of course, the theme you select will, in at least some subtle way, relate to your brand or what it stands for. However, the mission is *not* to pitch your product, but rather to provide a valuable service—in the form of a public forum—where like-minded consumers can share and communicate. Your brand is merely the (trusted) sponsor.

3. Listening Comes First

According to the Keller Fay Group, 22 percent of U.S. consumers have a brand-related conversation at least once online in an average day, versus 45 percent on the phone and 93 percent face-to-face.

Consequently, "social listening" is now a core competency that virtually all marketers must master. Companies, including large ones such as Dell, JetBlue, Starbucks, Whole Foods, and Comcast and small ones like local bakeries and ice cream shops, are excited about online social communities because they can help them get closer to their customers, quickly discover changing attitudes and perceptions, and learn valuable consumer insights that can be leveraged in ad campaigns and marketing programs, as well as to help refine product features and service offerings.

Some firms, like Dell and Kodak, for example, feel so strongly about the need to systematically listen to their customers that they have created a new role within the company dedicated to the practice of listening: chief listening officer (CLO). Principally, the CLO role involves a heavy amount of data mining and figuring out how to get the right information to the right people within the organization so that they can respond appropriately and quickly—often in real time.

Turning Listening into a Research Measurement Tool   The bottom line is that marketers who commit to ongoing social listening can tap into a powerful form of marketing measurement. Through active listening you will be able to understand your consumers on a deeper level, including their true perceptions, pain points, and passions. This, in turn, will help you better meet customer needs.

Critically, one of the greatest values of effective listening in social media is that it can help you identify what types of Magnetic Content will resonate best with your customers. In many cases, they will even give you specific ideas for Magnetic Content. In addition, marketers can use ongoing social listening to:

- Find out about problems or defects with a product that may need to be fixed.
- Discover if the customer service process is broken, and in what particular area.
- Learn if consumers have a misperception about the product or company and—even worse—are telling everyone about it on Twitter.
- Gain a better understanding of how consumers perceive or experience a competitor's product, service, or brand.
- Learn about the language consumers use to describe a product or brand, and then use those insights in offline and online advertising messages (e.g., your keyword search buys).
- Get a faster, more accurate read on how consumers feel about a company's advertising campaigns and then be prepared to change them on the fly.
- Create more effective forms of Magnetic Content that will drive further engagement with your brand.

Of course, listening is hardly a new concept in marketing. It's just that the traditional "listening" tools of the past—conducting focus groups, observing shopping behavior in malls, and offering toll-free help lines—are woefully inadequate compared with the digital tools marketers now have at their disposal. Today, marketers can easily monitor and track, often in real time, what vast numbers of consumers are expressing in blog posts, tweets, Facebook comments, videos, and other forms of social communications, many of which refer to brands and products. Mega coffee brand Starbucks was an early pioneer in using social media as a listening ear to the consumer with their MyStarbucksIdea.com forum, a branded social media community that solicits suggestions, comments, questions, and even votes from consumers. Importantly, Starbucks not only listens to the consumer ideas, they actually implement many of them as well.

Using a Social Media Dashboard for Listening Social media dashboards are relatively cheap and easy to implement—and they can be very effective. They provide an easy way to present and summarize data from all the social sites available in one place. You can look at the topics and keywords being discussed, provide visualization for trends, and get insights that will help you identify key influencers. Radian6 is a leading provider of such dashboards, and there are at least 50 other vendors when last we counted. The tool is less critical; what's more important is how you apply the learnings that result.

Is Your Listening Filtered or Unfiltered?   Depending on the marketer's objectives, social listening tends to fall into two camps: unfiltered and filtered with analysis.

Marketers who track *unfiltered* buzz are typically listening to ensure rapid-cycle response times to events—they simply cannot afford the delays entailed in conducting a detailed analysis.

The power users of real-time, rapid-response monitoring typically include public relations professionals who are trying to mitigate a company or brand crisis, exploit topical opportunities, blunt the effects of competitive or derogatory buzz, or quickly assess reactions to press releases and announcements.

Marketers choosing to monitor unfiltered posts want to gain immediate intelligence on specific market events, such as product launches, price changes, new promotions, or competitive introductions.

Marketers who use a *filtered* analysis approach pursue in-depth analysis of discussion threads to systematically absorb customer knowledge and glean more subtle consumer insights that can be used to drive overarching marketing and media strategies. These analyses typically address the following questions:

- Which topics precipitate customer buzz?
- What is the sentiment around these topics (positive, negative, neutral)?
- What are the customer perceptions of key product attributes such as product, quality, and service?
- Which elements of the value proposition and core benefits most resonate with consumers?
- What are the greatest areas of misperception where we need to defend the brand?

One company that takes social listening very seriously is global communications company Avaya, which uses third-party applications to continuously track mentions of its brand name on Twitter and other social platforms. The firm has automated alerts that go off when keywords for products and competitors are mentioned. If problems arise, say with technical issues related to the product, the company jumps into the fray to offer help within 15 or 20 minutes, thereby providing "killer support and customer delight," according to Paul Dunay, Avaya's global managing director of services and social marketing.

Listening is essential, but an even greater opportunity awaits those marketers who dare to take the next step: fostering and responding to consumer conversations.

4. Don't Just Barge into a Conversation; Add Value

Recall that one of the five factors, or criteria, for Magnetic Content asks this vital question: Is it useful? Strive to make every one of your social interactions, including blog posts and Tweets, useful.

Of course, participation in social media can offer many benefits for marketers, but it also requires some degree of caution—and likely a new mindset with regard to consumer messaging. Do not assume you can simply jump into a conversation consumers are already having and start pitching your products. For example, if your firm sells camera equipment, it would not be advisable for you to barge onto a blog where people are discussing photography techniques and announce that your "new XYZ model can solve all their camera needs." It would be far better to provide some helpful (non–product-specific) advice for how to take good pictures.

Marketers must look to create their own connections, be prepared to respond when they are mentioned directly, and earn the right to participate in existing communities when they have something of value to offer. Repeat: when they have something of value to offer. Here are tips on how to do this effectively.

Emulate How Consumers Interact with One Another Consumers are motivated to participate on social platforms by the constant stream of sharing, in the form of status updates, photos, links, and other forms of information and entertainment that their friends post. Marketers should take some cues from this, and act likewise. In fact, by this point, consumers pretty much expect their interactions with companies to be like their interactions with friends.

There are many ways to add value to digital forums. You might address specific problems that consumers bring up related to your product, service, or category, or you might provide information to address broader consumer needs, either individually or to the entire group. The key is to act more like a helpful friend and less like a corporation with a product to plug. When a consumer is looking for help deciding what kind of car to buy for his or her family, for example, it might be appropriate for you to share a link to a third-party source such as the results from a *Consumer Reports* rundown of automobiles that happens to favor your brand. In other situations, you might offer up factual information and links to correct a misperception or dispel a rumor.

If you ever have doubts about whether and how to contribute to a social media forum, refer back to our five-factor criteria for Magnetic Content; ask yourself, "Is what I'm about to share unique, useful, well executed, fun, and appropriate in the context of the social media environment?"

Adding Value to Ice Cream, Via Twitter

Many large national brands have huge numbers of followers on Twitter, but even a small family business can attract a sizable following—if it offers something of value. One classic Twitter success story comes from Humphry Slocombe, a modest 14-seat ice cream shop in San Francisco. Astoundingly, in the span of a year, the budget-challenged local firm amassed 300,000 Twitter followers, far exceeding those of larger competitors like Ben & Jerry's or Baskin-Robbins. The secret to their sweet success was twofold. First, Humphry Slocombe discovered that its patrons, scattered around San Francisco, were eager to be posted about what new flavors were being offered on a daily basis. Consumers were pleading for ice cream updates, and the Twitter platform addressed that need efficiently, and at virtually no cost. Second, the owners realized that it was important to stand out from the Twitter noise; through a stream of entertainingly edgy tweets, sometimes even bordering on rude, they established a Twitter personality that can best be described as "ice cream with attitude." Bottom line: the company's menu broadcasts on Twitter drive ice cream sales.

Get the Company Involved at All Levels   To keep up with the constant stream of conversations and do an effective job of responding and adding genuine value, most companies, especially large ones, will need more than one individual assigned to the task. Savvy companies today are empowering and carefully training select staff members from all over the organization to be the voice, and sometimes face, of the company, encouraging them to express their personalities on social platforms while also adhering to basic guidelines reflecting the culture of the brand or company.

Few industries are as constrained by and nervous about connecting with consumers in social media as health care. But that didn't stop health care maintenance provider WellPoint from embracing social media to the point of gaining a commitment from the entire company, including (and importantly) the legal department. To ensure that all of its associates were on the same page, the HMO created a companywide social media steering committee.

Even with a mostly decentralized approach, it is often a good idea to identify a particular group of employees to serve as the main hub for all social media interactions. Usually, this hub is spearheaded by an experienced person who

Figure 7.5

Corporate governance of social media

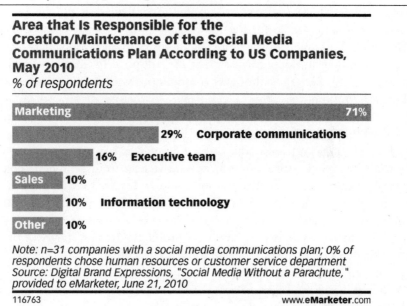

Area that Is Responsible for the
Creation/Maintenance of the Social Media
Communications Plan According to US Companies,
May 2010
% of respondents

Marketing	71%
Corporate communications	29%
Executive team	16%
Sales	10%
Information technology	10%
Other	10%

Note: n=31 companies with a social media communications plan; 0% of respondents chose human resources or customer service department
Source: Digital Brand Expressions, "Social Media Without a Parachute," provided to eMarketer, June 21, 2010

116763   www.**eMarketer**.com

serves as a kind of community manager. Technology can also play a key role here. At Dell, for instance, the company has created a social media "command center" that effectively monitors all the social media conversations that relate around Dell.

At Starbucks, nearly every department in the organization has a deputized representative charged with acting as a liaison between the consumers conversing on social platforms and the department. There are about 50 such representatives worldwide.

Although marketing is usually the primary group that engages with and manages social media, research shows that companies are empowering a wide range of departments to interact with consumers on social platforms (Figure 7.5).

Of course, if you're going to add value to digital conversations, you must also be prepared to adjust your tone—the way in which you speak.

5. Be authentic, transparent, and humble

Marketers have spent decades carefully crafting press releases, TV commercials, magazine ads, and other advertising messages to paint their brands in the best possible light.

We, as the authors of this book, have spent a combined three decades in the advertising business and can attest to the fact that each word of a client's copy is carefully crafted, refined, vetted, and then sent up the hierarchy, where it is subjected to further filtering, second-guessing, and testing. The problem is, consumers today aren't buying the corporate gobbledygook. They have too much outside information at their disposal (think Google) and too many ways to share their thoughts and opinions with countless others (think Twitter) to simply swallow a company's marketing drivel. So, as former Procter & Gamble CEO A. G. Lafley wisely advised several years ago, marketers need to "Let go!"

Part of *letting go* means adjusting, and yes relaxing, the corporate voice. In the social media space, consumers want to hear from genuine people, not disembodied corporate entities pushing a poorly disguised vested interest. Most important, social networks demand that you be very careful about what promises you make to consumers. When they see a disconnect between what you say and what you do, or how your product performs, they will find you out and alert others. Remember how important trust is!

So before you invite everyone in your company to "have at it" with Twitter and Facebook, we advise you to create and distribute a set of organizational guidelines that direct your employees on how to engage with consumers via social platforms. Roles also need to be established so that employees are clear on who does what, how, and when. Dell, the global computer firm, took this approach very seriously as they sought to embed social media into every function of the company. In addition to distributing rules and guidelines for how to use social platforms, Dell established in-house social media classes where nearly 4,000 employees were asked to undergo extensive training sessions; those finishing the program received certification, empowering them to use social media on the company's behalf.

Generally, the rules go something like this:

- Skip the "marketing speak" and talk in a conversational, natural tone— like a real person.
- Put forth real people and real voices, not a stilted corporate front.
- Speak in the first person singular, rather than the formal "we."
- Be willing to accept and acknowledge the negative comments as well as the positive.
- Be the first to acknowledge a mistake—and own up to it.
- Provide full disclosure as to who you are, what you represent, and what stake you might have in a given topic.
- Respond quickly if there's a crisis (ideally within 24 hours, or sooner).

This does not mean that those empowered to speak on behalf of the organization can ignore completely certain cultural, attitudinal, or tonal traits that are central to the company or brand's identity. These company- and brand-specific guidelines must be incorporated into the preceding list.

6. Recruit from Your Core: The Brand Enthusiasts Who Already Love You

This is one of the most important concepts to master with social media, so listen up!

Answer this question honestly: Is your company, product, or brand fortunate enough to have a sizeable following of brand enthusiasts—that is, consumers who are so engaged, loyal, and passionate that they want to share the good news with as many others as possible? If your answer is "yes," you have a ripe opportunity to exploit the viral power of social networks—as long as you proceed with patience, sensitivity, and tender loving care.

Digital communities allow marketers to: (1) find these coveted consumers (through listening/monitoring), (2) reward them, and (3) empower them to share their experience of your brand story with hundreds, thousands, or even millions of others. Millions *are* possible. According to the Facebook profile page of the Coca-Cola Company, the beverage maker enjoyed a fan base of nearly 22 million consumers as of January 2011.

Why are core brand loyalists so important? Two reasons. First, they represent your most important customers and likely account for a disproportionate share of your profits. Anything you can do to reward and reinforce their brand behavior will likely result in a healthy payback. The other reason is that these consumers are not only smitten with your brand, they are in a terrific position to sing its praises; they represent a trusted source that can influence others to join the core. Think of them as your product evangelists. Encourage them to do what for you is hard work, but for them comes naturally—recruiting others into the fold of your brand. Here are a few tips to leverage your brand fans.

Identify Core Brand Fans with Social Media Monitoring   By spending some time on social networks and using some of the more sophisticated monitoring tools available, you can begin to identify some of your greatest fans. Some of them will have created their own fan pages in tribute to your brand. Others will simply glow about you on their Facebook page or Twitter feed. Still others will rush to your defense on a blog post where your brand comes up. Take special notice of these people, as they represent your greatest asset in the social realm.

Consumer packaged goods firm Unilever used this approach successfully as they sought to identify brand enthusiasts and other likely prospects who could act as endorsers for a new skin care moisturizer product under the Vaseline brand. Unilever hired specialists to scour the Internet, including Facebook, Twitter, and blogs, for people who were conversing about topics such as "dry skin," "lotions," and "skin issues." After a lengthy culling and interview process, the brand identified several consumers who were eventually given free samples of the product and served as real-consumer spokespeople for Vaseline Intensive Rescue.

Nurture Brand Fans as You Would a Private Garden   Look for creative ways to reward your loyal fan base—with unique, personalized Magnetic Content. Often, this can come in the simple form of special discounts and coupons. As but one example, Starbucks, with more than 20 million followers, offers its brand enthusiasts downloadable vouchers for free food or music along with a purchase.

In addition to Starbucks, companies such as JetBlue, Southwest, DIRECTV, Dunkin' Donuts, Staples, and many small businesses use Twitter and Facebook as an efficient means to reward their loyal followers with special promotions and offers.

Dunkin' Donuts, for example, uses Twitter to dispense promotions and deals to its fan base of nearly 53,000 followers. In addition to special deals for munchkins and breakfast sandwiches, the company creates excitement through programs like the "create your own donut" contest. Such efforts come with an automatic feedback loop built right in, so they can evaluate which promotions are working best in real time.

Another obvious way to pay homage to your brand enthusiasts is to allow them to "fan" or "like" you.

Set Up a Brand Page on Facebook   Consumers who dig your brand are waiting for opportunities to broadcast their loyalty to the world at large. In fact, studies show that between 30 and 50 percent of social network users are fans of brands on platforms such as Facebook, Twitter, and the like.

If your brand is cherished by a loyal cadre of consumers, why not create a brand page where they can "like" you? In this way, they can not only associate with you but also evangelize like-minded friends and family to join the bandwagon. This is a no-brainer form of Magnetic Content that has a viral kick!

There are good marketing reasons for creating brand pages. First, it's a powerful form of permission marketing, since you're allowing your most valuable consumers to opt in at a deeper, more public level. Those consumers can, in turn, encourage their friends to opt in as well. Magnetism begets magnetism! Efficiency is also a strong consideration here: for example, once a consumer has "liked" a brand on Facebook, or begins to "follow" the company on Twitter, it costs nothing for the marketer to be able to continually "speak" to that consumer, who has essentially opted in.

There is also a good psychological reason for creating brand pages. It's called cognitive dissonance. As human beings, we like to have our beliefs internally consistent with each other, and that includes our beliefs about brands and products.

Cognitive dissonance often goes in gear when consumers purchase a product. For example, a consumer having purchased a Honda will, in his or her desire to remain internally consistent with personal beliefs and actions, seek to tell others about the car. The car owner will also tend to read articles that seem favorable to Hondas and avoid those that seem negative. In a sense, the consumer is post-rationalizing the purchase of the car.

Cognitive dissonance plays out in the social media realm as well. If a consumer publicly expresses an affiliation or "like" for a brand, say by friending it or putting its logo on his or her Facebook page, that person is more likely to purchase the brand and recommend it to others. How much more likely?

A research study by Chadwick Martin Bailey (March 2010) found that people who "like" a brand or become a follower of a brand on Facebook were 51 percent more likely to buy the brand and 60 percent more likely to refer it to others. Almost identical findings were found in a separate study among Twitter users. As more proof, a study by digital consulting firm Syncapse and research company Hotspex, found that people spend significantly more on products they are fans of, compared with consumers who are not fans. In the case of food and beverage marketers, fan spending is more than double that of nonfans (Figure 7.6).

Researcher Nielsen found that if Facebook users see that a friend of theirs "likes" an ad or has commented on it, they are up to 30 percent more likely to recall the ad's message.

Coffee company Starbucks has embraced social media marketing in a big way, primarily as a way to talk to its huge Facebook fan base of 20 million. It also works with foursquare to deliver coupons to consumers who become "mayors" of its stores (mayors hold the distinction of being the most frequent visitor of a particular establishment or brand space). Starbucks thus rewards its most loyal customers in a way that not only encourages deeper loyalty, but likely elicits word-of-mouth sharing as well, since mayors are likely to brag

Figure 7.6
Fans are often your best customers

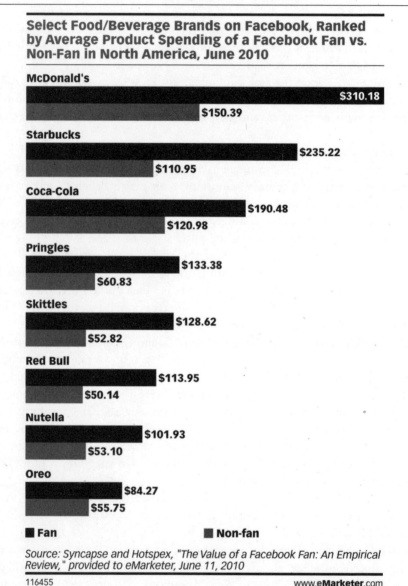

Select Food/Beverage Brands on Facebook, Ranked by Average Product Spending of a Facebook Fan vs. Non-Fan in North America, June 2010

McDonald's
$310.18
$150.39

Starbucks
$235.22
$110.95

Coca-Cola
$190.48
$120.98

Pringles
$133.38
$60.83

Skittles
$128.62
$52.82

Red Bull
$113.95
$50.14

Nutella
$101.93
$53.10

Oreo
$84.27
$55.75

■ Fan   ■ Non-fan

Source: Syncapse and Hotspex, "The Value of a Facebook Fan: An Empirical Review," provided to eMarketer, June 11, 2010

116455   www.eMarketer.com

about their elite status. Less obvious users of foursquare include publishing giant Simon & Schuster, which encourages readers to interact with authors by exploring physical locations mentioned in both fiction and nonfiction books, as identified on the publisher's website.

One more thing: even though brand pages can be incredibly easy and cheap to produce, you likely won't have any visitors if you don't spend money on paid advertising to make your potential fans aware. Social media does not work in a vacuum. It must be integrated with all of your other offline and online communications in order to direct your fan base to the channel.

Brand fans can exert great influence on others, but maybe not as much as so-called "influentials."

7. Target the Coveted Influentials

Some of us in this world have more clout than others. That's true in the social media realm, too. These so-called "influentials" or "influencers" have an undue influence on others because of their extensive digital networks and perceived expertise in a particular area.

According to research from the Keller Fay Group, influentials account for about 10 percent of the population, yet are 130 percent more likely than others to talk about brands on any given day. Forrester, on the other hand, believes that people it dubs "mass connectors" (those who maintain large social networks) account for just 6 percent of all online adults but a whopping 80 percent of so-called influence impressions on social networks. Influence impressions are posts on Facebook and other social networks that relate to products and services.

Influentials can move hundreds, thousands, or hundreds of thousands of consumers—to think, feel, or even act differently. Importantly, influence is less about the quantity of any individual's connections and more about the quality and duration of those interactions, as well as the degree to which the influencer is trusted. Someone may have a fewer number of overall connections, but if those connections are tightly grouped with each other, that person will have greater influence than someone else with a larger number of unconnected friends. Focus on the quality and tightness of the connections, not the absolute number.

Additional research from ICOM, a division of Epsilon Targeting, shows that influencers are most identifiable not by demographics but by behavior. In the ICOM report titled "The Influencer: A Consumer Voice with Legs," it was revealed that influencers exist across age, gender, and income breakdowns. Also, their use of media channels is not much different from the average user. The characteristic they do share is the desire to talk to others about their experiences with products, services, and brands.

Influencers are more likely than the general market to say others frequently take their advice and that it is fun to get people to try new products.

They look for new experiences, like to know about new products first, and tell their friends when they have problems with a brand. Importantly, influencers do not rely solely on social networks or even digital platforms to get their messages across. Much of an influencers' communications transpire offline, in conversations in living rooms and kitchens.

A couple of years ago, Ford Motor Company was looking to launch a new, highly fuel efficient car, the Ford Fiesta, to a target of digitally inclined consumers: millennials. Eschewing the usual media channels and strategies, the carmaker relied heavily on social media outlets such as Facebook, Twitter, and YouTube to recruit 100 "agents" who would get to receive and "test drive" a brand new Ford Fiesta for six months. Once the agents were selected, largely on the basis of their social influence, they were given access to the cars and encouraged to blog and post about their driving adventures throughout the trial period.

Said Scott Monty, Ford Motor Company's head of social media, "We put 100 cars in the hands of savvy digital influencers who are really excited about it, and [allowed] them to tell their story with the vehicle. People trust people like themselves, so we want to get cars into their hands." The influencer approach was successful on many accounts, not the least of which was the company's ability to humanize the brand through consumers who epitomized the target audience. In addition, the company was able to generate 60 percent brand awareness for a car that wasn't even officially on the market yet—that's roughly equivalent to the awareness for a car that's been on the market for two or three years. The program also generated 7 million views on YouTube and 4 million mentions on Twitter.

Another great example of leveraging influentials to create word-of-mouth marketing comes from Kimberly-Clark's diaper brand Pull-Ups, a product specifically geared toward moms with children who are being potty trained. Given the understandable apprehensions associated with potty training, especially for first-time moms, K-C realized that trust was a critical component in the sale of these specialized diapers. The company partnered with House Party to help organize 5,000 parties around the country, which in turn were hosted by selected moms who could act as influencers and evangelists for other moms. K-C jump-started the parties, which all occurred on the same date (February 20, 2010) by providing the host mothers with kits, coupons, fun activities, and gifts (like a "Potty Dance training mat") to further empower the influencers and get the parties rolling.

Although the parties were held "offline" in people's homes, the second iteration of the House Party concept will scale even larger by extending the program online, using social media. Specifically, K-C will allow partygoers to continually share supportive ideas, conversations, videos, and success stories via digital channels.

Now that we understand the critical consumer trends behind social media and we have a basic grasp of the seven best practices for marketers looking to master it, let's delve into the area few marketers have dared to tread: measuring social media and achieving ROI.

Social Media Performance Measurement That Works

The seven best practices discussed represent practical ways to impact and *engage* with consumers by tapping into the power of peer-to-peer networks. But are these efforts worth the cost, as measured in time, effort, and direct financial investment?

One compelling study that substantiates social media's potential payoff comes from the Altimeter Group, in conjunction with Wetpaint. In their joint study looking at the top 100 global brands, they found a financial correlation between those companies that are "deeply and widely engaged" in social media and those that significantly outperform their peers in terms of both revenue and profit performance.

At the moment, there is no widely accepted applicable metric for social media measurement, such as page rank for organic search or open rate for e-mail. In the absence of a simple, direct link between investment in social media and resulting impact, only a relatively small portion of marketers (less than 20 percent currently) even attempt to justify the dollar investments in their social media programs. Identifying the right metrics and discovering the true return on social investment have been elusive.

No Game Plan

According to a May 2010 study by Digital Brand Expressions, 52 percent of marketers using some form of social media marketing say they are operating "without a game plan." In a separate survey, conducted in April 2010 by R2integrated, a similar figure of 50 percent was found for those claiming they did not have a defined social media strategy.

As we'll see, measurement and the calculation of ROI for social media initiatives is complicated by three factors: (1) it's a channel that can serve both branding and direct response goals; (2) it's a consumer-centric channel where the marketer may be able to only indirectly influence results; and (3) there are numerous qualitative benefits to social media programs that defy simple numerical measurement.

How Social Media Is Measured Today: The Cheap Way Out

When it comes to attempting to measure social media success, there is a strong tendency among marketers to gravitate toward the inexpensive

Figure 7.7
How social media is measured today

Analytics/Measurement Tools Used by Social Media Marketers Worldwide, September 2009
% of respondents

Free analytics software (e.g., Google Analytics, Quantcast or YouTube Analytics)
74.5%

Free buzz-monitoring service (e.g., TweetDeck, Facebook Stream Search or Google Alerts)
51.1%

Tracking Twitter clicks and retweets (e.g., Bit.ly)
47.5%

Polls of social media friends/fans/connections to estimate effectiveness
37.8%

Paid analytics software (e.g., Omniture)
30.8%

Scientific control/exposed surveys of friends/fans/connections to determine effectiveness
29.8%

Paid buzz-monitoring service (e.g., Nielsen Buzz Metrics, Cymphony or Radiant 6)
19.7%

Note: n=1,513
Source: MarketingProfs, "The State of Social Media," provided to eMarketer, December 10, 2009

109988   www.eMarketer.com

solutions (Figure 7.7). Typically, marketers prefer the free analytics software (such as Google Analytics, Quantcast, etc.), rather than paying for third-party services (e.g., Omniture) or building out measurement systems themselves.

For some businesses, particularly smaller ones with limited or no budgets, the free analytics software tools might be "good enough." But many larger marketers who use them often complain they get the value of what they pay for. More sophisticated tools cost money, but they often pay for themselves in terms of time savings—you'll spend far less time trudging through reams of data and more time acting on the data and taking advantage of its insights.

How Do I Measure Thee? Let Me Count the Ways You might be wondering: How many different metrics are there for measuring the performance of social media? 20? 50? 100? 1,000?

If you answered "100," you're in agreement with at least one influential marketing blogger—David Berkowitz, senior director of marketing and innovation at ad agency 360i. On his blog, he provides a list of 100 ways to measure social media. The list ranges from soft metrics, such as the number of fans, followers, or friends, to more substantial measurements, such as impact on online and offline sales, market share, and leads generated. And then everything else in between.

While the 100-metric list highlights the many exciting ways in which social media can be evaluated, it also explains why marketers are so confounded. Too many choices—without clear objectives and a framework for success—is a recipe for paralysis and/or failure.

Among this large array of metrics, guess which is most often used by marketers to measure the impact of social media efforts? According to several independent surveys and studies, website traffic appears to be the default metric. On a consensus basis, about two-thirds of marketers, including both business-to-consumer (B2C) and B2B firms, use site traffic (hits, visits, page views) as their primary measurement metric for social media.

Even though site traffic can be an important barometer of consumer interest for a brand, it cannot, on its own, justify heavier investment spending in social media. Most marketers would agree with this statement but have yet to make the transition to more effective, relevant metrics; instead, they are clinging to what's quick and easy to measure (Figure 7.8).

Creating a Framework for Measuring Social Media

Given the abundance of measurement choices available (100+) and the gravitational pull toward quick and easy methods, it is imperative to establish the correct framework for organizing social media metrics. The measurement

Figure 7.8

Measurement techniques by sector

Social Media Metrics Used, by Sector, Aug 2010
% of US B2B and B2C marketers

	B2B product firms	B2B service firms	B2C product firms	B2C service firms	Total
Hits/visits/page views	63.4%	58.3%	76.2%	55.1%	47.6%
Repeat visits	43.8%	42.4%	61.9%	40.6%	34.7%
Conversion rates (from visitor to purchase)	30.7%	33.8%	39.7%	30.4%	25.4%
Number of followers or friends	20.9%	27.2%	50.8%	46.4%	24.0%
Sales levels	25.5%	19.9%	30.2%	18.8%	17.9%
Revenue per customer	21.6%	21.2%	34.9%	14.5%	17.2%
Buzz indicators (web mentions)	16.3%	17.2%	25.4%	33.3%	15.7%
Customer acquisition costs	13.1%	14.6%	19.0%	18.8%	11.8%
Profits per customer	11.1%	11.3%	17.5%	13.0%	9.4%
Online product/service ratings	9.8%	7.3%	20.6%	11.6%	8.2%
Customer retention costs	10.5%	7.3%	11.1%	13.0%	7.7%
Net promoter score	11.1%	3.3%	17.5%	13.0%	7.5%
Other text analysis ratings	9.8%	6.6%	11.1%	8.7%	6.6%
Abandoned shopping carts	4.6%	2.6%	9.5%	5.8%	3.8%

Source: Duke University's Fuqua School of Business, "The CMO Survey" commissioned by the American Marketing Association (AMA), Aug 30, 2010

119319   www.**eMarketer**.com

framework from Chapter 2 once again provides a quick way to select appropriate metrics. For measuring social campaigns, we recommend using the following sets of metrics.

Exposure Metrics for Social Media

Metrics to evaluate the short-term aspects of a campaign for developing an engaged audience on social media platforms go much further than merely counting followers or fans.

1. Qualified Social Reach A key goal of social media is to reach a large number of people, get them intrigued in your brand's Magnetic Content, and then motivate them to interact with the content, as well as share it with others. Along the way, you want them to opt in to your brand's social media presence as a friend, fan, follower, or even a member of your brands' blogs or social communities. Our definition of Qualified Social Reach is *the number of consumers who opt in to your social media presence,* which, depending on the social platform, can include any and all of the following:

- Number of fans or friends
- Number of followers
- Number of subscribers/members—this would include your brands' own blogs and other social communities created around a specific product or brand

Although these numbers are a good indication of the overall popularity of your brand, as well as general interest in the social Magnetic Content you offer, it does not give you the entire story. You need another view into whether your audience is actually immersing itself and engaging with your Magnetic Content. This leads to our second exposure metric for social media.

2. Social Interaction Rate   The previous metric gave you insight into how many people have opted in to your social content, which is a critical factor for the success of your social media program. The Social Interaction Rate is a metric that will help you determine whether your consumers are *actively engaging* with the content—do they comment on it, do they pass it along? Fundamentally, you want to find out if the Magnetic Content is striking the right chord with the target audience. Here again, depending on the social platform, this metric represents interaction/engagement with the content, and it can be any or a mix of the following:

- Number of comments
- Number of tweets or retweets
- Number of posts or repostings—brands' blogs or related social communities
- Number or percentage of comments in response to photos/videos/posts

This interaction metric is important, because it also represents the ability of the social content to spread; the more interaction you have, the greater likelihood it will spread virally and in turn drive the earlier metric of Qualified Social Reach.

The next metric goes a step further and informs you whether all this discussion and engagement with the content is culminating in positive impacts on your brand. This is the strategic area of metrics for social media.

Strategic Metrics for Social Media

One of the most desirable outcome metrics with social media is getting a measurable lift in recognition and other brand and product attributes.

3. Engagement Score (ES)   As discussed in Chapter 2, the Engagement Score (ES) is actually a series of metrics all bundled into a score. It represents the degree of magnetism of the social content. It is vital for brands looking to evaluate the degree of engagement of their social content.

The ES defines engagement based on what each member does during a visit. It is based on actual behavior aligned to the objectives of the brand. The methodology is based on ascribing a value score to the type of activity that is performed in social media. For example, a status update or tweet will have a lower value than adding a fan or follower. We have recommended a hierarchy of seven different levels of engagement in Chapter 2, with a recommended point value for each level in the engagement hierarchy. This is how you can start to identify the most engaging content and help your brand optimize content for its particular audience.

4. Brand Perception Lift   Brand lift transcends the various individual social media channels and has great meaning for marketers committed to branding initiatives. Brand lift is calculated by determining the change in a brand perception among consumers measured before and after their interactions with social media content, as compared with a control group that did not interact with social media content. The most commonly used brand-lift metrics are:

- Brand awareness
- Brand attribute lift
- Brand favorability
- Purchase intent

The specific metric to be selected is based on the marketer's objective. The idea is to identify and segment those individuals within your target audience who were *exposed* to programs and content and compare their brand perception with a *control* group of consumers who were not exposed to the program and content. The "lift" created within the exposed group is used to calculate the metric.

Test and control measurement was explained in Chapter 2. Many companies provide the survey capabilities for test and control approaches. Some of the major players now involved in social media are Dynamic Logic, comScore, InsightExpress, and Nielsen.

Financial Metrics for Social Media

Finally, we arrive at the third area of the measurement framework for social media. These metrics quantify the efficiency and return on investment, or other financial outcomes, of your social media expenditures.

5. Efficiency Metrics of Cost per X   Efficiency metrics are simple and easy to work with. They represent the cost to get a particular unit that is measurable. The unit can be any one of the following metrics we have discussed earlier:

- Cost per fan/friend/follower/member
- Cost per comments/tweets
- Cost per brand perception lift

We recommend using *all* of these metrics to evaluate your social media efforts. They are critical in helping you determine whether you can efficiently scale your social media efforts.

6. Return on Investment (ROI)   One of the main issues with social media measurement is how to link activity to financial value or ROI. It is well and good to get a handle on the number of fans and their engagement level, but unless you can translate numbers into financial value, your organization's social media strategy will be flying blind.

At the time this book went to print, less than one-fifth of marketers implementing social media strategies said they were systematically measuring it to the point of determining actual ROI, according to a variety of sources. Even understanding the basic value of social media has been elusive. According to a global study by Econsultancy, 47 percent of companies say they are not able to measure the value gained from social media investments. So for nearly half of marketers, the jury is still out.

Why is ROI measurement of social media so rare? There are three basic reasons.

First, marketers are intimidated even by the prospect of attempting to measure ROI, which many view as nearly impossible. Second, clarity is hard to achieve because there are so many soft metrics available to be counted: it can be confusing to choose which ones are the most important. Last, in their enthusiasm, marketers tend to jump into social media before establishing clear marketing goals. This makes it far more difficult to measure success.

All this is changing in 2011 and 2012, which will be the years marketers begin to create effective measurement systems to gauge how well they're doing there. Those who invest the time, money, and strategic thinking to perfect their social media strategies—and tie those efforts to bottom-line results—stand to gain significant competitive advantage over those in the purely experimental stages.

As outlined in Chapter 2, to estimate social media ROI requires setting up test and control analytics. You want to identify and segment those individuals who were *exposed* to social media programs and content and compare their purchase history or purchase intent with a *control* group of consumers who were not exposed to the program and content. The "lift" created within the exposed group, measured before and after the campaign, is used to calculate the return on your investment in the channel or in a specific social venue.

If a lift or increase in the metric is identified, it can be translated into an ROI calculation as follows:

$$\frac{VALUE\,(\text{Exposed}) - VALUE\,(\text{Control})}{\text{Full Costs}} \times 100\%$$

If you are using social media listening tools in your ROI calculations, don't overlook the value of market research cost savings that can result from social listening and tracking. Social media monitoring is far more efficient than organizing focus groups, and you get a much larger pool of people.

Follow the Customer Pathway to Purchase   Another way of getting to hard ROI numbers with social media is to map out the pathway from consumer engagement to purchase. This methods works best if you have e-commerce on the site that enables you to directly track the consumers engagement with your social content and then purchase.

This metrics-driven approach is used by pizza chain Papa John's International. Jim Ensign, vice president of marketing communications at Papa John's, told eMarketer in an interview, "We look at the percentage [of Facebook fans] that convert to customers, the percentage increase in their frequency [of visits], projected increases in their average ticket and what their tenure is with us. . . . We can project their future value. Are we 100% right? No. But are we directionally correct? Absolutely."

Savvy marketers could take this approach a step further and develop sophisticated models that include the lifetime value of a customer and then determine what kinds of social engagements bring in new customers, and, more specifically, which engagements drive long-term loyalty to the brand.

Social Media Data and Metrics Tools

Now that we have identified the critical social media metrics organized into a framework of tiered actions (i.e., Exposure, Strategic, and Financial), let's discuss the tools and data sources required for collecting these metrics.

The current state of data availability on social media platforms reflects what one should expect from a relatively new digital medium. Being digital, the platform provides data—and lots of it. Being nascent, the various data capture tools, definitions, and formats of the platform are inconsistent. The good news is that, despite being inconsistent, the current social media platforms are able to provide data for calculating the majority of the metrics we discussed earlier. In addition, third-party tools can be used to compare and integrate with other social media platforms and digital channels as shown in Table 7.1.

How Useful Are Softer Metrics?   While most companies will ultimately want hard ROI metrics versus the softer ones, such as the number of friends or followers, these can serve as valuable proxy measures when the harder

Table 7.1
Tools for Social Media

Source	Overview	Examples
1. Social media property reports	Provide basic metrics: followers, fans, subscribers, interaction metrics (e.g., likes, photos, video views, posts, comments, tweets)	Standard administration reports from Facebook, MySpace, YouTube, Flickr
2. Third-party social media tracking tools	Provide top-line information on a marketer's community or blogs and enable broad comparison of trends across social media platforms	Radian6, TwitterAnalyzer, TweetBeep
3. Site analytics tools	Enable integration of social media data sets into other digital channels for a comprehensive digital marketing view	Site Catalyst, Google Analytics

Source: Vipin Mayar.

metrics are elusive. This assumes, of course, that the soft metrics can be linked to business outcomes.

An emphasis on softer metrics might be entirely appropriate for some marketers given the strong branding benefits attributable to social interactions. There are certainly many nonprofit organizations and educational groups whose ultimate goal is to spread information, rather than collect e-mails or sell a product. And there are many instances where a commercial enterprise might have a marketing goal that, in the short term, does not directly relate to profitability.

In another light, there are many cases where the cost of doing social media outreach is so incredibly low, that any outsized impacts can lead to an obvious, if not specifically quantifiable, ROI. Cell phone manufacturer RIM took this view with their flagship Blackberry brand. Their vice president of Global Digital, Brian Wallace tells the story of how his typing of a single, humorous tweet (less than 140 characters long) resulted in a huge public relations bonanza on the Twitter channel. Said Wallace in the November 29, 2010, issue of *Advertising Age*: "I remember getting emails from my peers asking me why we would post such a thing. My response was that this post reached over 150,000 people, 98% of the posts were positive and it drove a 15% increase in our followers. Now what's the value of that to our company? For the cost of $0.00 we have increased positive brand sentiment, generated a measurable earned-media value and now have 20,000+ more people who I can share product-related information to. Not a bad ROI."

Or, take the example of a negative situation where an influential blogger is trashing your brand and spreading false rumors. What is it worth to your company if these inflamed comments are extinguished by a cadre of brand enthusiasts who come to your rescue by speaking out on your behalf? As the MasterCard commercials would say, that could be "priceless."

Conclusion

Clearly, if a company is not actively participating in social media and engaging in a two-way, ongoing dialogue with consumers, it will eventually lose touch and fall behind its competitors.

Write this on your bathroom mirror: *Consumers are the owners of my brand.* What consumers say about your product, service, or brand is more important than what you say about it. Therefore, you must listen carefully to what they have to say and, as appropriate, respond—if you are adding value to the conversation. Staying out of the picture, or not engaging with social consumers in an appropriate manner, will cause them to eventually lose trust in your brand, the kiss of death for any marketer. Social media continues to grow rapidly and is now permeating every aspect of the web. Social connections are being woven into every kind of website and every kind of device, including mobile phones, tablets, and digital readers.

It is early days in social media measurement. There is an abundance of metrics from which to select. We have outlined a measurement framework and provided a point of view on the key metrics with some practical guidelines for getting to that elusive ROI.

Keep in mind that the key building blocks that make up a consumer/ brand relationship—consideration, trial, purchase, trust, brand loyalty, and consumer advocacy—have strong emotional components that cannot be established overnight. Social media demands that marketers adopt a patient approach that encompasses a long series of graduated interactions that, depending on the product buying cycle, could last weeks, months, or even years.

CHAPTER 8

Mobile: The Always On, Anytime, Anywhere Channel

"For over 10 years in my career conducting analytics around customer satisfaction and loyalty, I have found that the biggest driver of loyalty is an unexpected positive experience. The mobile channel is uniquely equipped to provide this unexpected delightful experience, especially with fast 3G and 4G speeds and highly contextualized location-based services. For example, imagine the value to a consumer of being able to find an item of interest in stock at a convenient location with comparison pricing in seconds. The value of mobile as a local driver of satisfaction and loyalty should not be discounted."

—*Vipin Mayar*

It's a small screen, but it can pack a powerful punch. With mobile devices, the variety of opportunities for delivering Magnetic Content to consumers is perhaps greater than for other media. But so too is the danger of alienating them—all because of the close, personal nature of the device, which is typically strapped somewhere on their bodies for 16 hours or more a day. This puts a huge premium on an offering that will magnetize the consumer with clarity, timeliness, and relevance.

How then to make the most of mobile? This chapter will answer the following questions:

1. What are the best practices for marketers to deliver Magnetic Content via mobile devices?
2. What are the best strategies for driving Performance Measurement of mobile efforts?

3. Where are the most exciting opportunities in mobile channel marketing today?

The mobile consumer can choose to engage with marketers in multiple ways today, including via phone call (such as a customer service 800 number), click to call, e-mail, click to text, application downloads, and numerous other ways. Mobile ad network Greystripe, for example, suggests 10 different ad-stimulated actions that can be performed on a phone screen to drive consumers down the conversion path through mobile:

- Branding/information dive
- Data collection by survey
- Click to web/WAP
- Click to call
- Click to YouTube/QuickTime (sample video)
- Click to iTunes (sample or download)
- Click to download (variety of assets, including apps)
- Click to maps
- Click to buy
- Click to poll

The Mobile Marketing Landscape

Today the mobile phone ranks third to television and radio in terms of U.S. market penetration, but it is rapidly replacing the personal computer as the platform of choice for many Internet applications. While eMarketer estimates that 73 percent of Americans regularly access the Internet on a desktop computer, more than three-quarters (76 percent) own a mobile phone, which they use and interact with multiple times a day. Among the younger half of the adult population, the mobile phone is even more ubiquitous, with more than 90 percent of those aged 18 to 44 owning one. Further, more and more Americans are "cutting the cord"—replacing their landline phones with exclusive use of cell phones. Data from the Nielsen Convergence Audit suggests that nearly one-quarter of U.S. households do not have a landline.

Or consider the global picture. There are 6.8 billion people on the planet. A total of 1.3 billion can access the Internet on a personal computer, but 4.6 billion people, or two-thirds of the entire population, have cell phones—all with the capability of delivering your marketing message. For many people in the world, their only experience of the Web is through their phone.

Within the vast population of mobile users, a growing proportion own so-called smart phones, which greatly facilitate activities such as Internet browsing, mobile commerce, mobile video, mobile search, and mobile social networking. Smart phones also offer unique features such as geo-location services and specialized applications (aka apps) that are absent, or at best unwieldy, on a standard-feature phone. In the United States, nearly one-third (31 percent) of mobile phone users possess a smart phone, such as an iPhone, Droid, or Blackberry. This percentage will rise to one-half of phone owners over the next several years, according to eMarketer analysis and research.

Consumers are also spending greater amounts of time with their mobile devices. U.S. consumers increased their time spent per day with mobile by nearly 40 percent in 2009, according to the Yankee Group. eMarketer estimates they currently spend 50 minutes per day on mobile devices—equal to the amount of time they spend reading newspapers and magazines—combined.

Why Marketers Love Mobile

With mobile devices evolving rapidly in capability, feature sets, and screen resolution, and with consumer adoption quickly overtaking use of standard phones, marketers are overcoming their reluctance to embrace mobile messaging. And consumers are getting more and more comfortable with seeing ads on their mobile devices. According to an August 2010 study by ad network InMobi and comScore, 38 percent of the nearly 4,400 U.S. mobile consumers surveyed felt mobile ads "serve an important purpose," and an additional 25 percent stated they are getting accustomed to viewing mobile ads. Consumers younger than age 25 were the most comfortable. Brand health benefits often follow (see Figure 8.1).

According to an early 2010 survey by Omniture, 23 percent of marketers at the time were using mobile in their marketing efforts. Another 2010 study by R2integrated found that nearly half of marketing professionals describe mobile as important or very important to their overall marketing strategy. A third study, from the American Marketing Association, revealed that 64 percent of marketers expected to increase their focus on mobile media in 2010. Particularly with the proliferation of smart phones, marketers are drawn to the mobile channel for several reasons:

- The ubiquitous, always-on nature of mobile phones means broad potential reach and accessibility.
- With mobile, two-way interaction between marketers and individual consumers is possible.

Figure 8.1
Mobile drives response

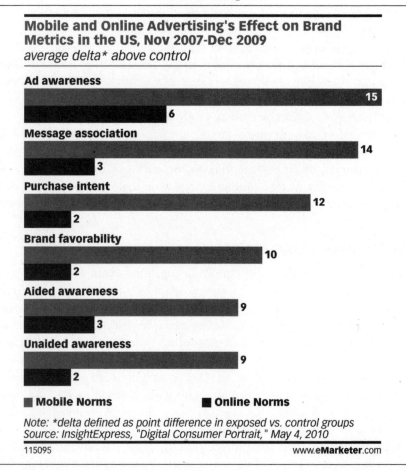

Mobile and Online Advertising's Effect on Brand Metrics in the US, Nov 2007-Dec 2009
average delta* above control

Ad awareness
15
6

Message association
14
3

Purchase intent
12
2

Brand favorability
10
2

Aided awareness
9
3

Unaided awareness
9
2

■ Mobile Norms   ■ Online Norms

Note: *delta defined as point difference in exposed vs. control groups
Source: InsightExpress, "Digital Consumer Portrait," May 4, 2010
115095   www.**eMarketer**.com

- Although most desktop web campaigns allow marketers to target the right message to the right person, the mobile device, through geo-location targeting technology, allows marketers to add two additional dimensions: space and time (that is, you can target the right message not only to the right person, but also at the right time and place).
- Mobile marketing efforts allow for the possibility of extremely granular targeting—given the highly personalized nature of the devices (particularly with smart phones, which often contain highly personal information).
- The mobile screen may be tiny, but it's usually far less cluttered than the typical computer screen, offering marketers a "cleaner" environment for their ad message.

- Mobile devices offer seemingly endless possibilities for engagement with consumers—at all stages along the consumer buying cycle, from awareness and interest, to information-gathering and purchase, and finally to loyalty and retention for customer relationship marketing (CRM) programs.
- Likewise, the mobile phone offers marketers unprecedented opportunities for measurement—not only of the mobile components of a campaign but of the entire campaign, including traditional media.
- Mobile ad campaigns consistently enjoy higher recall and response rates than do those on desktop computers.
- Finally, marketers can barely resist the allure of mobile apps, which allow for untold engagement opportunities!

With all these exciting benefits, mobile must be a huge advertising market, right? Well, not quite.

Mobile Advertising Dollar Trends

The joke in mobile marketing circles is that every new year ushers in the "year of the mobile." And yet, like Godot, it never seems to arrive. But mobile's time may have finally come. eMarketer sees mobile advertising spending in the United States virtually doubling over two years, from $743 million in 2010 to $1.1 billion in 2011 and up to $1.5 billion by 2012. A few researchers estimate that mobile spending could be double or even quadruple that figure in 2012 (Figure 8.2).

On a global basis, mobile ad spending could reach as high as $10 or $12 billion in a couple of years, according to several researchers and investment banks.

Those numbers may seem large, but some perspective is needed. Considering the substantial size of the mobile audience—which is typically 75 percent or more of the entire adult population in any given market—advertising spending on mobile devices is relatively small in comparison. The dollar investments in mobile, like the size of the screens, are small. In the United States, for example, mobile marketing is only one-twenty-fifth the size of the online advertising market.

Despite a small base, mobile ad spending rose nearly 80 percent in 2010, and the growth rate will continue to rise in the high double digits for years to come, according to projections by eMarketer.

The Mobile Tipping Point   Four factors are converging to create a tipping point for mobile advertising and marketing in the United States. First, there

Figure 8.2
Mobile ad spending on the rise

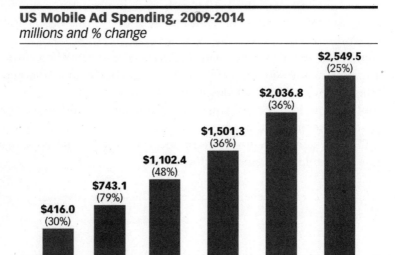

US Mobile Ad Spending, 2009-2014
millions and % change

Note: includes display (banner, rich media and video), search and
messaging-based advertising
Source: eMarketer, Sep 2010

120009   www.**eMarketer**.com

is now a critical mass of smart phone handsets—slightly less than one in
three mobile users are carrying a phone that can perform most of the same
functions as a desktop computer, including web commerce, search, video,
social networking, and e-mail.

Second, largely because of the growing use of smart phones, nearly
40 percent of all U.S. cell phone users can now surf the web on their phones,
according to eMarketer. By 2014, web access through the phone will reach
half the U.S. mobile population. With more and more consumers having
the ability to surf the web on their phones, this means that marketers can
begin to apply the most popular forms of desktop computer–based Internet
advertising—banner ads, video units, search, social media, sponsorships, and
so on—on the mobile handset or tablet device.

The third factor, also driven by smart phone adoption, and in particular the
iPhone, is the explosion of applications for mobile phone users. Apps provide
marketers with exciting new ways to engage their audiences, whether through
sponsorship of existing apps or branded apps that marketers create themselves
to serve some consumer need or interest, aka Magnetic Content.

But the fourth factor is the most important: a new breed of players is fueling greater competition, innovation, and excitement in the mobile category. Until recently, the U.S. mobile market was dominated by legacy telco players—carriers such as AT&T, Sprint, T-Mobile, and Verizon. But now that two powerful and innovation-driven rivals have entered the picture— Google and Apple—the market is being reenergized. Both Google and Apple have introduced new operating systems, Android and iOS, respectively, and have directly entered the mobile advertising network business through their acquisitions of AdMob (by Google) and Quattro Wireless (by Apple). Intense rivalry, world-class execution, and a zealous fixation on customer-focused innovation by these dominant players suggest a market about to bubble over with opportunities.

Magnetizing with Mobile: Six Strategies for Success

If you are looking to magnetize customers, providing them with relevant brand messages, information, and services that reflect their intentions and interests, the mobile phone offers up a wide variety of promising and unique opportunities. However, with so many different kinds of tactical opportunities for engaging with customers, getting your strategy right is all the more important. With mobile, it's easy to get sidetracked by the latest trends, without firmly establishing the broad brand objectives you are trying to achieve.

You will first need to clearly map out the experience you want consumers to have with your brand via the mobile platform. The following provides a set of six best practices for magnetizing consumers in the mobile environment:

1. Identify and understand your mobile audience to discover what may attract them.
2. Make the best use of the channel with precise targeting.
3. Design and execute mobile as an integral, but *additive,* channel.
4. Use geo-location technology—judiciously.
5. Make it measureable and actionable with mobile couponing/shopping.
6. Think before you app!

There are a lot of working parts entailed in each of these strategies, including the need to coordinate the technical aspects with your information technology (IT) and technical resource partners, both internal and external. You will also need to be diligent in your approach. Because of the intense personal nature of phones, any clumsy efforts on your part, such as inappropriately targeted ads, or an overly simplistic or poorly executed app, can significantly harm your brand. The bar for what constitutes good or acceptable brand interactions on the mobile device is much higher than for any other medium, simply because it's so personal. Proceed with caution.

The best news is that all of these mobile magnetic strategies can be applied to the goals of both acquiring new customers and keeping existing ones loyal and happy. The key is to realize that although consumers are increasingly accepting of marketing messages on their mobile phones, they also expect something valuable in return for their attention. That's where Magnetic Content comes in!

1. Identify and Understand Your Mobile Audience to Discover What May Attract Them

Different demographic groups do different things on their mobile phones, and in different ways and on different kinds of phones. They also have different attitudes toward marketing messages delivered via the phone. Understanding the demographics and preferences of mobile users and how they use their devices is an essential first step in determining what will appeal to them as useful, unique, and magnetic. So, arm yourself with all the data you can find to understand your particular mobile target. A basic question is whether your target uses a conventional feature phone or a smart phone, such as an iPhone, Blackberry, or Droid. The more sophisticated your users, the more sophisticated you can be with your marketing approaches. By age group, young adults are not only heavy users of mobile phones, especially the latest smart phones, but are also more open to mobile marketing initiatives. And generally, smart phone owners are wealthier than their standard-feature phone-owning counterparts.

One example of a company that successfully did its homework is Kraft, maker of the popular iFood Assistant app for the iPhone. The company subsequently created a new, specialized app for the iPad called Big Fork, Little Fork, which was born out of research showing that there was strong demand among families for kid-friendly recipes and related educational games.

If you don't have this kind of market research information, try to find a way to get it. If you are going to lay out a clear path from the mobile consumer to your brand, the consumer should always be the starting point—not your product.

2. Make the Best Use of the Mobile Channel with Precise Targeting

Because of the extremely personal nature of phones (many consumers even sleep with them), as well as the small screen size, precise targeting of ad messages is even more important in the mobile environment. Marketers should take full advantage of the latest targeting technologies that allow for the delivery of more relevant messages, including those that reflect time and location status. Just make sure you are adhering strictly to opt-in, permission-based marketing principles.

The targeting capabilities of mobile ad networks, especially those that partner with the carriers and thus have access to rich subscriber data, make for campaigns that convert faster and at higher rates than on the desktop web. For example, consider the information that Vipin's mobile provider knows about him—he's a 45- to 50-year-old male who travels frequently to San Francisco, Detroit, and internationally and who predominantly uses American Airlines and Hertz. In addition, his location and personal calling pattern information can be analyzed and passed on to an appropriate marketer at the moment he's engaging with a given application to make a value-added offer on the spot. This can all be accomplished without compromising his individual identity, and it will be possible in the near future. The mobile phone can become the ultimate targeting device for marketers!

But also consider what certain mobile marketers do not know about Geoff. One of his favorite mobile apps is called RunKeeper; when he goes out for a daily run with his iPhone, it conveniently tracks his time, running pace, and distance and even maps out his course visually. Given all this customized information, no wonder Geoff was surprised to see the sponsored ad that appeared prominently on his RunKeeper app while training for his first half-marathon: a McDonald's promotion for "Chicken McNuggets smothered in Sweet Chili Sauce." Not to begrudge anyone for enjoying the occasional fast food treat, but the targeting of this ad seemed, well, hardly appropriate. An ad for Nike shoes, or better yet a sports drink, would have perhaps made more sense.

Better targeting and more personalized experiences are certainly possible. With the Point Inside iPhone app, for example, visitors to large shopping centers can find their way around much more easily and enjoy a customized experience reflecting their physical surroundings. When the app is launched, the floor plan of the respective mall appears on the iPhone; the integrated GPS module in the phone then locates the user's position and displays a visual map of where all the retail stores are located. Point Inside also displays the phone numbers of the shops and even remembers where the user has parked his or her car.

Mobile platforms now have the ability to collect user data on location and preferences, store this information in a database and create real-time campaigns segmented by interests around specific themes. As a result, mobile ad networks are reporting average click-through rates (CTRs) that exceed those on the desktop web by a factor of 10 or more.

3. Design and Execute Mobile as an Integral, But *Additive*, Channel

Don't put mobile in a silo! Mobile marketing works best when it is carefully integrated with other online and offline media channels. Even when it takes the backseat role, which is often the case, mobile can serve as a powerful catalyst, accelerator, enhancer, and even barometer for an integrated media campaign. The mobile phone, because it's always on and follows consumers along wherever they go, has the unique ability to bridge the gap between the digital and physical worlds. It can also serve dual marketing roles, lending itself to both direct response and brand image campaigns that rely on multiple exposures to reinforce a marketing message.

Bottom line: We advise taking a holistic view of your entire media plan and accompanying messaging to determine what role, if any, mobile should play in the mix. Many times, mobile works best as the punch line for a setup in traditional media, such as a TV commercial, radio spot, or even a billboard ad. For example, big brands like Nike and Dove have run massive interactive billboard ads in New York's Times Square that allow passersby to interact with the ads by typing in text codes into their mobile phones. This is personalized marketing—in a public way.

In this complementary, assistive role, mobile should be thought of as an ongoing series of opportunities to potentially connect with the consumer, rather than a one-time, stand-alone interaction or campaign. We believe you should bring in mobile at the earliest possible stage of planning and budgeting your media, rather than trying to tack it on at the end. It's fruitful to ask these two vital questions at the very beginning:

- How can mobile be used to reach audiences in ways and places that other media cannot?
- Where can mobile support and enhance other media placements and marketing efforts?

Mobile is not only complementary to other media channels; it can act as an accelerator for stimulating desired consumer behaviors. The always-available accessibility of the mobile phone makes it possible for marketers to stimulate an immediate response from consumers, which can also be quickly measured. Mobile is one of the easiest ways to measure consumer engagement, and it can happen anywhere, at anytime.

Use Mobile to Alert Consumers to Your Magnetic Content   While there are plenty of opportunities for delivering Magnetic Content directly through the phone (such as through apps), another strategy is to use the mobile phone as a messaging device to alert the consumer about Magnetic Content that lies waiting on other platforms, such as your brand website, YouTube, or a branded Facebook page. Even a brief text alert can be used as a trigger mechanism for pushing consumers further along on your engagement map toward Magnetic Content—where they can become engaged at a deeper level. In this way, SMS not only is efficient and cost-effective, but can also be carefully timed to coincide with key events or promotions. (It is essential, of course, to garner the appropriate permissions from the consumer to send such messages.)

Lending credence to this SMS strategy is a research study from Harris/Placecast (Figure 8.3). Among the mobile users who signed up to receive text alerts, 34 percent said they would be more likely to visit the company's website in response to the alert, and 33 percent indicated they would visit

Figure 8.3
Mobile customers are receptive to commercial messages

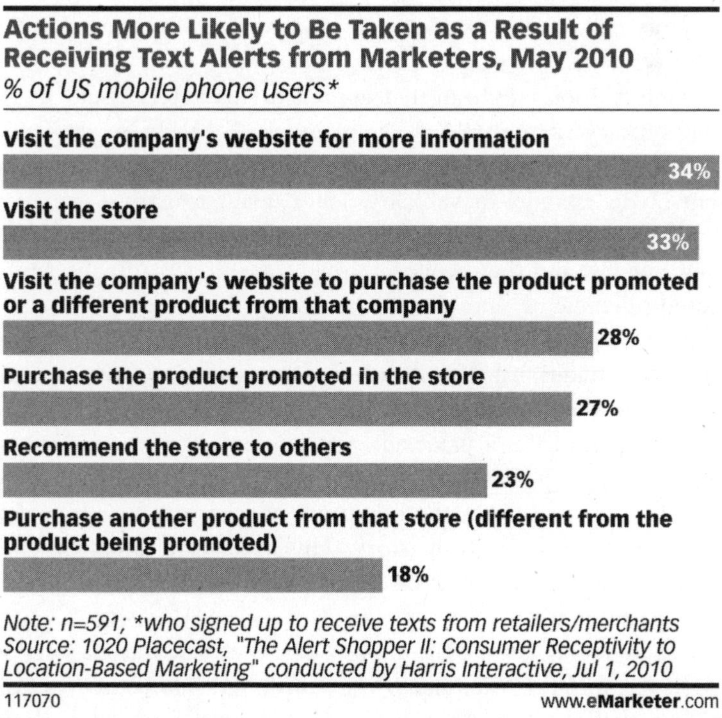

Actions More Likely to Be Taken as a Result of Receiving Text Alerts from Marketers, May 2010
% of US mobile phone users*

Visit the company's website for more information
34%

Visit the store
33%

Visit the company's website to purchase the product promoted or a different product from that company
28%

Purchase the product promoted in the store
27%

Recommend the store to others
23%

Purchase another product from that store (different from the product being promoted)
18%

Note: n=591; *who signed up to receive texts from retailers/merchants
Source: 1020 Placecast, "The Alert Shopper II: Consumer Receptivity to Location-Based Marketing" conducted by Harris Interactive, Jul 1, 2010

117070   www.**eMarketer**.com

a physical store. Imagine how much higher these response rates could be if you were offering truly Magnetic Content for their efforts.

Further substantiating the strategy of using mobile advertising to draw consumers to your Magnetic Content, consider the results of a survey by InMobi and comScore. Respondents to the August 2010 survey said the number one benefit (47 percent) of having seen mobile advertising was that it introduced them to something new; the second-rated benefit, at 35 percent of respondents, was helping them learn more about something. Both responses suggest consumers would welcome ads leading them to valuable Magnetic Content by a marketer.

Use Mobile to Track, Measure, and Enhance Other Media   Jiffy Lube provides a classic, textbook case for how to incorporate mobile as a call-to-action measurement tool for a traditional media campaign promotion. The oil-change service ran a radio spot that invited consumers to text on their mobile phones for a chance to win a year's worth of oil changes. Each listener who entered received a $5 coupon via SMS, and Jiffy Lube found that 50 percent of those redeeming the SMS coupons were new customers. By adding the mobile call to action to the existing media buy (at very little additional expense), Jiffy Lube made its radio dollars work harder and was able to track the results far more effectively.

For a slightly more sophisticated approach, marketers could use mobile to test the efficacy of multiple media channels. By including different key-words or numbers for consumers to text in to a short code, each representing a different media channel or vehicle (such as print magazine or newspaper), marketers can determine which publications perform better in terms of generating opt-ins, and then reallocate media spend accordingly. Mobile can thus be used to efficiently measure the health of other media channels.

Mobile can also be used to enhance other media. Even an insurance company using a traditional print format like newspapers can perk up consumer interest through the integrated use of mobile. One high-profile insurance company in Belgium ran a print ad in a newspaper showing a street scene of a massive car pileup. The ad's headline read, "To find out what happens, put your iPhone here." Once the consumer obliges and the app is activated, they get sent a video that tells the story. This multistage campaign effectively combines video on top of mobile on top of print—all to engage the consumer in a branded experience.

As with social media, the mobile phone can also serve marketers as a powerful, one-to-one channel for listening to the consumer. Think of ways to make it easier for mobile consumers to provide you with feedback—about your product, ad campaign, customer service, competitive offerings, and so on. Allow your customers to reach you, not just by dialing your customer service 800 number on their mobile phone (who has time for all those mindless menu trees!), but via other, more efficient means such as click to call, mobile e-mail, or text or by engaging with a branded customer-talk-back app. This is all part of the magnetism approach—making it easier for consumers to reach and engage with you.

Consider also the growing popularity of quick response (QR) codes and snap-tags. These are images (in printed form or online) that can be scanned by a mobile device. Once scanned, the code allows the consumer to interact with mobile content, or perhaps with a mobile-optimized website, and provides access to tools, rewards, and goodies such as exclusive videos, polls, brochure downloads, discount coupons, contest entries, and much more. The big advantage is that they do not require any text entry for the consumer to bring up the mobile content. Physically, a QR code is a two-dimensional visual code that is readable by QR scanners, smart phones, and even standard-feature phones if they incorporate a camera. Snap-tags are similar. The codes create a bridge between offline media and a mobile device; consumers can access desired mobile content by simply pointing their mobile phones toward a QR code which can be placed within a newspaper or magazine, on an outdoor billboard, in a sign within a shopping mall, on a decal in a restaurant or shop window, or even a tote bag or event giveaway.

Younger adults and teens find QR codes and snap-tags very easy to use and increasingly expect to see them. There are, however, some technical issues with QR codes in the United States due to the lack of a universal standard. In some instances, this requires the consumer to download a specific scanner software app, which is an extra step that can hinder QR code marketing to the broader public. However, some marketers view such downloads as another way to tally or qualify a prospective customer. Snap-tags, which can be read by a phone camera, often incorporate vivid color patterns to attract consumers to snap.

4. Use Geo-Location Technology—Judiciously

Geo-location technology offers a powerful capability to engage with consumers based on knowledge of their physical whereabouts. Location-based services, using GPS technology, can also provide marketers with compelling data that can enable them to present relevant offers and rewards right when consumers are at the point of decision. For example, product information or coupons can be instantly delivered to consumers when they check in at a retail store with their cell phones.

Geo-location services such as foursquare and Facebook Places represent the next evolution in our concept of Magnetic Content. They allow marketers to deliver offers, coupons, information, and even entertainment to consumers at the very moment they're likely to need it—before they even think to look for it or perform a search. Even a simple ad, if it's delivered at a time and place that is likely to be of use to the consumer, can be viewed as welcome Magnetic Content.

One technology company, Shopkick, has created a location app that allows customers to get points (called kickbucks) when they physically enter a participating retailer's store; they get more points as they continue to engage with the retailer, say by stopping in the dressing room or visiting another floor. The prevailing idea behind these promotions is that they are more likely to be effective because they are delivered to shoppers who are clearly in a buying frame of mind, as well as the fact that they have opted in at the retailer.

These and other location-based services, such as foursquare, Gowalla, and Loopt, get a lot of press attention, and marketers seem enthralled about the prospects of deploying the technology to connect with consumers in real time and space. However, the market penetration numbers tell of a smaller opportunity, at least for the time being. According to numerous sources, well under 10 percent of the mobile population currently engages with check-in services. And among the small portion that do engage, most of them are young males. This is hardly the kind of reach most marketers are seeking. But as these technologies proliferate and become absorbed by the bigger social platforms like Facebook, Twitter, and Yelp, the floodgates will open and virtually every website and service will be able to tell where you are.

Practically speaking, geo-location targeting is mostly limited for marketers as a local point-of-purchase (POP) opportunity. It helps you reach out to existing customers, particularly young males, and for those looking for nearby food and entertainment services such as bars, restaurants, clubs, and concerts. For example, the English mobile music provider Shazam has enhanced its iPhone app Shazam Encore and (Shazam) RED to allow iPhone and iPod Touch users to use Pandora and Last.fm to create Internet radio stations from their tagged music. When a song is tagged, an icon will be displayed that, when tapped, provides tour and ticket information for that band or artist. Users can also find out where their favorite tagged artists are performing locally, with automated geo-location functionality.

One local firm that uses geo-location technology effectively is Pacific Catch, a small chain of seafood restaurants in the San Francisco Bay Area. In addition to Twitter and Facebook, Pacific Catch relies on the foursquare application to retain customers through rewards like special discounts tied to their number of visits. A patron who checks in to one of Pacific Catch's stores five times, for example, will see a timely offer pop up on their phone, such as for a free shrimp appetizer or other fish dish. Customers receiving such rewards are not only likely to remain loyal but also be motivated to tell others, and this drives new business for the chain. As cited in an October 6, 2010, *New York Times* article, 1,400 people checked in at Pacific Catch a total of 2,800 times. Many local businesses end up using foursquare and similar check-in services as a digital replacement for coupons, buy-one-get-one-free offers, and loyalty cards.

The future for location-based mobile technologies is great. Soon, we'll see the experience of checking in to take advantage of an offer serving as the direct-response end point (the End Action) of a longer and larger campaign effort that started with branding and awareness building. Location data will help guide brand messaging at each stage of the purchase funnel, with success turning on the combined power of reach, relevancy, and the ability to drive local offer redemption. As eMarketer analyst Noah Elkin says, "The company with the richest social graph and the most extensive geo-location information has the upper hand in providing a better value proposition to the consumer."

We also offer a word of caution: if marketers as a group are not judicious with their use of geo-location technology, they can end up creating a geo-location apocalypse—a situation where the consumer is inundated with messages every time they walk into a shopping mall or particular area of town. Just as we've seen with e-mail, even consumers who are selective when they opt in to marketers' messages can end up, over time, being bombarded with promotional messages from even well-meaning marketers. Keep it opt in; keep it sparing.

5. Make It Measurable and Actionable with Mobile Couponing/Shopping

Although actual purchasing of products and services on the mobile phone is a relatively recent and limited occurrence, at least in the United States, marketers should be paying a great deal of attention to the growing consumer trend of mobile shopping and couponing. Geo-location technology allows companies to market to consumers at or near the point of sale, potentially reducing the time barrier and friction between shopping activity and an actual transaction.

Consumers are warming to using their phones as shopping aides. Many are pulling out their smart phones right in the midst of shopping at a physical store to access information, such as to compare products and prices, that will help them decide on a given purchase, which may or may not transpire in the store. Increasingly, too, consumers are embracing the convenience advantage of mobile coupons. Based on numerous sources, including mBlox and IHL Group, approximately 15 percent of U.S. mobile subscribers have redeemed a mobile coupon, although this number will grow rapidly over the coming years. All this provides unique promotional opportunities for savvy marketers.

Mobile coupons—delivered to customers while in or near the store—can be used to accelerate purchase activity. A coupon delivered right at the point of purchase can be just the incentive to push a hesitant customer over the fence. Consumers can also download relevant coupons on their phones for redemption at a more convenient time. The best news? All of this coupon activity can be monitored by the marketer in real time.

According to a 2010 survey by PriceGrabber.com (Figure 8.4), 35 percent of consumers with web-enabled phones participate in mobile shopping, but only 13 percent said they made purchases (Pew Internet & American Life Project puts the purchase number at only 11 percent of mobile users). Similarly, according to Retrevo, Internet users are three times as likely to research or compare prices on their mobile phones as they are to make a purchase. Another source, ATG, claims the factor is fourfold.

Correspondingly, from the seller side, although 12 percent of multichannel retailers in 2010 were using mobile advertising to promote sales and special offers and 3 percent distributed mobile coupons, the vast majority, nearly 80 percent, said they were not offering any m-commerce services. We believe, however, that retailers and other marketers may be missing a big opportunity to engage with mobile consumers who are in shopping mode. According to Forrester, about half of all retail sales in the United States are influenced by online researching and browsing, a growing portion of which is taking place on the mobile phone. Make no mistake; the bulk of these digitally influenced sales will actually take place in a store, but the impact from shopping via handheld devices is huge and growing.

Recent research shows that mobile coupons tied to location technology deliver redemptions rates that are far superior to any other delivery mechanism. Coupon redemption rates for print tend to hover around 1 percent, whereas those for online top out at around 10 percent; mobile coupon redemptions rates, though, often reach 20 percent. There are a growing number of local-mobile ad networks to choose from, including Where, LocalAdXchange, Chitika, and CityGrid.

Mobile coupons work particularly well for retailers, because they control the product inventory, the point-of-sale (POS) positioning, and can directly

Figure 8.4
Web commerce activity is growing over time

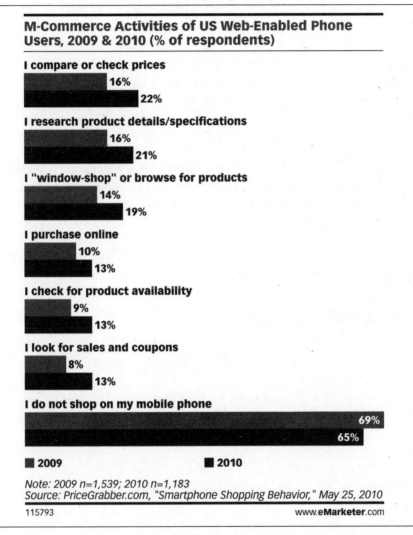

M-Commerce Activities of US Web-Enabled Phone Users, 2009 & 2010 (% of respondents)

I compare or check prices
16%
22%

I research product details/specifications
16%
21%

I "window-shop" or browse for products
14%
19%

I purchase online
10%
13%

I check for product availability
9%
13%

I look for sales and coupons
8%
13%

I do not shop on my mobile phone
69%
65%

■ 2009   ■ 2010

Note: 2009 n=1,539; 2010 n=1,183
Source: PriceGrabber.com, "Smartphone Shopping Behavior," May 25, 2010

115793   www.**eMarketer**.com

manage and train their employees to accept mobile coupons from customers. However, for manufacturers, mobile coupons present a bit of a challenge given the complexities of retail distribution. For example, Pampers, the global disposable diaper brand, cannot issue a mobile coupon and expect that the consumer can walk into any store in the country and redeem it. First, it is quite likely that the clerk has never even heard of mobile coupons, much less been trained in how to handle them. Second, the retailer may not be participating in the offering, thus preventing the coupon from being redeemed. Consequently, it's best for manufacturers to establish partnerships. As one option, the manufacturer could find a retailer who has a mobile program and create a mobile coupon specifically for that retailer.

The other option is to partner with a retailer who does not have a mobile program but can participate in a co-sponsored campaign that delivers mobile coupons driving people into the store. For example, in the case of the Pampers example, the brand could partner with a grocery chain such as Safeway, which does have a full-fledged mobile coupon program, and create co-sponsored campaign such as "Buy one pack of Pampers at Safeway, and get the second one free! Text Pampers to 80800 now!" As another option, manufacturers can search for applications that have aggregated retailers into a network to deliver mobile coupons from various manufacturers. There are currently several applications on the market, such as Cellfire, Groupon, and Daily Savings, which work with retailers to provide mobile coupons. This allows the manufacturer to place coupons with retailers who are already using mobile coupons and quickly get in front of an existing coupon-hungry mobile audience.

6. Think before You App!

So your CEO walks into your office, pounds his fist on the table and exclaims, "Where the heck is our app?!" What do you do?

Try to buy some time.

Apps are certainly cool. However, with literally hundreds of thousands of apps flooding the market—none of which works on every kind of device, but all of which must vie for the consumer's limited attention—you'd better think really hard about the purpose of any app you create, or whether you should even have one at all. They can be a powerful way to engage consumers with your Magnetic Content—if you first do your homework.

> According to FutureSource Consulting, consumers worldwide will download 10 billion apps in 2011 and 16 billion by 2013.

The Magnetic Content opportunities for apps are endless—limited only by your imagination! With smart phones and now tablets becoming a growing presence within the mobile device landscape, apps may become an indispensable means for brands to engage consumers at various stages of the purchase funnel.

The in-app ad market is tiny now but will likely grow quickly. Borrell Associates estimates that in-app ads accounted for only 5 percent of total mobile advertising in 2010. The research firm calculates in-app advertising skyrocketed by 667 percent from 2009 to 2010.There are two basic marketing approaches for brands desiring to take advantage of apps. You can either develop an original app yourself, or you can sponsor an existing app that has already proved to be popular. With the do-it-yourself (DIY) strategy, you will likely enjoy a deeper engagement with the consumer, but the latter strategy is far easier to implement (for example, insert your brand ad here).

If you're building a brand app from scratch, rule number one is to keep the customer and his or her needs firmly in mind—before you start designing. If your app is really just a thinly disguised ad for your product and doesn't solve any consumer need or want, no one will care and you won't draw people in. On the other hand, you can also fail another way. If you create a nifty app that manages to hit a home run with consumers but does a poor job of linking back to your brand in a way that either indirectly reinforces a key brand attribute or directly leads the consumer to seek information on your company or product, it's useless.

When creating apps, marketers must strive for Magnetic Content that is unique, useful, fun, and well executed and that clearly leverages the special properties of the mobile platform. The two key words here are *portability* and *utility*— does the app provide something useful for the consumer on the go? Often, utility comes in the form of providing timely information or content that somehow relates to your brand positioning, promise, or personality.

An apt example of an app comes from Benjamin Moore, the paint company. Their Ben Color Capture app for the iPhone lets consumers take a picture of an object with their mobile phone. Then the app delivers the closest color match in Benjamin Moore's catalog of more than 3,300 hues. To get complimentary color matches, users shake their phone and four coordinating colors and a harmonizing palette pops up. Color matches can also be saved for a trip to the store. And, of course, GPS technology facilitates the process of finding the nearest store.

Even a car insurance company can use mobile apps to delight its customers with utility. Nationwide built a mobile app, the Nationwide Mobile App for iPhone, that enables customers in an accident to manage all the necessary paperwork on the spot, thereby reducing the irritation and hassle of having to fill forms out the old-fashioned way.

More examples of branded apps providing consumer utility that is enhanced by their portability are:

- Clorox, the consumer packaged goods company, provides an app called iStain that allows consumers, especially busy moms, to quickly determine the best means of eradicating a stain while on the go; importantly, many of the tips do not use Clorox products but instead rely on common household items.
- The Gap's StyleMixer app invites mobile users to virtually mix and match pieces of clothing by combining existing wardrobe items and pairing them with new items from the Gap; it uses the iPhone's camera feature and links to Facebook friends to further engage the user.

Besides utility, another way to engage consumers through apps is by offering entertainment, which can come in the form of games, puzzles, videos, or contests. One such example is the free iPhone app called iButterfly; it represents a playful combination between augmented reality and location-based coupons, cleverly using the iPhone's GPS. The user has to try to catch a flying, virtual butterfly on the screen by aiming and shaking the iPhone. Only then will the user get to see the location-based coupons and other information. A variety of companies, including Japan's largest electronics store Yamada Denki, are currently testing the iButterfly to see if they can use it as a new e-commerce tool.

Plan and Budget for Discoverability   One often-overlooked challenge with apps is discoverability. You can build a great app, but consumers won't necessarily find it. Discoverability, or the way in which consumers browse, search for, or learn about an app, presents challenges for any brand in such a crowded environment. Understanding how a consumer will discover your app is a key consideration and probably represents the more expensive proposition. Getting onto Apple's Top 25 Free Apps or other app lists of the week are avenues for discoverability, but they can't be the only ones. Recommendations from family and friends via Facebook and other social networks can play a role, too. Of course, a search campaign and accompanying landing page should also be part of the mix. But, most likely, you will need to extensively promote the app using online, offline, and mobile display media. In other words, paid media. A general rule of thumb is to allocate at least two-thirds of the app budget to its promotion. If you are thinking about spending $20,000 on developing an app, plan to spend at least $60,000 on marketing to make sure it gets some penetration.

It is also critical to track consumer engagement with your app—and not just with raw download figures. Do consumers use it, or lose it? Even if you are lucky enough to score a significant number of downloads initially, you can expect that, over time, there will be some kind of attrition rate. Initial downloads are an important data point, but they don't offer insight into actual usage, engagement, and retention. The nature and intensity of the interactions, as well as the frequency of use over time, must be factored into your ROI calculation. Ultimately, you are better off with 1,000 highly engaged consumers who stick with you than you are with 10,000 consumers who download the app once but never return. Kraft's iFood Assistant, for example, ties directly into the company's CRM program. By linking the app across all of its CRM channels over an extended period, Kraft gets a holistic view of its users, is able to measure high-value tasks, and can use this information to begin to understand lifetime customer value.

Ed Kaczmarek, director of innovation and consumer experiences for Kraft Foods, describes the value of the many-sided app:

> Engagement means using it and repeat usage. It means that they're going into the app, using the different functions—whether that's saving recipes to their recipe box, e-mailing to a friend, touching the Recipe of the Day idea, browsing recipes, doing a search—it's engaging the platform. When they're engaging the platform, they're seeing the utility we're providing but they're also engaging our brand throughout the experience.*

Mobile Performance Measurement

Building a forward-looking mobile strategy and measurement process requires two things at the outset: making sure the mobile strategy plugs into your overall marketing strategy and creating a Performance Measurement plan to justify the investment in additive mobile initiatives. If you're not sure how to do this, don't worry. The lack of understanding that surrounds mobile measurement is common in the industry. It's a newer channel, and many of the popular digital analytic tools don't yet include capabilities to integrate mobile channels.

Reliable data collection for mobile measurement can be a challenge. The United States alone has hundreds of different devices and carriers, as well as numerous mobile operating systems, each with different mechanisms for data collection standards. All this creates nonuniformity, service gaps, and issues

---

*Source: interview with eMarketer, February 2, 2010.

in obtaining accurate data. A measurement tool and solution would ideally be able to accommodate data from all these different platforms, carriers, and devices.

Further, existing web analytics tools do not extend into tracking unique visitors on mobile sites, which impedes accurate measurement. Web analytics tools that track individuals or visitors based on cookies and/or JavaScript tags are not supported by feature phones, which account for the about 70 percent of phones in the United States. Only the leading smart phones (like the iPhone, Android, and some Nokia phones) support tags for tracking visitors.

Cookies, useful for tracking individuals on the web, also fail on mobile devices. Placing cookies on handsets is not reliable; some phones, including the Apple iPhone, will either wipe off cookies or turn them off when the phone is switched off.

Another mobile measurement challenge is tracking the source of your consumers viewing your site. Not all devices enable geographic detection. Some newer devices can inherently enable tracking of who you are, where you live, and where you are at any given point in time. However, this requires that the mobile operator not only collect all this data but also be willing to share it with marketers in some useful form.

As a marketer, you have to decide whether you need to get a custom mobile measurement tool that is able to address these mobile challenges or work with the limitations of your current web analytics tools. The good news is that many vendors are working out the details to integrate mobile data more seamlessly, and the date is not too far away when that will happen. A few promising ones to try out are discussed here.

PercentMobile is a mobile analytics tool with an expansive and accurate database and detection mechanism. It has a simple user interface and reporting layer and is appropriate for small-business owners. Some of the other ones that we like are AdMob and Webtrends Mobile Analytics.

Of course, what to measure with mobile depends on the objectives of a given campaign, and the array of possible metrics can be a daunting alphabet soup. Our measurement framework once again provides a quick way to choose appropriate metrics. For measuring mobile campaigns, we recommend using four of our seven recommended digital campaign metrics.

Exposure Metrics for Mobile Platforms

Exposure metrics on mobile are but a slight variation from measurements for other channels, which is helpful if you are employing mobile media to boost traffic or stimulate engagement elsewhere.

1. Qualified Reach This metric is defined as *the number of mobile users who may have seen your messaging AND then choose to have some interaction with branded content.* Qualified Reach is very appropriate to the mobile channel and can be used to measure the success of your ads (or other Magnetic Content) in terms of driving consumers to your mobile sites. It is especially useful given that mobile customers are opting in for ads to access rewards, coupons, and special offers. As we mentioned in Chapter 2, Qualified Reach is different from pure impressions, which is incomplete, because it does not contain any element of actual engagement with the ad or message unit.

2. Use Click-Through Rates (CTRs) as a Diagnostic Aid CTR is calculated by dividing the number of users who clicked on an ad by the number of times the ad was delivered (that is, impressions). It reflects potential interest to learn more about your products and services. It should never be the primary metric or the main objective of a mobile campaign. As discussed in Chapter 2, it is most useful as a diagnostic metric.

Mobile enjoys unusually high click rates, often five times or more higher than that of Internet display ads. CTR for text messaging can be as high as 15 percent. As an opt-in channel, texting (or SMS) is used by marketers to drive traffic, often by including a link to rich media or a video. Text campaigns integrated with offline media like TV can use codes to track the number of clicks or hits being generated by your campaign, broken out by medium. For example, if you are running TV and radio ads, you could insert different text codes for each, for example, "VMGR001" and "VMGR002," to distinguish response rates for each medium. Of course, if you are using SMS coupons (delivering coupons through SMS), you will have a great way to track the effectiveness of your campaign.

Strategic Metrics for Mobile

Evaluating customer and brand growth through mobile channels is likely to become more important as more and more consumers use smaller devices as their primary or preferred access to the Internet.

3. End Action Rate End Action in the mobile space often relates to the number of people who download an application, sign up for an offer, or continue on to buy something. The End Action rate is often referred to as the conversion event because it represents the conversion, or any desired outcome for the mobile content.

Given the importance of the End Action, you should conduct the appropriate analytics to understand what drives the highest conversion. For example:

- Are there certain ads, messages, or placements that drive the highest conversion?
- Does a specific time of day deliver higher conversion rates?
- Are there any handsets or devices delivering higher conversion rates?
- Which target segments and audiences are most likely to convert?

Financial Metrics as Applied to Mobile

As mobile is a new area for many marketers, financial metrics that help you quantify your return on investment, or other financial outcomes, of a mobile marketing activity should be set in place early on.

4. Return on Investment (ROI)   A recent survey by R2integrated indicated that 43 percent of marketers were concerned about how to track their mobile ROI. We can verify that marketers also find it hard to predict incremental usage and revenue. This should be expected with a relatively new medium.

Our ROI methodologies and concepts are built upon our principle of *incrementality* and are particularly applicable to new mobile initiatives. As we have suggested, all marketing, whether it is offline or online, should show results as *an incremental improvement*—in *acquisition, retention, loyalty, key perception(s),* or *sales.*

The critical question in the estimation of ROI for mobile becomes, "How do you determine 'incrementality' in such a new medium?" To do this, you need to first identify your own goals for incremental revenue from the mobile channel.

What are common goals of incremental revenue for mobile that other marketers use? We've identified three familiar areas of source data you can use to calculate your ROI:

1. *Increase in the number of transactions and in the transaction size.* Mobile is a "purchase accelerator." It accelerates conversion from shoppers to buyers through targeted coupons, offers, and the use of location-based services to their mobile devices.

   But how do you know whether or not the mobile service actually drove the additional trip to the store or increased order/basket size?

You can determine this by offering a short-term test promotion with a mobile-specific coupon or an up-selling or cross-selling offer. The resulting incrementality can be computed by comparing redemption rates, number of transactions, and total transaction size during the promotion period versus the nonpromotion period. Through this comparison we can show how much of a transaction lift took place during the promotion and use that as part of the ROI calculation.

2. *Increase in the number of customers.* Mobile can help a brand acquire new customers. Many mobile users will interact with a brand's application, especially if it is magnetic and offers some kind of utility or valuable service. Furthermore, for marketers trying to reach younger adults, a mobile presence can play an increasing role in their selection of a brand or a product.

3. *Additional revenue from mobile commerce.* Mobile coupons, tickets, and auctions are all beginning to generate additive mobile commerce, referred to as m-commerce, and you'd be hard pressed to find an online retailer who has not adapted their home page and website to work quickly on the small screen of a mobile device. All major retailers are investing in m-commerce sites and retail-oriented applications to get consumers to buy their products and services through their mobile phones. These sales can be easily separated out to determine how they are contributing incremental revenue for your ROI.

The next step is to simply calculate the ROI from the preceding data. We go back to the ROI equation and plug in the source data of incremental revenue, based on three sets of useful numbers:

- Increased revenue generated from increased number of transactions and basket size estimated from the test
- Increased revenue from new customers purchasing on mobile media
- Increased revenue generated from mobile-only services and m-commerce

Just sum these three sources of revenue and then divide by the total cost to estimate ROI.

For example, for a mobile campaign, a company spent $500,000 when launching a mobile coupon program to prospects and customers. It drove new customers and resulted in a larger basket size. The company estimated the increased revenue from new customers was $1,500,000. Generating a larger transaction size and basket size from existing customers provided an additional estimated $800,000, for a total of $2,300,000 in incremental revenue.

ROI in this instance was:

$$\frac{\$2,300,000 - \$500,000}{\$500,000} \times 100\% = 3.6\%$$

Tablet Mania?

The iPad and other tablets are changing the meaning of mobility and present a new alternative to the smaller mobile phone screen. Laptops and netbooks have served consumers as mobile Internet access and media consumption devices for years. But the success of the iPad has put renewed focus on tablets, which are predicted to skyrocket in sales over the next several years; by 2015, they are projected to account for a greater share of computer sales than netbooks or desktops. Already, according to eMarketer, 24 million Americans own a tablet, representing nearly 8 percent of the population. For advertisers and marketers, tablet devices provide a one-two punch of a bigger screen with touch capability, both of which promise more immersive experiences for content and advertising alike.

Conclusion

Brands today need mobile marketing to stay relevant. Mobile devices are not likely to do away with desktop computers or big-screen TVs anytime soon, but they are becoming a more widely used conduit to web-based content, services, and even ads, simply because of their omnipresence. The amount of time consumers spend with their mobile devices is also growing at a far quicker pace than time spent either using computers or watching TV, meaning that marketers who want to travel along with their audience (and who doesn't?!) will have to focus more attention on mobile advertising and Magnetic Content. As eMarketer mobile analyst Noah Elkin says, "Half the battle of staying relevant is showing up in the right place, at the right time and on the right device."

Finding Opportunity: A Summary of Trends in Mobile Marketing

The mobile phone provides marketers with a wide range of opportunities for engaging with consumers and prospects, many of which are unique to the mobile device. The following section highlights the key numbers, trends, and pros

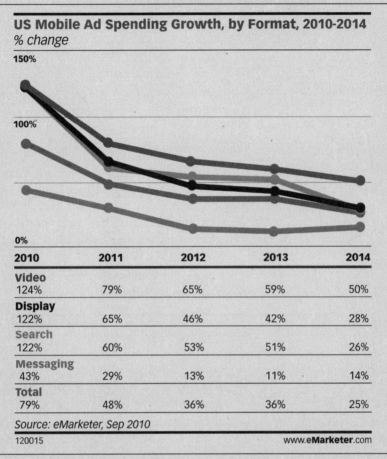

Figure 8.5

Multiple growth opportunities for mobile

US Mobile Ad Spending Growth, by Format, 2010-2014
% change

	2010	2011	2012	2013	2014
Video	124%	79%	65%	59%	50%
Display	122%	65%	46%	42%	28%
Search	122%	60%	53%	51%	26%
Messaging	43%	29%	13%	11%	14%
Total	79%	48%	36%	36%	25%

Source: eMarketer, Sep 2010

120015   www.**eMarketer**.com

and cons for each mobile ad format. Keep in mind that most of the individual opportunities represent a relatively small market in terms of audience reach. However, know this: (1) the audience size will grow; (2) the audience you do reach is likely to be highly engaged; and (3) it is the integration of these mobile subformats with other online and offline ad platforms (see Figure 8.5) that creates the real opportunity, what we call the "additive" effect.

Text messaging currently accounts for the bulk of spending on mobile advertising in the United States—about 55 percent of the U.S. mobile ad market in 2009, according to eMarketer.

(continued)

Figure 8.6
Texting activity

Mobile Content Activities, by Age, May 2010
% of US mobile phone users

	18-29	30-49	50-64	65+
Send/receive text messages	95%	82%	57%	19%
Take a picture	93%	83%	67%	34%
Access the internet	65%	43%	18%	10%
Play music	64%	36%	13%	6%
Play a game	60%	37%	17%	9%
Record a video	60%	39%	14%	5%
Send/receive email	52%	37%	22%	11%
Use a social networking site	48%	23%	8%	3%
Send/receive instant messages	46%	35%	17%	10%
Watch a video	40%	20%	6%	4%
Post a photo or video online	33%	15%	5%	2%
Use a status update service	21%	9%	3%	2%
Make a purchase	20%	11%	4%	5%

Note: n=1,917
Source: Pew Internet & American Life Project, "Mobile Access 2010," Jul 7, 2010

117353   www.e**Marketer**.com

Along with taking pictures, sending and receiving text messages is the most popular content activity on mobile phones today. According to Pew Internet & American Life Project, nearly three-quarters (72 percent) of all U.S. adults engage in texting activity, which can be done on both a standard-feature phone as well a smart phone (Figure 8.6). As expected, there is also a strong skew toward younger people.

Messaging is as close to a universal activity as there is for mobile users, and high interaction rates mean that SMS will remain a mobile marketing staple. That said, given the proliferation of other, more exciting ways to engage with consumers on mobile devices, we believe messaging-based advertising will decline but continue to be an effective way for marketers to reach the mobile masses. Currently, a large majority of U.S. mobile users still rely on feature phones, so SMS and MMS remain an important channel to reach them. As with many ad formats on mobile phones, SMS and MMS ads will be far more acceptable to consumers if they feel they are being offered something of value in exchange for the messaging.

Mobile Video

Particularly for those marketers targeting the always-on-the-go youth market, the benefits of using mobile video as an advertising platform are compelling. While the screen is small, video advertising on the mobile phone can replicate the best attributes of the television experience, including sight, sound, and motion. These elements, in turn, provide rich opportunities for conveying emotion, excitement, and deep engagement—critical for most brand marketers.

However, the audience today is still relatively small and fragmented, and there are complications involved in delivering video on a range of incompatible devices and operating systems, all to a tiny screen.

The population of U.S. mobile users watching video on their phones is 31 million today (2011), representing 12.5 percent of mobile phone users and 10 percent of the entire U.S. population, according to eMarketer. Among smart phone owners the penetration rate, as you would expect, is much higher, at 37 percent, according to Initiative (June 2010). By year-end 2014, the total number watching mobile video will rise to 57 million, or 22 percent of U.S. mobile users. Other sources, like Pew Internet & American Life Project, estimate mobile video penetration at a higher level; Pew reports that 20 percent of mobile users were accessing video on their phones as of May 2010 (Figure 8.7).

Not surprisingly, the heaviest consumption of video on phones is done by younger demographics, particularly young males. Although 40 percent of mobile users aged 18 to 29 view video on their phones and 20 percent of those aged 30 to 49 do so, only 6 percent of those 50 to 64 years old engage in the activity, according to Pew Internet & American Life Project. Hispanics are also heavy users of mobile video; 33 percent of mobile Hispanic users watch video on their phones, whereas only 15 percent of non-Hispanic whites do so, also according to Pew.

Figure 8.7
Video on the small screen is increasing

US Mobile Video Viewers, 2008-2014
millions and % of population

	2008	2009	2010	2011	2012	2013	2014
Mobile video viewers	**12.3**	**18.4**	**23.9**	**31.4**	**40.0**	**47.9**	**56.7**
% of mobile phone users	5.4%	7.7%	9.7%	12.5%	15.7%	18.5%	21.5%
% of population	4.1%	6.0%	7.7%	10.0%	12.7%	15.0%	17.6%

Note: CAGR (2009-2014)=22.8%
Source: eMarketer, July 2010

117990   www.**eMarketer**.com

(continued)

Still, it helps to remember that hours spent watching video on mobile devices pales in comparison to traditional TV watching. Even among the most avid demographic group of mobile video watchers, namely teens aged 12 to 17, the average time spent watching mobile video is only seven hours per month, versus 108 hours spent watching TV, according to the Nielsen Company (June 2010 statistics). A study by KPMG International in July 2010 found that only 5 percent of consumers prefer mobile phones as a platform for watching video, compared with 77 percent who prefer the experience on personal computers—no doubt because of the larger screen.

The mobile video viewer market is still highly fragmented, because consumption can take place on paid and free applications, mobile websites, pay-per-view downloads, and subscriptions through mobile carriers. Market growth has also been impeded by the quality of the viewing experience as well as the costs associated with subscriptions. But with expected steady improvements in the devices, the increase in mobile broadband availability, and the emergence of viewing options outside the carrier networks, the mobile video audience is set for rapid expansion.

eMarketer projects that growth in mobile video revenues will be fueled primarily by consumers paying directly for content in the form of subscription-based and pay-per-download services, as opposed to ad-supported video. The ad-supported mobile video market is estimated at less than $60 million in 2011 and is expected to rise to only $206 million by 2014. Growth, however, should be rapid. Ad-supported mobile video revenues will post a 60 percent compound annual growth rate (CAGR) between 2009 and 2014.

Mobile Display

Just as display ads are heavily deployed on desktop computers, particularly by brand marketers, look for more display ads to appear on mobile phones. The number one factor driving increased use of mobile display ads is the increased prevalence of Internet surfing on the mobile channel. More Internet surfing means more possibilities for brand exposure.

eMarketer estimates that 40 percent of U.S. mobile users will access the Internet on their phones in 2011, and this figure will rise to just over 50 percent in 2013 (Figure 8.8).

As mobile Internet use increases and the screens on the devices get larger and sharper, display advertising will grow. But current actual consumption of web pages on the mobile device may still be in its infancy. According to analytics firm StatCounter, mobile accounts for approximately 2 percent of total web traffic in the United States, as of August 2009. Quantcast puts this figure at about 3 to 4 percent.

Figure 8.8

Internet access by phone

US Mobile Internet Users and Penetration, 2008-2014

	2008	2009	2010	2011	2012	2013	2014
Mobile internet users (millions)	**50.9**	**68.6**	**85.5**	**101.1**	**115.2**	**129.7**	**142.1**
% of mobile phone users	22.3%	28.7%	34.7%	40.3%	45.2%	50.1%	53.9%
% of population	16.7%	22.3%	27.6%	32.3%	36.4%	40.6%	44.1%

Note: CAGR (2009-2014)=15.7%
Source: eMarketer, July 2010

117979   www.**eMarketer**.com

Another factor driving mobile display ads is increased usage of mobile applications, specifically free, ad-supported apps. All the available data suggest they will continue as a central facet of the mobile ecosystem, meaning that in-application display advertising will likewise grow in importance.

A third factor is the increasing array of attractive inventory options available to marketers. These include interstitials, takeovers, and rich media interactive ads. Apple's iPad demonstrated its first ad apps in the last weeks of 2010, and Apple is expected to have continued influence in how ads are designed and delivered for digital publications and other participants in this platform

These options, and especially in-app display ads, provide marketers with some of the most engaging and effective formats on mobile. Consumers tend to find them influential and unobtrusive as well. When InsightExpress split out the most active 15 percent of mobile users, dubbed "mobile intensives" in the research firm's Digital Consumer Portrait, it found that group—which is affluent and likely to own a smart phone—was more likely to respond to mobile Internet banners than any other type of mobile advertising and did not consider such ads annoying.

Mobile Search

The most important thing to realize about mobile searchers is that they are going to be even more likely to have an immediate intent in mind. Mobile searchers are often looking to complete an action in the very short term, as opposed to the longer-term, information-gathering mode you typically see with desktop search.

Marketers have made search on the desktop computer a key part of their marketing arsenal for reaching consumers—most particularly hand-raisers—who

(continued)

express their personal interest in a particular product or service category by typing keywords into a search engine. Obviously, as more mobile consumers are able to easily search on their mobile devices, marketers will invest likewise.

About one-third of searches on mobile devices have a local intent, according to Google executive Paul Feng, group product manager of Google Mobile Ads.

For advertisers looking to use mobile search, achieving a prominent search ranking is of paramount importance given the limited screen size of mobile devices. In addition, because mobile users tend to browse fewer results than desktop searchers, appearing above the fold is more critical in the mobile environment.

eMarketer expects mobile search advertising to grow even more quickly than display, with U.S. spending climbing at a compound annual growth rate of nearly 59 percent between 2008 and 2013. By that year, search will account for 37 percent of the mobile advertising market—the largest share of any format, just as it is on the desktop computer.

Other researchers, such as The Kelsey Group, expect even more rapid growth, with search leaving mobile display and SMS marketing in the dust over the next several years.

Mobile Social

The iPhone revolutionized the concept of mobile social networking, making it as easy as installing an app to interact with social networks and send updates. Social networking is also the fastest-growing category of mobile applications, according to comScore MobiLens, which reported a 240 percent year-over-year growth rate for mobile social app users in April 2010. It was also the fastest-growing content category for mobile web browsing.

Not surprisingly, social networking is a much more prominent activity for smart phone owners than for people who use standard-feature phones. In the three months ending in January 2010, 31 percent of U.S. smart phone owners accessed social networking sites via their mobile device, according to comScore, compared with just 6.8 percent of standard-feature phone owners. eMarketer predicts that the number of mobile social network users in the United States will reach 42 million by the end of 2011, or 43 percent of mobile Internet users. *Consider this: by late 2010, social giant Facebook had amassed 200 million mobile users on its global platform.*

Marketers looking to double their opportunities by combining mobile with social—a powerful duo—must keep in mind that the demographics of mobile users often differ from those on a computer. Many teens, for example, still have standard-feature phones, so their usage of mobile social networking is lower than their overall usage of sites such as Facebook. Just 23 percent told the Pew Internet & American Life Project in September 2009 that they used mobile social networks, compared with 88 percent of teens who texted. By contrast, eMarketer estimates nearly four in five Internet users aged 12 to 17 visit social networks at least monthly on any device.

Marketers also need to rethink their value equation in the intersection between mobile and social. Mobile is the most personal communication platform, and social networking is a highly personalized activity. We recommend marketers tread lightly and focus heavily on how they can add value—by providing some combination of utility, relevance, and fun. (See Figure 8.9.)

Figure 8.9
Social network users have been slow to pick up the phone

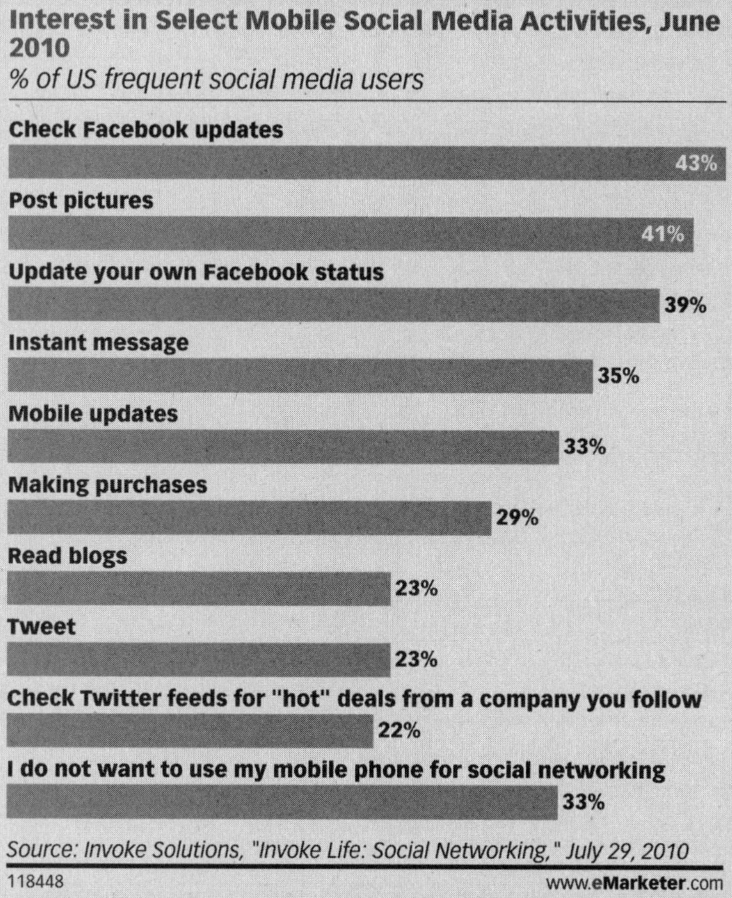

Interest in Select Mobile Social Media Activities, June 2010
% of US frequent social media users

Check Facebook updates
43%

Post pictures
41%

Update your own Facebook status
39%

Instant message
35%

Mobile updates
33%

Making purchases
29%

Read blogs
23%

Tweet
23%

Check Twitter feeds for "hot" deals from a company you follow
22%

I do not want to use my mobile phone for social networking
33%

Source: Invoke Solutions, "Invoke Life: Social Networking," July 29, 2010

118448   www.eMarketer.com

(continued)

Mobile Apps

Mobile applications are a central part of the smart phone experience, with usage growing rapidly. Recent data from the Pew Internet & American Life Project survey shows that among the 82 percent of adults today with cell phones, 43 percent have software applications on their devices. However, having an app and using one are not synonymous. Of those who have apps on their phones, only 68 percent of this group actually uses that software. This means that only 29 percent of U.S. adults are active app users. Separately, according to comScore MobiLens, by April 2010 there were nearly 70 million unique U.S. users of mobile applications, up 28 percent over the previous year (Figure 8.10).

The opportunity for marketers who succeed at the app value proposition can be great. Smart phones are in the hands of ever-increasing numbers of mobile users, and smart phone owners tend to be wealthier and better educated than the average consumer, making them an attractive target. Furthermore, in-app advertising has relatively high recall rates and is well tolerated by many mobile users, considered less annoying or intrusive than tactics such as messaging-based ads.

Figure 8.10
Most popular apps for the phone

Fastest-Growing US Mobile Application Categories, April 2009 & April 2010
thousands of unique users and % change

	April 2009	April 2010	% change
Social networking	4,270	14,518	240%
Weather	8,557	18,063	111%
News	4,148	9,292	124%
Sports information	3,598	7,672	113%
Bank accounts	2,340	4,974	113%
Maps	8,708	16,773	93%
Movie information	3,296	6,359	93%
Online retail	1,416	2,701	91%
Search	5,434	10,315	90%
Photo- or video-sharing service	3,131	5,950	90%
Total application users*	**54,414**	**69,639**	**28%**

Note: ages 13+; three-month average for period ending April 2009 and April 2010; *excludes games preloaded on device
Source: comScore MobiLens as cited in press release, June 2, 2010

116260   www.eMarketer.com

Location-Based Services

Many marketers have wondered about the potential of location-based services like foursquare and Gowalla, which have relatively small user bases despite their supercharged publicity. Research data from multiple, credible sources indicates a market of miniscule proportions:

- Only 7 percent of U.S. consumers say they have even heard of social location apps that allow you to post status updates of your current location (Edison Research, February 2010).
- Just 4 percent of online U.S. adults have ever tried mobile geo-location applications, and even fewer, a mere 1 percent, use them weekly (Forrester Research, 2010).
- Only 4 percent of online Americans ever use location-based services and even fewer, 1 percent, use it on any given day (Pew, November 2010).
- Only 5 percent of U.S. mobile phone users say it is important for them to be able to use location-based social networking services on their phones (1020 Placecast, 2010).
- Usage of location-based services is skewed heavily toward young males. According to Forrester, 80 percent of those who have tried them are men, and 70 percent are between the ages of 19 and 35 (Forrester Research, 2010).
- Location-based marketing spending reached only $43 million in 2010 and will still represent a relatively small market, at $1.8 billion by 2015 (ABI Research, 2010).

But social media powerhouse Facebook may help the trend reach critical mass with its August 2010 rollout of the Places feature. In addition, it is highly likely that other big players, like Yelp, Twitter, and even Google, will help location-based services become mainstream. Furthermore, research suggests that mobile owners are getting used to sharing their location in many ways, regardless of their privacy worries.

Location-based data can be highly valuable to marketers who can offer targeted and relevant messages and deals, especially to younger consumers. Harris Interactive and Placecast found in May 2010 that many mobile users thought a location-based component to text alerts would make them more useful and interesting. Wi-Fi provider and mobile ad server JiWire found in April that nearly half of Wi-Fi users would share their location to receive more relevant advertising, although even more were willing to do so in exchange for local content as well. And research from the Mobile Marketing Association in March found that although relatively few mobile users recalled seeing location-based ads, they had the highest response rates.

(continued)

Marketers want to reach consumers when they are close to making a purchase. Location-based services enable them to deliver a compelling offer or reward just where consumers are at the point of decision. This is very powerful. "Checking in" is still a fairly niche activity, but as more consumers are introduced to the concept, they may find it benefits themselves, as well as marketers. Ads can be pushed to people the moment they are engaged with something, rather than after they have taken an action, and the ability to find friends—and their local tips and advice—can also ease the decision-making process.

In-Store Mobile

Mobile shopping from inside a store is just beginning to achieve its vast potential. The promise for consumers is an interactive and personalized store experience—without the pressures of a salesperson breathing down your neck. Currently, in-store mobile shoppers can easily retrieve customer product reviews. In the future, they will receive promotions based on their past purchase history and what they are interested in at the moment.

Retailers will benefit from this technology by converting more store visitors into buyers and improving customer loyalty. Mobile shopping makes it easier for stores to accommodate information needs that consumers have while in the store.

A December 2009 study by Motorola found that North Americans were behind the rest of the world in adoption of in-store mobile shopping activities such as calling or texting to ask someone about a potential purchase, checking online for further information, or searching for coupons and special offers while shopping (Figure 8.11). Worldwide, younger mobile users lead the way on all these activities, with members of Generation Y looking to their mobile devices for in-store shopping help at nearly twice the rate of baby boomers.

Retailers and third-party developers have introduced mobile applications with capabilities aimed at in-store shoppers; these include barcode scanning and quick access to customer reviews. More such offerings are in development and will launch in the upcoming year. Overall, these apps help retailers increase in-store purchases and fend off competitors' and third-party developers' price comparison apps.

At the same time, several third-party developers offer mobile apps that enable shoppers to get competitors' prices for an item they see in a store. These apps can also help customers extract a price concession from the retailer whose store they are in, as in, "Can you match *this* price?"

Such levels of price transparency may worry retailers, but if they fail to get on board with in-store mobile offerings, they can be sure their competition will do so. Retailers can target their most loyal customers with their own retailer-specific application, keeping their brand on deck and in front of the mobile

Figure 8.11
In-store mobile activity by age group

In-Store Mobile Shopping Activities of Internet Users Worldwide, by Generation, December 2009
% of respondents

	Gen Y	Gen X	Boomers
Called to ask someone about a product I might purchase	38.2%	29.7%	20.5%
Texted to ask someone about a product I might purchase	30.5%	19.2%	9.4%
Sent a picture of a product I might purchase	23.0%	15.2%	7.2%
Used mobile phone to access Internet to compare prices	21.4%	11.9%	5.8%
Used mobile phone to access Internet to look at product reviews or other product information	20.6%	13.7%	4.9%
Made an Internet purchase directly on the mobile phone	10.1%	6.2%	3.0%
Used mobile phone to access Internet to get coupons or special offers while shopping	13.6%	7.2%	2.1%
Used mobile phone for at least one of the above shopping-related activities	**64.0%**	**50.1%**	**33.2%**

Note: in the past two weeks
Source: Motorola, "2009 Retail Holiday Season Shopper Study" conducted by e-Rewards and TNS International, January 1, 2010

116173   www.**eMarketer**.com

user's eyeballs, or opt to work with a third party. Some, such as Shopkick, have ambitious location-based components that can allow stores like Macy's to find out what department shoppers are in and push out highly targeted offers when consumers are at the point of purchase.

CHAPTER 9

Online Video: Delivering Emotional Engagement

"As soon as I could see we were making as much or more money each day than we spent on ads on YouTube, I knew we had something."
—*Jeffrey Harmon, CMO, Orabrush, as quoted in the* New York Times, *September 27, 2010*

Only about 40 percent of large U.S. marketers are using online video today, and the percentage is much smaller among small businesses. Similarly, the investment in advertising dollars in the video channel is relatively small. However, marketer participation and spending levels will grow rapidly over the next few years as broadband penetration rates continue to climb, technologies and ad formats converge, and more advertiser-friendly content pours online.

In fact, no other advertising channel—online or offline—is growing faster than online video. And for good reason. Using online video, marketers can bring together the powerful emotional elements of television—featuring sight, sound, and motion—with the uniquely interactive capabilities of the Internet. Moreover, compared with traditional television, web video promises better audience measurement, improved targeting, and, of course, rich opportunities for viral sharing of your message across the web. At least that's the potential.

Done correctly, an online video presence can help you foster a rich, emotional connection with your consumers, boost your brand awareness, lure prospective customers, and help solidify support among your brand loyalists.

In this chapter, we will:

1. Discuss the trends, opportunities, and barriers marketers need to know before investing in online video.
2. Learn how Magnetic Content strategies can attract and engage consumers in ways not possible with other digital channels.
3. Describe the measurement challenges and opportunities with online video.

The Online Video Landscape

Online video advertising is ranked not only as the fastest-growing online format today, but also for years to come, according to eMarketer. In 2011, online video advertising in the United States will reach nearly $2.0 billion, more than doubling from $1.0 billion in 2009. By 2014, online video advertising will top $5.7 billion in spending and account for more than 14 percent of total online advertising. Most researchers and investment banks peg the growth rate for online video ad spending in the double digits for the next several years.

Online video ad spending, as a portion of total online display advertising, will also grow significantly over the next few years, from 13 percent in 2009 to nearly 36 percent by 2014 (Figure 9.1).

The global picture is also promising, as researchers predict worldwide online video ad spending climbing from $4.0 billion in 2010, according to Caris & Company, to a substantial $11.3 billion by 2014, according to IDC.

Of course, when you compare online video ad dollars to the television markets in any given country, TV wins hands down. In the United States, online video spending of nearly $2.0 billion in 2011 represents only a small fraction of the $60 billion television market. Nonetheless, online video is slowly gaining dollar share.

The same pattern plays out with consumer usage of online video. While 70 percent of Americans watch online video, the time they spend with the channel is minimal as compared with time spent watching TV. Actual weekly time spent viewing video online is—even for the heaviest-viewing demographic groups—a mere fraction of their total time spent watching all video in the home. The bulk of overall video consumption continues to take place on the television set. eMarketer estimates that, in 2010, time spent watching Internet video represented only 2 percent of total time spent watching video in America.

Figure 9.1

Online display advertising is trending toward online video

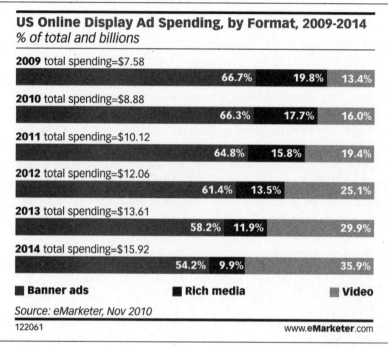

US Online Display Ad Spending, by Format, 2009-2014
% of total and billions

2009 total spending=$7.58

66.7%   19.8%   13.4%

2010 total spending=$8.88

66.3%   17.7%   16.0%

2011 total spending=$10.12

64.8%   15.8%   19.4%

2012 total spending=$12.06

61.4%   13.5%   25.1%

2013 total spending=$13.61

58.2%   11.9%   29.9%

2014 total spending=$15.92

54.2%   9.9%   35.9%

■ **Banner ads**   ■ **Rich media**   ■ **Video**

Source: eMarketer, Nov 2010

122061   www.**eMarketer**.com

Looked at another way, the average American watches approximately five hours of television every day, according to Nielsen. In contrast, numerous sources, including Nielsen and comScore, confirm that the average Internet user watches less than four hours of online video—*every month*. So, if you are looking to reach a large number of consumers on a consistent basis, the much bigger opportunity still lies on TV—at least today.

Despite the limited reach potential, though, online video offers some unique advantages that marketers looking to engage with digital consumers should consider.

Better Than TV? If So, Why?

The potential for creating an emotional lock with consumers through online video, just as with TV, remains an attractive benefit to advertisers. After all, it is emotions and feelings that drive consumers to buy and stay loyal to a brand, much more so than cognitive beliefs. A wealth of research studies provide

compelling evidence that consumers are far more attentive and engaged with
online video than they are with television ads:

- Viewers are 2.5 times more likely to be "fully engaged" in online video
  than their counterparts who watch traditional television programming
  (source: Frank N. Magid Associates, 2010).
- The ability of consumers to retain messages from online video ads is
  higher than for traditional TV ads (source: Magna Global and Turner
  Broadcasting Corp, 2010).
- Viewers are 28 percent more likely to pay attention to online video ads
  than they are TV ads (source: Interpret LLC, 2009).
- Online video ads are more effective than TV ads based on several key
  brand measures, including general recall (at 65 percent vs. 46 percent),
  brand recall (at 50 percent vs. 28 percent), message recall (at 39 percent vs.
  21 percent), and brand likability (at 26 percent vs. 14 percent) (source:
  Nielsen IAG, 2010—based on 14,000 surveys).
- More than half (55 percent) of consumers deem online videos ads as
  acceptable/more acceptable than TV ads (source: Frank N. Magid
  Associates, May, 2010).

Numerous studies also show that online video ads are more appealing to
consumers than are TV ads (Figure 9.2). These improved recall rates are
driven by four factors: (1) there is less ad clutter (thus far) with online video
programming; (2) consumers are in a lean-forward (as opposed to lean-
backward) mode when watching videos online; (3) with most long-form
online video content, the consumer is not given the option to skip the ads,
whereas one-third of television viewers can now fast-forward through ads; and
(4) there is still a novelty effect, since video ads are relatively new on the scene.

Since online video is generally less cluttered with ads than is television,
your marketing messages are more likely to be noticed. According to com-
Score, although ad units comprise about 8 percent of the typical hour's worth
of online video content (excluding user-generated content), ads on television
account for 25 percent (15 minutes) of a given hour's worth of viewing time.
As a case in point, Hulu, the dominant website for free viewing of television
shows, deliberately restricts its so-called ad-load factor to between one-fourth
and one-half the number of ads placed in traditional television programming.
Research conducted by Hulu indicates that advertising spots placed on their site
are at least 55 percent more effective than the same ads shown on traditional
TV channels. They claim this is due to a combination of the lighter ad load
and that the ads are more tailored to audience interests.

Figure 9.2

**People are more tolerant and appreciative of video ads
on a computer screen**

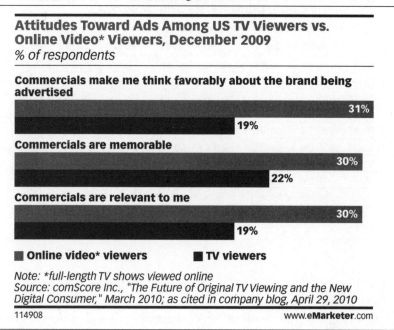

Attitudes Toward Ads Among US TV Viewers vs.
Online Video* Viewers, December 2009
% of respondents

**Commercials make me think favorably about the brand being
advertised**

31%

19%

Commercials are memorable

30%

22%

Commercials are relevant to me

30%

19%

■ Online video* viewers   ■ TV viewers

Note: *full-length TV shows viewed online
Source: comScore Inc., "The Future of Original TV Viewing and the New
Digital Consumer," March 2010; as cited in company blog, April 29, 2010

114908   www.**eMarketer**.com

As another benefit for marketers, online video allows for greater measurability and makes it possible to reach more precise demographic targets, compared with traditional television. Online, for example, you can reach people who, by their past surfing and searching behavior, reveal an intention or interest in your product or category.

In addition, online video is cheaper to produce, on average, than a typical television spot. The cost of video cameras and related equipment today has democratized video production so that all companies, large and small, can make quality videos without busting their budget. And spending for broadcast television spots can also be amortized when TV spots are redeployed or archived in online channels.

Who Watches Video Online?

People of all ages watch online video, but the younger demographic groups, especially teens and millennials, are by far the heaviest users (Figure 9.3). In 2011, eMarketer estimates that more than 90 percent of those aged 18

Figure 9.3
U.S. online viewers by age, 2008–2014

US Online Video Viewers, by Age, 2008-2014
% of Internet users in each group

	2008	2009	2010	2011	2012	2013	2014
0-11	50.0%	54.1%	58.1%	61.9%	67.0%	70.8%	75.1%
12-17	70.0%	74.9%	79.0%	82.8%	87.1%	90.1%	91.8%
18-24	80.1%	83.2%	86.0%	90.1%	93.0%	94.1%	95.2%
25-34	75.1%	80.0%	84.1%	88.0%	91.1%	93.1%	93.9%
35-44	69.1%	74.0%	77.1%	79.9%	82.9%	85.9%	88.0%
45-54	50.2%	54.9%	58.1%	60.9%	64.0%	66.1%	68.1%
55-64	35.1%	40.2%	43.8%	49.1%	53.1%	55.9%	59.0%
65+	18.8%	22.7%	25.8%	28.8%	33.2%	36.2%	39.0%

Note: individuals who watch video content online at least once per month
Source: eMarketer, April 2010

114439   www.**eMarketer**.com

to 24 will watch online video, and 88 percent of those 25 to 34 will do so; in contrast, only 61 percent of those aged 45 to 54 and 49 percent of those aged 55 to 64 will watch online video, suggesting that growth will continue to skew to younger viewers. The Nielsen Company also reports that 18- to 24-year-olds watch more than five hours of online video per average month, while those in the 50- to 64-year-old age bracket watch less than half that amount.

However, over the next few years, usage levels across all age groups will begin to even out somewhat, with penetration exceeding 50 percent for every age cohort, except for seniors aged 65 and older.

The bottom line is that online video watching is already a mainstream activity that appeals to nearly every segment of the population. The fact that younger people are more likely to watch videos online today speaks directly to their comfort level with technology, including their proclivity toward viewing video segments on smaller, phone-sized screens.

What Are Online Video Viewers Watching? Currently, most online video viewing falls under the loose heading of "digital snacking"—typically characterized by two- or three-minute snippets on YouTube or a similar length movie trailer or news segment. According to Nielsen, more than 80 percent of online video was labeled by the researcher as "short-form" in 2009. It's important to note that this short-form content is predominantly user generated,

Figure 9.4

What's watched most online today

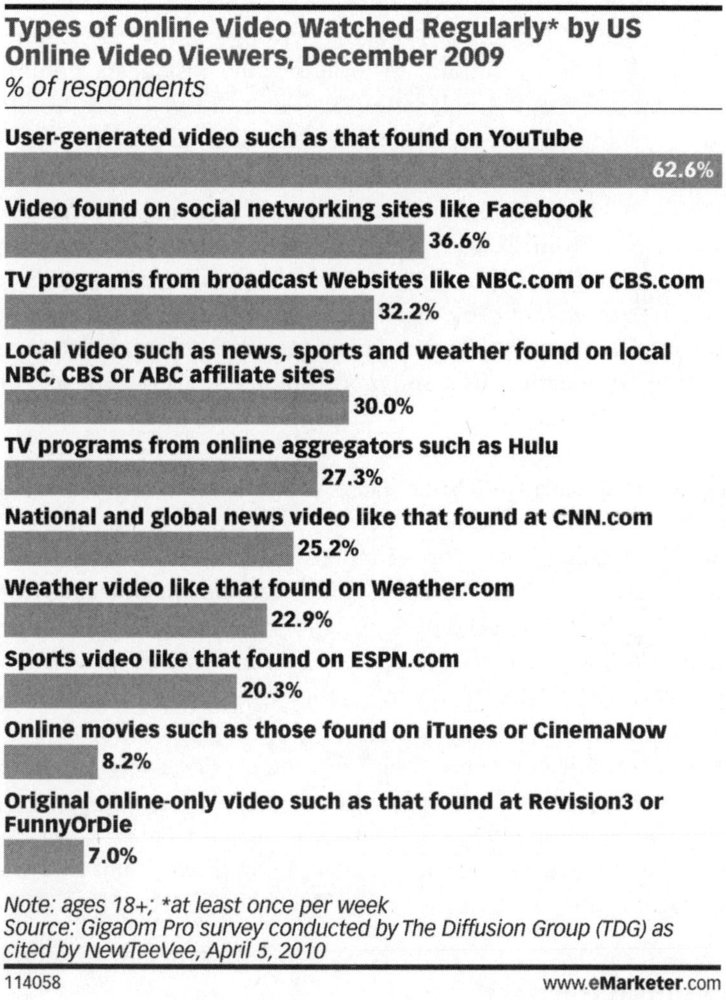

Types of Online Video Watched Regularly* by US Online Video Viewers, December 2009
% of respondents

User-generated video such as that found on YouTube

62.6%

Video found on social networking sites like Facebook

36.6%

TV programs from broadcast Websites like NBC.com or CBS.com

32.2%

Local video such as news, sports and weather found on local NBC, CBS or ABC affiliate sites

30.0%

TV programs from online aggregators such as Hulu

27.3%

National and global news video like that found at CNN.com

25.2%

Weather video like that found on Weather.com

22.9%

Sports video like that found on ESPN.com

20.3%

Online movies such as those found on iTunes or CinemaNow

8.2%

Original online-only video such as that found at Revision3 or FunnyOrDie

7.0%

Note: ages 18+; *at least once per week
Source: GigaOm Pro survey conducted by The Diffusion Group (TDG) as cited by NewTeeVee, April 5, 2010

114058 www.**eMarketer**.com

as opposed to professionally produced video material. Other sources confer with the short-form skew (Figure 9.4).

With digital snacking being the primary use of online video today, it should be no surprise that YouTube is the 800-pound gorilla in the video space. In every survey and study, YouTube comes out as the king of video, whether measured by number of audience viewers or sheer tonnage of videos viewed.

But the video dial is turning, and Americans are increasingly supplementing their online video snacking habits with main course fare, namely full-length television shows and entire movies. eMarketer estimates that in 2011, 72 million adult Internet users will regularly watch full-length TV shows online, accounting for 39 percent of adult Internet users and 29 percent of all adults in the United States. This growth is being driven by a number of factors, not the least of which is a profusion of professionally produced, premium TV and movie content from popular sites like Hulu, VEVO, and the broadcast TV sites.

The Hulu video site is a joint venture between News Corp's Fox and Comcast's NBC that aggregates both old and current episodic television shows and movies from their respective inventories, as well as from a variety of partners. At roughly 45 million visitors, Hulu attracts an audience the size of a major television cable network. In terms of online videos viewed, Hulu is a solid number two to YouTube. Hulu employs a hybrid model of monetization, supporting its content through both ads and an emerging subscription-based model.

"My Time" Is Replacing "Prime Time"   Marketers should keep in mind that the main reason consumers choose to watch video online is for the convenience of being able to watch their favorite content, especially TV shows and movies, on their own schedule. In the on-demand video era, "prime time" is being replaced by "my time." Younger people, in particular, don't want to follow the dictates of a television network as to when they can watch their favorite shows. Increasingly, they expect to be able to watch any program they desire both when and where they desire to watch it.

That said, consumers rate the actual viewing experience of video online as inferior to watching it on a standard television screen. In a survey by comScore, consumers rated online video highly in terms of convenience (for example, "watch the show whenever I want," or "on my own time") but gave television high marks for sound and picture quality (Figure 9.5).

Online Video Barriers

Although a critical mass of consumers now enjoy online video, as we've seen, their actual consumption of video on the Internet is still a mere fraction of the time they spend with TV on the big screen; thus, the exposure opportunity right now is somewhat limited. But beyond the scale limitations, there are other obstacles for marketers to face as well, such as:

- There is nowhere near enough quality (premium, long-form, safe) inventory for marketers to buy.

Figure 9.5

Selective viewing preferences across platforms

Preference of Online vs. TV for Select Activities According to US Cross-Platform TV Content Viewers, December 2009
% of respondents

	Online	TV
Watch the show wherever I want	75%	25%
Watch the show on my own time	74%	24%
Ability to stop and play show when I want	70%	30%
Less interference from commercials	67%	33%
Overall convenience	61%	39%
Overall viewing experience	32%	68%
View show as soon as it's released	31%	69%
Sound quality	28%	72%
Picture quality	25%	75%

Note: n=535; respondents were asked "For each attribute below, please select whether online or TV is better."
Source: comScore, Inc. as cited in press release, April 1, 2010

113899   www.**eMarketer**.com

- The cost–per–thousand (CPM) rates are overpriced versus standard television spot pricing; on a CPM basis, television delivers audiences at approximately $8 to $15 CPMs, whereas online video is closer to the $20 to $40 range on premium sites and typically $10 on lesser-known ones. Many marketers believe that pricing is too high given the lower numbers for viewership.
- Marketers are concerned about the appropriateness of the context in which their video ads are placed, particularly when buying through video ad networks.

Some early issues in web video advertising are being resolved. This includes some pro forma standardization of technologies, unit sizes, and formats (pre–roll, mid–roll, overlay, etc.) as the collective mind of the industry has discovered what works and what does not. Measurement and metrics for the video channel have also matured; later in this chapter you'll find the metrics we recommend for driving results from this channel.

How to Magnetize Customers with Online Video

Of all the digital channels discussed in this book, video offers marketers the most promising opportunities for engaging with consumers in an emotional way, just as they've done for decades with television. What's more, online video is flexible and can be used in a variety of effective and creative ways that span paid media, owned media (Magnetic Content) and earned media.

The majority of marketers using online video produce their own branded video content, and this is the most popular use by far, followed by product or service demos, editorial video content, and customer/employee testimonials, according to TurnHere, an online video production company (Figure 9.6).

We recommend marketers follow three basic strategies for making use of online video, as well as adhering to the general criteria for Magnetic Content outlined in Chapter 3—make it unique, useful, fun, well executed, and appropriate for the channel in which it appears.

Figure 9.6

How marketers use video messaging

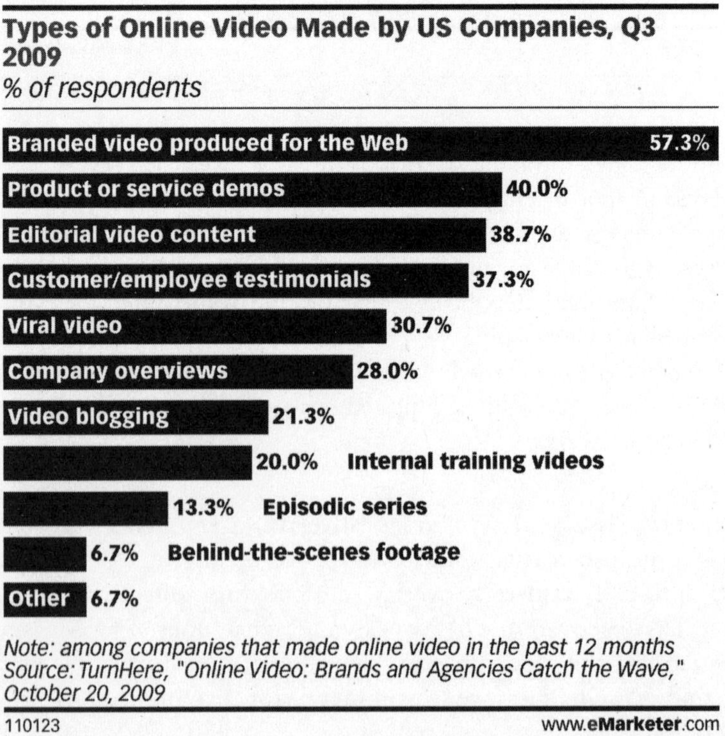

Types of Online Video Made by US Companies, Q3 2009
% of respondents

Branded video produced for the Web	57.3%
Product or service demos	40.0%
Editorial video content	38.7%
Customer/employee testimonials	37.3%
Viral video	30.7%
Company overviews	28.0%
Video blogging	21.3%
	20.0% Internal training videos
	13.3% Episodic series
	6.7% Behind-the-scenes footage
Other	6.7%

Note: among companies that made online video in the past 12 months
Source: TurnHere, "Online Video: Brands and Agencies Catch the Wave," October 20, 2009

110123   www.eMarketer.com

Sponsor Existing Video Content

One of the simplest ways to get started with online video is to place video ads on contextually relevant content sites that feature video content. This is a paid media approach similar to buying commercial time on television.

The temptation will be to repurpose television spots you've already produced and simply run them online. Try to resist that temptation. Remember that Magnetic Content needs to be unique, pertinent to the channel, and offer something that's inherently useful, informative, fun, and/or entertaining. Online video ads generally do better if they're specifically made for the online environment, including some form of interactivity that allows consumers to engage more fully, if they choose.

Reminiscent of the early days of television, there are a growing number of well-known brands paying to sponsor video content online. Food maker ConAgra, for instance, paid for a one-year deal to sponsor video content on Yahoo!'s "What's So Funny" video program. Included in the program are post-roll video ads, display ads, and product placement opportunities for ConAgra Food's brands, including Marie Callender's, Healthy Choice, and Orville Redenbacher's popcorn. Yahoo!'s "What's So Funny" program is a series of three-minute episodes, run every weekday at lunch hour; it features celebrity co-hosts Mike Bachmann and Shira Lazar presenting their selections for the funniest moments from the previous evening's television lineup. Viewers also have the chance to vote on their favorite TV moments. As an example of how the sponsorship works, the first episode featured a segment called "Ingredients for Good Comedy," which focused on what goes into making a TV show funny. The sponsoring brand, Marie Callender's salad dressing, was tied into the theme by emphasizing the product's fresh-tasting ingredients. Commenting on the sponsorship was Brett Groom, vice president media, social and digital marketing at ConAgra Foods, who said, "This is a great example of our commitment to finding new ways to more deeply engage with our consumers, reaching them over the lunch hour when they visit Yahoo! to get a recap of last night's funniest moments on TV."

There is much debate in online marketing circles about which formats work best for online video ads. Some swear by pre-rolls, which are video ads set up to run automatically before the chosen video content. Others insist this approach is annoying for consumers, since it interrupts the content they chose to view; instead, they propose placing the video ad unit at the end of the chosen content, which of course runs the risk that the viewer will abort the viewing experience just as the ad starts. Another group maintains that video overlays are preferred by consumers because they can choose to view, or not view, the ad that hovers over the selected viewing content.

However, there is one strategy that has proved effective across the board, and it is currently being used on a number of video platforms. It entails giving viewers the opportunity to choose which advertiser's brand message they want to view. For example, on the popular long-form video content site Hulu, the consumer often gets to choose from among three advertisers. (Note: they must watch the selected ad in pre-roll form in order to view the desired program material.) Several independent studies have proved this "consumer choice" model to be the most effective for prompting consumer engagement. Even the click-through rates for this approach are double that of standard pre-roll ads, where the consumer does not get to select the advertiser or brand. When consumers gets to choose, they have more ownership in the ad experience and are therefore more likely to be engaged. It also assures some degree of relevance for the consumer.

> "Having to select an ad makes consumers more engaged."
> —*Beth Uyenco, global research director,*
> *advertising and publisher solutions group,*
> *Microsoft, as quoted in the* Wall Street
> Journal, *February 3, 2010*

From a creative standpoint, your goal should be to create video ads (or other forms of branded video content) that act as a magnet for consumers—so entertaining, compelling, and/or relevant and informative that they will not be seen as a disruption, but rather as a welcome complement to the content they came to see in the first place. If your video ads are really exceptional, consumers will want to share them with others. According to a 2010 survey by Chadwick Martin Bailey, 63 percent of Internet users say they are "somewhat or very likely" to share "funny videos"; remarkably, this was the third-ranked form of content likely to be shared, behind "news about a family member or friends" (81 percent) and "family pictures or videos" (80 percent).

Ideally, you want to create a multistage Engagement Map (see Chapter 3) where your video ad acts as the initial "hook" to pull consumers in and then you use other forms of Magnetic Content to keep them engaged. You can achieve this by including a link at the end of the video ad that directs consumers back to a dedicated landing page where they can view more video ads or other forms of branded video content, play a fun game, enter a contest, or vote on a product feature, all at increasing levels of engagement.

Note: if you're going to place video ads on third-party sites or ad networks, be aware of the context or environment in which they appear. Most brand marketers strongly prefer to skew their media placements toward premium content sites offering professional, full-length TV shows or movies, such as Hulu or the television network sites. Consistently, user-generated content is seen as too risky an environment for most brands.

Cost, of course, remains a factor. Magnetic video content needs to be well executed, so the wish to reuse broadcast TV ads is understandable. Do brand marketers benefit more from using recycled TV commercials or from videos made especially for online viewing? A study by Dynamic Logic research, released in September 2010, found that "repurposed TV spots result in higher brand awareness metrics; however, video content produced specifically for the online space is far more likely to influence purchase decisions."

Create Your Own Branded, Highly Magnetic Video Content

If the first strategy of creating and deploying video ads falls under the "paid media" camp, this next strategy is squarely in the "owned media" camp, or as we view it, "Magnetic Content." It involves a wide range of video formats, objectives, and tactics, all of which share a common goal; their purpose is to attract consumers by providing some kind of genuine, value-added experience. They aren't designed so much as to "sell product," but rather to enhance the brand—creating engagement and engendering long-term loyalty with the consumer. As "Magnetic Content," these videos are typically placed on a marketer's own website or special microsite, but they are often also distributed through YouTube and other free, video-sharing sites.

Following are several suggested forms of magnetic video content. The first two approaches are more product-focused, whereas the other three are designed to provide consumers with some kind of utility or entertainment that transcends the product offering, but nonetheless support the brand's overall proposition.

Product Demos: Show versus Tell   Video demonstrations of a product or service in action have been used by marketers for decades. It is one thing to "tell" your consumers how well your product works; it is quite another to "show" them using online video.

Probably the most famous example of using online video to demonstrate a product's unique features comes from Blendtec, the blender manufacturer. The company's quirky video vignettes, under the provocative theme "Will It

Blend?" have tallied up millions of views on sites like YouTube; they are highly entertaining to watch and thus invite consumers to come back for more. However, they also manage to subtly drive home the point that Blendtec blenders are supremely robust and can seemingly blend just about anything.

Another great example comes from Apple. The company of iconic brands like Mac, iPod, iTouch, and iPad, creates polished, highly engaging video tutorials to show customers all the many ways they can enjoy the product they have just purchased. But each of these tutorials does double-duty, because they also act as powerful selling demos for those who have not yet purchased the product. With video, seeing is not only believing, it can be highly persuasive!

Customer Testimonials   If you have customers or clients who like to rave about your product or service, why not put them in front of a camera and let them share their passion with hundreds, thousands, or even millions of your prospects? Beyond words, video testimonials can convey the emotion consumers experience in their loyalty toward your brand.

As one example, Procter & Gamble selected video testimonials as a means of communicating the benefits of its new Scope Outlast, a mouth-freshening product that apparently works up to five times longer than a standard oral care routine. By having real consumers tout the personal, emotional benefits of the product in front of a video camera, the company was able to tap into the power and trustworthiness of a (pardon the pun) word-of-mouth strategy, with positive statements such as, "My breath stayed fresh for hours"; "I feel very kiss-able!"; and "I felt confident." Such comments delivered in a video format allow viewers to fully appreciate the confidence-boosting benefits of the product.

How-To, Helpful, or Learning Videos   These are videos you create to help the consumer accomplish some task or learn something of value, presumably in an area that relates to your product or encompasses your brand values. Again, it isn't about selling product, but rather helping the consumer in a way that will, indirectly, reflect positively on your brand. This approach is really only limited by your imagination:

- A fishing reel manufacturer produces a video segment demonstrating the best practices for fly-fishing.
- A financial services firm creates a series of videos that profile various investment approaches based on stage of life.
- A gardening supplies catalog company invites customers and prospects to share videos of their own gardens and how they created them.
- A fast-food chain seeking to improve its image delivers a series of online videos that educates on healthy eating and exercise habits.

- A floor cleaner manufacturer produces a video showing homeowners how to take care of their floors.
- A car insurance company creates a series of videos providing tips on how to maintain a good driving record.

Clearly, with a little creativity, and a relatively small budget, you can come up with a video offering that will serve a need for your customers while also moving your brand higher up on the consideration ladder.

General Mill's Betty Crocker brand provides a good example of deploying video content as an instructional tool. Specifically, Betty Crocker created 1,485 helpful videos for preparing delicious treats—covering everything from how to make chocolate peanut butter cookies, which runs a little over two minutes, to whipping up gluten-free marble cake, at a little over four minutes. As a result of the series, Betty Crocker saw traffic to its site more than double to over 5 million per month after the videos were posted. Plus, through an aggressive syndication and distribution effort involving video ad networks and other partners, as well as organic search efforts on Google, Yahoo!, Bing, and YouTube, Betty Crocker was able to position itself as the go-to guide for birthday cakes and party desserts.

As one example involving a small business, Original Skateboards produced a series of videos demonstrating skateboard skills and then placed the videos on YouTube along with a coupon offer that enabled the company to carefully track sales. Clearly, instructional videos can be highly magnetic as they seek to solve a consumer problem; if done well, they are also likely to draw in the very consumers who are ripe for your product.

Entertaining Videos, Including Webisodes   If you want to take engagement to a higher, more sustained level, consider the investment of creating entertaining videos, or a series of such videos, usually called webisodes. Webisodes are scripted video vignettes that entertain or amuse consumers and keep them coming back for more. Many consumer packaged goods firms like Procter & Gamble, Unilever, and others have tried this approach, sometimes hiring expensive TV directors and actors to ensure quality and attract strong interest. For the smaller enterprise, there are a growing multitude of web video studios and boutiques offering their video producing and editing services for hire. In many cases, they employ the talents of veterans who have long-standing professional experience creating corporate videos, training films, and B-rolls.

On the other hand, small businesses on a shoestring budget can also produce fun-to-watch videos in-house at a relatively low cost; what's more, if the videos are entertaining enough, they can spread virally on sites like

YouTube. As one example, consider the word-of-mouth success story of Robert Wagstaff, an entrepreneur with a product called Orabrush that eradicates mouth odor with a special brush designed to remove bacteria from the tongue. Wagstaff was able to establish a solid retail presence at major drugstores by placing a highly amusing video on free websites such as YouTube and Facebook. After only one year, the Orabrush video series was viewed 24 million times. The cost to produce the original video? A paltry fee of $500 to a student at a local university. The original branded video was so successful that the Orabrush founder created a new installment every week in a series entitled, "Diaries of a Dirty Tongue."

Key to the brand's success was the fact that consumers chose to click on the videos and, in doing so, self-selected themselves as potential customers. According to the *New York Times,* almost 40,000 consumers who watched the entertaining videos on the YouTube channel (called Curebadbreath .com) have signed up to get e-mail updates every time Orabrush posts a new video, "making it the seventh most-subscribed channel, ahead of brands like Disney, BMW and Nintendo Wii."

As another example, Nestle's candy division created an entire branded video community around its Butterfinger chocolate bar. At their dedicated microsite, which is also linked to Facebook, community participants can view humorous video clips, upload their own videos, comment on the videos, and share them with friends.

Importantly, if your creative approach is strong enough with online video, you can achieve the seemingly impossible dual objective of both entertaining and magnetizing consumers while directly promoting your brand's name and positioning. In our opinion, the best example of this comes from Evian, French maker of bottled spring water. The company created a captivating video using computer-generated animation to portray babies, in diapers no less, break-dancing and performing amazing stunts on inline skates in a park. While the "Live Young" video is one of the most popular on YouTube ever, accumulating more than 30 million views, the brand message comes through loud and clear—that Evian helps you stay young. What's more, Evian managed to inextricably link its brand name with the popular video by including a clever scene where one of the rollerblading babies weaves in and out of a line of Evian bottles. In essence, Evian used product placement within its own branded video content. The viewer is not likely to miss the sponsoring brand.

A third example of a successful webisode series comes from Kmart. The retail giant created an eight-episode series of short, four- to six-minute videos focused on the story of Cassie Mitchell, a teen girl who is new to a school and can't seem to get her look right. Lifting humorously from the movie

Groundhog Day, Carrie is doomed to repeat her first day of school over and over again, as she tries to experiment with new looks and impress a boy that she has a crush on. According to *Advertising Age*, the "First Day" video program accumulated an astounding 8 million episode views by the time the initial series was over. Critically, one of the most important factors for its success relates directly to one of our five criteria for Magnetic Content: it was extremely well executed. Said *Advertising Age*, "It could be cheesy, but instead it's incredibly winning (and as smartly produced as anything you'd seen on Nick or Disney Channel). And given that the fashion-as-self-expression angle is integral to the plot, the Kmart branding—and the 'Featured Products' sidebar—feels servicey, not overbearing. It's like reading *Lucky* magazine if *Lucky* had a plot." Notably, Kmart enlisted the professional expertise of Alloy (which also produced the *Gossip Girl* and *Pretty Little Liars* book series). In other words, had Kmart pushed too hard on the product sell and/or failed to execute at the highest level, the video series would have flopped.

One cautionary note here: when seeking to create online branded videos, do not have as your main goal to create a viral video sensation. Rather, seek to create quality, magnetic videos that will enable you to develop a more intimate, genuine relationship with consumers than is possible with standard advertising. It is also important to note that, with owned media, you usually have more control over the environment in which your content appears, such as on your own website, but it can be harder to achieve sufficient scale. This is why you need a multichannel approach.

Social Video Forums   Video can also be combined effectively with social media to create a branded online community forum focused on a particular life stage, demographic, interest, or passion. Often such video/social mash-ups include a mix of professionally produced videos with those created and uploaded by community members.

An excellent example comes from a partnership of First Response pregnancy test, made by Church & Dwight Co. and TLC, part of Discovery Communications. The two groups co-produced a web video series called "A Conception Story: Six Journeys to Pregnancy," which chronicles the stories of six women and their pregnancies over a 10-episode arc. According to *Advertising Age*, the show offered an innovative blend of professionally produced segments and DIY content. Each mom-to-be was given a Flip camcorder so she could capture her own video-diaristic thoughts on her own time and terms. The series was embellished and made more engaging through the inclusion of weekly blog posts, an active message board community, and other supportive elements.

The fact that the women created the video segments themselves added an element of authenticity, in addition to the emotionally powerful story lines.

The Multichannel Approach to Online Video

The most effective recipe for leveraging online video involves a powerful mix of paid media, to drive immediate traffic and reach, with owned media, to engage with consumers and communicate a key brand message, plus earned media, to get the branded message authenticated and more widely distributed. When the benefits of all three approaches are combined holistically, your online video program will pack a powerful one-two-three punch.

Placing video ads on third-party websites (paid media) gives you control over your message—and to some extent, where it is placed—while also enabling you to quickly reach a large enough audience to achieve scale. With owned media, in the form of branded video assets (aka your Magnetic Content), you have full control of the message as well as where it's placed, but you also have the opportunity to deepen emotional engagement with the consumer. Although owned media tends to attract a smaller, niche audience, the consumers who do choose to participate are, by definition, more engaged. Finally, earned media provides you the least control over both the message and where it's delivered, but it allows you the possibility of not only massively extending your reach but creating credibility around your message through viral sharing by consumers.

All three forms of media feed off each other in both predictable and unpredictable ways. In addition, you can amortize the cost of your video assets by distributing the videos over multiple points of distribution.

For an example of paid media working in synergy with owned and earned media, let's go back to our tongue brush maker, Orabrush. After the founder saw success with his free placement of videos on YouTube and Facebook, he began purchasing paid media ads on these sites to expand his reach; the ads linked back to his e-commerce website to drive more video viewing, and eventually sales.

Another example of combining paid and owned media comes from financial marketer TD Ameritrade Holding Corporation, which created a series of informative online videos designed exclusively for the web. The multiseason series is called "The Invested Life" and matches consumers with independent financial advisors—not TD Ameritrade employees—to tackle issues related to retirement, taxes, real estate, debt management, college savings plans, and, of course, investing. The video show is hosted by television celebrity Suzanne Sena and runs in the "Money" section of msn.com at a cost of $8 to $10 million; it is also promoted on blogs, Facebook, and Twitter.

Performance Measurement for Online Video

Online video has the potential to be far more measurable than its traditional, and much larger, counterpart, television. On the other hand, the sheer number of metrics available for measuring the effects of online video can be paralyzing. Marketers also realize they need more robust and reliable measurement systems to help them successfully evaluate the impact of digital video advertising across the three screens—Internet, television, and mobile. Too often, the massive data-filled spreadsheets that marketers get from their researchers cloud the picture more than clarify it.

A 2010 survey of more than 100 marketers by Tremor Media and DM2PRO found that inadequate ROI measurement was a major reason for holding back on web video advertising; other factors included a lack of quality content and insufficient reach.

What makes video measurement particularly challenging is that it's not just the particular effectiveness of an individual ad that marketers need to evaluate but also several related factors, including:

- The ad's placement, such as the site, the video stream, or the network
- The quality of the ad inventory
- The type of video ad, in-stream (like a pre-roll) versus in-banner (which a user must start in most cases)
- The source of the video ad—repurposed TV commercials versus made especially for the Internet
- The quality of the ad's creative
- The length of the ad, such as 15 seconds, 30 seconds, 34 seconds, or a 4-minute video that's branded content
- The time of day when the ad runs
- The location of the viewer
- The accuracy of the ad's targeting
- The degree that both the ad's creative and the product were relevant to the target audience

Building Performance Measurement for video requires not only tracking the engagement or interaction of the consumer with the video but also building in a way to measure how and to what extent consumers *share* the videos. Generally, video sharing drives engagement far beyond the intended audience, driving greater reach and lowering the cost of viewer acquisition.

Of course, what to measure with video depends on the objectives of a given campaign, and as noted before, the array of possible video metrics can be daunting. The measurement framework from Chapter 2 once again provides a quick way to choose appropriate metrics. For measuring video campaigns, we recommend using the following five metrics.

Exposure Metrics for Online Video

Exposure metrics for online video typically relate to the successful dissemination and placement of video ads or content.

1. Qualified Reach, or Qualified Visits For online video, this metric is defined as *the number of visitors who have viewed the video ad or branded content.* A key consideration in defining this metric is *how much* of the video should the consumer have watched. What if someone started the video and then stopped it within seconds? Should that consumer count in this metric? We believe you should look at only those consumers who have completed the video for this metric. Thus, another important Exposure metric is completion rate.

2. Completion Rate For online video, marketers gravitate toward completion rates and associated metrics because they provide critical input on whether the audience has viewed and fully engaged with the video ad or branded content. The completion rate is the percentage of times a video clip is played in its *entirety*, as measured across all viewers of the video.

According to several studies, including those by DoubleClick, Media-Mind, and others, the average completion rate for video ads is about 50 percent

Figure 9.7
Benchmarking shows the wide gulf between click-through and completion rates

US Online Ad Campaign* Metrics, Dec 2009	
Clickthrough rate (CTR)	0.1%
Interaction rate	2.5%
Expansion rate	2.8%
Video complete rate	50.0%
Average interaction time (seconds)	9.0
Average display time (seconds)	34.6
Average expanding time (seconds)	4.7

Note: *image, flash and rich media campaigns
Source: DoubleClick, "2009 Year-in-Review Benchmarks," July 19, 2010

118096   www.eMarketer.com

(Figure 9.7). This is a good benchmark to use if you consider completion rate as one of your primary metrics for video ads.

A variety of factors can potentially influence video completion rates, including:

- The quality of the video ad or branded content in terms of its creative execution, or how compelling it is.
- The type of video creative (Figure 9.8), whether recycled from a TV spot or created exclusively for the web.
- The site where the video is placed, in terms of both audience demographics and degree of page clutter.
- The video content in which the video ad is streamed, and how much viewers value that content.

Figure 9.8
Completion rates of video message types

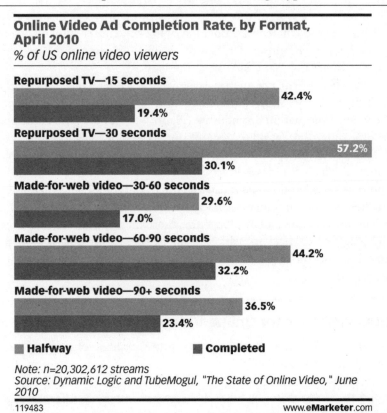

Online Video Ad Completion Rate, by Format, April 2010
% of US online video viewers

Repurposed TV—15 seconds
- 42.4%
- 19.4%

Repurposed TV—30 seconds
- 57.2%
- 30.1%

Made-for-web video—30-60 seconds
- 29.6%
- 17.0%

Made-for-web video—60-90 seconds
- 44.2%
- 32.2%

Made-for-web video—90+ seconds
- 36.5%
- 23.4%

■ Halfway   ■ Completed

Note: n=20,302,612 streams
Source: Dynamic Logic and TubeMogul, "The State of Online Video," June 2010

119483   www.**eMarketer**.com

- The way in which the ad is initiated (user-initiated video ads get a higher completion rate than do those that start automatically).
- The size of an in-banner video ad, and whether or not it's expandable.
- The advertiser's industry, and the extent to which the products are high or low engagement.

3. Time Spent   Obviously, the more time consumers spend with a video ad or other form of branded video content, the more engaged they are likely to be. For that reason, many marketers regard the duration of time consumers spend with video as another important metric. However, while some consumers view only a portion of an online video ad, clicking away before completion, that does not mean they are not influenced by the brand and its messaging. That said, because of the consumer tendency to drop out at some point before the ad is completed, marketers should aim to place their key communication points, including the advertiser's brand name, as early within the video as possible.

Marketers should also understand where large numbers of consumers are dropping off in the video; this is easily determined by bar charts or simple graphs. Pinpointing where in the duration of the content the drop off begins can help you determine causes for it. Is it too long? Is the section not interesting, or is there something that is alienating the viewers?

A series of performance metrics calculated by digital analytics marketing services firm Unicast shows how video time spent can vary significantly by industry and even within an industry (Figure 9.9). For instance, the average video play time peaks at 48.61 seconds for technology ads, but drops to less than 10 seconds for ads from the advertising/marketing, automotive, and consumer electronics industries.

This type of video time spent data has important implications and questions for marketers. Do consumers spend more time watching video ads for technology products because it takes longer to absorb the complexity of the message? Are ads targeted to those in marketing fields viewed for only a short period of time because these people are technologically savvy and know how to escape the ads?

Strategic Metrics for Online Video

Again, Strategic metrics are those that capture strategic objectives related to customer and brand growth.

4. Brand Perception Lift   As with TV ads, web video ads offer the potential for a high degree of emotional engagement. Further, the best way to gauge

Figure 9.9
Viewing time varies by industry

Performance Metrics for Rich Media and Online Video Ad Campaigns for Select US Industries, Q1 2010

1 Clickthrough rate   4 Average video play time (seconds)

2 Interaction rate   5 Average engage time (seconds)

3 Average ad display
time (seconds)

	1	2	3	4	5
Pharmaceutical	0.89%	1.66%	131.65	25.45	21
Telecom/utility	0.66%	1.00%	71.01	22.70	20
Technology	0.63%	1.04%	83.78	48.61	36
Advertising/marketing	0.53%	3.90%	124.45	8.84	33
Restaurants	0.43%	0.38%	63.78	14.18	15
Travel/tourism	0.29%	2.99%	110.06	24.38	28
Automotive	0.28%	1.05%	67.14	9.95	9
Education	0.27%	0.02%	81.07	11.50	14
Finance/insurance	0.23%	2.12%	63.17	17.30	10
Internet services	0.15%	0.26%	53.40	12.32	12
Politics/government	0.15%	0.04%	92.15	11.53	24
Consumer electronics	0.14%	1.02%	63.96	9.60	20

Source: Unicast, "Analytics Benchmark Report Q1 2010," Jul 7, 2010

117726   www.**eMarketer**.com

the emotional connection a consumer has with a brand is to look at brand health scores, which are typically calculated by measuring lifts in commonly used brand metrics. In the video channel, brand lift is calculated by determining the change in a given brand perception metric measured before and after consumers interact with a video and then comparing those results with a control group that did not view the video. Many companies provide these kinds of survey-based measurement capabilities, including Dynamic Logic, comScore, InsightExpress, and Nielsen.

The following are the most commonly used brand-lift metrics:

- Aided awareness
- Brand attribute lift
- Brand favorability
- Purchase intent

The specific metric or metrics to be selected are based on the marketer's objectives. Any particular online video advertising campaign will tend to stimulate better results for one brand metric over others; for example, awareness might get a greater lift than purchase intent based on the advertiser's objectives.

Financial Metrics as Applied to Video

Recall that Financial metrics quantify the return on, or financial outcomes, associated with a given marketing activity. These kinds of metrics go beyond capturing the degree of brand health, as measured by consumer perceptions, and tell you whether you are affecting sales. In the vernacular of American football, the former can get you to the 10-yard line, but the latter gets you a touchdown.

5. Return on Investment (ROI)   The Holy Grail of measurement for brand marketers is to be able to determine an ROI; accordingly, those running online video advertising want to know how it affects both offline and online consumer purchases. Just as television advertising has been proved to "move product," innovative marketers are finding ways to connect their online video advertising with subsequent consumer behaviors, primarily through the use of panel-based survey methods—often looking at intent expressed online and then linking it back to offline sales.

Research firm Experian Simmons found that 1.7 percent of total Internet users in a recent survey made an online purchase at least somewhat or more often after viewing a full-motion video ad (Figure 9.10). While that figure may seem tiny, with enough reach, even a small percentage of the audience can translate to reasonably good sales.

As we outlined in Chapter 2, to estimate ROI you will need to identify and segment those individuals who were *exposed* to video ads and/or branded content and compare their purchase history or purchase intent with a *control* group of consumers who were not exposed to the content. The lift created within the exposed group is used to calculate ROI. The test-and-control research approach can be done cost effectively using consumer panels.

Video is the fastest-growing channel in the media landscape, and it provides marketers with the ability to connect with online audiences in a more emotional way that can lead to deeper engagement, lifts in brand metrics, and ultimately, higher sales. However, because online video also happens to be one of the more expensive digital channels, it puts a greater burden on marketers to

Figure 9.10
Video ad viewing and purchase behaviors

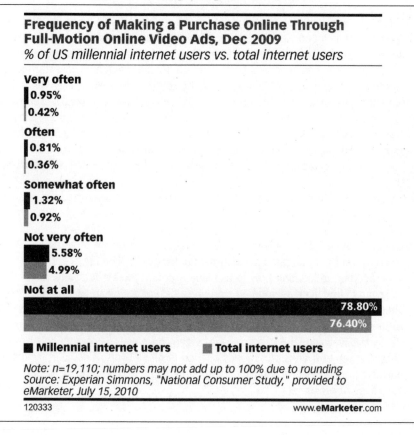

Frequency of Making a Purchase Online Through Full-Motion Online Video Ads, Dec 2009
% of US millennial internet users vs. total internet users

Very often
0.95%
0.42%

Often
0.81%
0.36%

Somewhat often
1.32%
0.92%

Not very often
5.58%
4.99%

Not at all
78.80%
76.40%

■ Millennial internet users   ■ Total internet users

Note: n=19,110; numbers may not add up to 100% due to rounding
Source: Experian Simmons, "National Consumer Study," provided to eMarketer, July 15, 2010

120333   www.**eMarketer**.com

carefully calculate an ROI and determine whether the benefits are worth the greater costs.

Conclusion

The online video audience has reached critical mass. And it's not all teens and 20-somethings, either, although they are by far the heaviest users. Over the next several years, online will take a greater share of video viewing time: eMarketer predicts online will capture more than 6 percent of video time by just 2012. Marketers desiring to make an emotional connection with consumers should not overlook the online video channel.

The Future of Web Video

If there is one single factor that would cause consumers to significantly ratchet up their online video viewing time—and correspondingly result in huge sums of advertising dollars being siphoned away from the $60 billion television market—it is convergence. The seamless connection of TV and personal computer would create consumer Nirvana—combining all the control and variety of online video with the vastly superior experience of watching favorite shows and movies on the big screen. Today, only about 2 out of 10 (20 percent) households in America even have the capability to watch Internet content on their television screens. But far fewer, only about 5 percent, watch online video on their TV sets weekly, according to Leichtman Research. That's soon going to change, though.

Large, innovation-driven companies, with exemplary track records at streamlining and simplifying consumer interactions with technology—like Apple, Amazon, Google, and Netflix—have entered the online video fray. Soon, the blurry line between a TV and a computer video experience will be all but gone. This will open up the floodgates for television dollars to flow online.

In addition to learning how to use video content more effectively, marketers will need to formulate appropriate strategies for syndicating and distributing their video content through convergent channels. They will need to stay abreast of content syndication tactics as viral applications and platforms are upgraded, or fall by the wayside. The viral nature of video content—the potential for it to be passed along to friends and friends of friends, on all kinds of devices, including portable phones—is enticing to marketers as they try to become integral to the daily lives of consumers.

PART III

PART III

CHAPTER 10

Integration across Online and Offline Channels

"We have proven that digital media can work harder when it's used with other media. [That's why] we sit together at the table to ensure that we are integrated from the very start of the media plan."
—*Doug Chavez, senior manager, digital and integrated marketing, Del Monte Foods, in an interview with eMarketer, August 28, 2009*

$\mathbf{M}$ost marketers know intuitively that digital channels work best when they're integrated with other, traditional media. Just think of the consumer—the person you're trying to engage and establish a relationship with. Today's consumer moves seamlessly between offline and online media channels, often dividing their attention between two or more at the same time. But unless you, as a marketer, can keep up, following and measuring the activity and points of impact along the consumer's engagement path, you will not be able to spend your media dollars wisely. But we don't need to tell you that.

Optimizing spending across multiple media and measuring the resultant effects were hard enough when there were only three television networks and the Internet did not exist. But now with hundreds of television channel choices and millions of websites to choose from, integration and measurement across media is mind-bogglingly complicated.

In this chapter, we will address the multimedia integration and measurement questions facing companies of all sizes and across industries:

1. What channels should I select to reach my consumers?
2. How much should I spend in each?
3. How should my spend be allocated between online and offline channels?
4. How do I properly attribute credit and adjust for cross-channel effects (for example, TV and search)?

Read this chapter to gain understanding and insights about how to plan, allocate, and measure spending across online and offline channels. It represents one of the most critical, and yet challenging, aspects of marketing in the digital world.

Media Integration—A Challenge Still Unmet

Can applying integration strategies give you a competitive edge? Independent research studies reveal that only about 1 of every 10 marketers now address the importance of media integration across offline and online channels. Yet a 2010 survey of U.S. senior-level marketers by Alterian found that nearly 90 percent said they considered campaign integration either "vital" (46 percent) or "extremely vital" (43 percent). The Alterian study also reported that 60 percent of respondent marketers agreed that *most customer engagement happens both offline and online*. And an April 2010 survey by Aprimo and Argyle Executive Forum found that U.S. marketing executives considered integrating and tracking multiple channels to be the single biggest challenge for chief marketing officers (CMOs) today.

Integrated campaigns may work better for business-to-business (B2B) marketers as well. According to researcher Outsell, although 39 percent of B2B marketers say that a single media channel by itself is "extremely or somewhat effective," 73 percent say that multiple ad formats working together are considered "extremely or somewhat effective."

Despite all this perceived importance, only a small portion of marketers routinely measure cross-channel media campaigns. According to a 2009 TNS and Eyeblaster* study, only 12 percent of marketers claimed to measure digital cross-channel performance data all the time; an additional 25 percent of marketers said they measure cross-channel data often and want to do more. But tellingly, more than 40 percent said they do it rarely or never due to the complexities and lack of confidence in the numbers. So, if you've been hesitant, know you are not alone.

---

*Eyeblaster is now known as MediaMind.

Barriers to Cross-Channel Measurement

According to U.S. online marketers surveyed in June 2010 by interactive marketing agency Zeta Interactive, "organizational structure" was cited as the top problem preventing integration, suggesting that many companies are still keeping their marketing activities in silos rather than working to coordinate them. Technology issues and the challenges of working with multiple vendors and agencies were also cited as problems, along with a sheer lack of cross-channel expertise. In an earlier survey, conducted jointly by the Association of National Advertisers (ANA) and the American Association of Advertising Agencies (the 4A's) in 2009, blame was similarly placed on internal organizational silos. As with most marketing initiatives, silos impede a focused enterprise-wide approach, and there is similar difficulty in getting multiple agencies to collaborate on integration.

Today, there is greater urgency to finding solutions. Best-in-class marketers—those 1 in 10—are moving ahead. Consider the following digital trends, which demonstrate the critical need for an integrated approach*:

- The scale of online has reached mass media proportions—73 percent of Americans are online.
- Facebook alone has more than 600 million users worldwide.
- In the United States, 24 percent of consumer media time is now spent online, second only to television (40 percent).
- Marketers are continuing to divert increasing portions of their media budgets from traditional channels to digital channels, and online now accounts for 17 percent of total U.S. media spending.
- There is an explosion of user-generated content pouring online, in the form of blogs, social media postings, status updates, videos uploaded to YouTube, photos uploaded to Flickr and Shutterfly, and 140-character tweets pushed out onto Twitter; all of this user-generated content competes with traditional, "professional" content for the consumer's time and attention.
- Consumers have become rabid multitaskers—three-fourths of Internet users have engaged in simultaneous TV and Internet usage, and 57 percent do so on a monthly basis, according to Nielsen.
- Search is a particularly critical part of the media integration mix, because it is so often used by consumers to find out more about a product after seeing an ad for it in other media, such as television.

*Source: All statistics are from eMarketer, unless noted otherwise.

- Finally, mobile phones allow consumers the ability to potentially engage with marketers wherever they happen to be, and often in reaction to ads seen in traditional media, including television, outdoor, and radio.

Want an example of how the interactions and effects between online and offline channels can create complications for marketers? Consider a consumer who watches an ad during a televised football game and then goes online to search to learn more about the product advertised; eventually, the consumer buys the product online. How much of the credit for that sale should go to TV versus search? Currently, in most measurement reports, search ends up claiming total credit for the sale. Unjustifiably so, of course. In this chapter we will explain the methodologies and provide concrete guidelines to assign appropriate attribution for sales across multiple channels.

Allocating Spending: Two Models

There are two methods for allocation of optimal spending between offline and online channels. We have outlined them here and provide guidelines to you (marketers) on how to successfully deploy them within your organization:

1. Marketing Mix Models, or True Attribution Models
2. True Insights Model

These are two reliable methods for addressing the offline and online integration challenge. Several large and small companies are using them. Read on and see how you can bring them into your organization.

Marketing Mix Models, or True Attribution Models

The most *reliable* and *accurate* way to perform this allocation modeling is using econometric analysis, commonly referred to as marketing mix models. We call them *True Attribution Modeling (TAM)*, because that accurately describes their purpose. TAM measures and attributes sales to specific marketing channels, using regression models that help marketers understand the true impact of each channel.

So, what are the questions that TAM answers? True Attribution Models can answer *all* of your key channel allocation questions:

- What is the right spend between online and offline channels?
- What is the return on investment (ROI) of different marketing channels and tactics?

- Do certain types of markets respond to varying levels of investment?
- What is the impact of competitive spending and activity?

TAM has been around for years and can provide a competitive edge to companies that use it wisely. It is interesting to note that a recent McKinsey & Company study showed little evidence of use of TAM for spend allocations, which suggests that even your biggest competitors may not have this edge:

> In response to a question about how budgets are allocated across different media, 80 percent of the respondents say that their companies either use qualitative measures—that is, subjective judgments—or simply repeat what they did last year.

First, a bit of history: you may know these models as "marketing mix modeling," a phrase coined by American Marketing Association (AMA) past president Neil Borden in an article he wrote back in 1949. He recognized that marketers could experiment with varieties of marketing "recipes" to determine the effectiveness of each marketing input. But at the time, the utility of many of these efforts to isolate the recipe was limited by the availability of suitable data. Constrained by data, these models were able to occupy only a niche among theoreticians. It wasn't ready for use in the real world.

Today, with data virtually exploding out of every digital channel, just about any organization can begin driving business decision making using quantitative assessments of marketing effectiveness derived from these models. *The digital age has removed the barriers for True Attribution Modeling.*

Building TAM or marketing mix models requires considerable technical expertise. However, the initial work toward building such models relies on a marketer's basic skill set and familiarity with the channels and strategies in use by your organization. We recommend the following steps to begin this process:

1. Select the right marketing objectives.
2. Verify that you have the necessary data.
3. Hire an expert to build the models.
4. Develop TAMs that are dynamic and forward-looking.
5. Test, test, and test.
6. Blend in business judgment to refine your approach.

1. Select the Right Marketing Objectives   Where do you start? Identify the right business metric to model. The metric can be any one of the key

Figure 10.1
Lower funnel metrics are preferred for cross-channel analysis

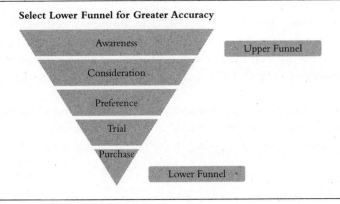

Source: Vipin Mayar.

business metrics from the ones that occur higher up in the consideration/ purchase funnel that identify early signs of marketing impact, such as interest and awareness, to the ones that occur lower in the funnel closer to purchase activity (see Figure 10.1). If you can, select lower funnel objectives, as they are closer to purchase. Lower funnel metrics are also easier to obtain, even if you have to reach across silos, and may be more reliably accurate, or at least agreed upon by other stakeholders within the organization.

2. Verify That You Have the Necessary Data   Getting the data is the most critical step to build these models. The accuracy of the models is based on the quality of the data. So, getting this right is a vital step. Keep in mind that key data factors drive the accuracy of the models:

- Obtain a wide variety of data from media inputs, macroeconomic factors, pricing, and promotion history, as well as all call center/digital activity. A list of the types of data we recommend is provided in Table 10.1.
- Look for granular data, at least weekly. Typically you need to examine a year's full history. Summary data will not work.

3. Hire an Expert to Build the Models   This is not something you can likely pass off to your internal analytics group to build. However, your internal quantitative experts can help you evaluate and choose the right modeling partner. There is no shortage of companies with expertise to build these models. Some of the well-known brands include MMA, Hudson River

Table 10.1

Inputs Table

Response Channel	Media	Base Factors	External Factors	Competition
Direct mail	TV	Product mix	Seasonality	Advertising
Telemarketing	Radio	New products	Weather	Pricing
E-mail	Print	Price	Macro-economic	Store concentration
Catalogs	Internet	Point-of-sale activity		Promotions
Circulars	Public relations	Inventory		
Coupons	Sponsorships			
In-store events	Events			
In-store displays				
Discounts				
Loyalty program				

Source: Vipin Mayar.

Group, IRI, Accenture, and MarketShare Partners. Most media and large agencies have a specialized marketing mix group that provides these services. And a ton of offshore companies like Infosys and Mu Sigma have started delivering marketing mix models as well.

It usually takes four to eight weeks to collect the data and another four to six weeks to build the models. So, about three months from launching a project you should have the models built by the experts providing you accurate insights into sales contribution of each channel as well as the ROI of each channel.

Armed with these very powerful results, you are now ready to take action and move forward. The next set of guidelines will help you with the deployment of these models.

4. Make TAMs Dynamic and Forward-Looking   True Allocation Models need to be an active and ongoing part of the marketing planning process. It's dispiriting to see the models sitting in a nice hardbound binder, not being used for ongoing planning and forecasting. Not only should the model be able to tell you how you are doing, it should be able to help you see what you should be doing next year and beyond. You should make sure that your modeling provider has strong expertise in building forward-looking simulators.

These models can be integrated into a forward-looking "what-if" business scenario simulation tool that enables marketers to forecast sales under different scenarios—high spend, low spend, or changing some other assumption. For example, you can reallocate your marketing budget in different proportions and see the direct impact on sales/value. We recommend that you try scenarios with a 20 percent increase or decrease in budgets. A 20 percent shift can make a significant impact in results, and at the same time, it does not entail taking a large risk.

5. Test, Test, and Test   Often, when marketers are faced with recommendations from TAM for the first time, they experience lack of confidence to implement the recommendations. It is prudent not to place "big bets" initially without actual in-market testing. For example, the TAM may suggest moving significant spending to online banners. Although that may be the right recommendation, the organization internally may not be able to move the spending so quickly. A structured test where you take 20 percent of the actual recommendation is very prudent. These tests vary in complexity from simple A/B tests to more complex multivariate tests. We discussed testing considerations and process in Chapter 2, if you need a refresher to get started.

6. Blend in Business Judgment to Refine Your Approach   With every predictive analytics implementation, there is a balance between pure judgment and pure science. To find that right balance with allocation models, organizations must understand the underlying strengths and limitations of the models. There is a lot of merit in starting small and evolving with each application of modeling. We firmly believe that any recommendations contrary to prevailing wisdom should be investigated! Business judgment should always be applied in these situations.

The desired maturity level where all the decisions are made with proven models may take years. Your modeling partner should also be a great advisor for you as you decide how best to deploy the recommendations from these models, such as shifting money from one channel to another.

True Insights-Based Allocation—A Waste Reduction Approach

Creating True Allocation Models is a powerful tool that enables you to align your online and offline spend and reduce wastage in your marketing spend. These models allow measurement of marketing effects by disentangling the various factors that affect sales. Managed well, they can yield significant improvements in ROI and provide a significant competitive edge.

However, there is another approach that does not require the same degree of data dependency, is quicker, and can be a very effective allocation method for smaller businesses. This approach uses consumer research data for allocation, as opposed to actual market performance data. We call it "True Insights-Based Allocation." Although it can never be as precise as TAM, it is still a very useful first step to get into cross-channel analytics. It is quick, inexpensive, and actionable! The entire program can be completed within four to six weeks.

True Insights-Based Allocation also works across both emerging and traditional communications channels, and it is applicable to a wide range of marketing categories.

Our recommended guidelines for building True Insight Models are similar to those recommended for marketing mix models or TAMs:

1. Select the right marketing objectives.
2. Select the right channels, especially emerging channels.
3. Hire an expert agency to conduct the study.
4. Get the survey design right, as this is critical.
5. Get the cost data right.
6. Run several scenarios.

While the timeline for this process is shorter, being deliberate and disciplined in the early stages will go a long way to developing models that are easy to use and easy to understand.

1. Select the Right Marketing Objectives   The first step is determining your key objectives for each brand. Each of your marketing channels serves different marketing purposes, and the answer to the optimization question will vary based on the selected objective(s). It is not necessary to select just one objective; it's okay to select the few most important ones and then assign them weights based on their relative importance.

2. Select the Right Channels, Especially Emerging Channels   Select appropriate online and offline channels. There are really no limits to the number of channels that can be selected in this approach. However, each channel must meet the following criteria:

- It is used by your target segment.
- It is used, or (for emerging channels) at least considered for use, as part of your marketing programs.

Feel free to include all the emerging channels, and any relatively new channels, such as social media channels like Twitter, Facebook, and so on, if you are wondering about their effectiveness with your target segments. Don't forget the niche channels appropriate for the category. For example, include recommendations from physicians if you are selling in the pharmaceutical industry, "package design" if you're in the beverage industry, and so forth.

3. Hire an Expert Agency to Conduct the Study   This will be a huge time-saver for you. All agencies with strong channel planning skills have expertise in implementing True Insights–Based Allocation. Most of them have given this methodology their own proprietary names. For example, some of the well-known ones are Fusion from McCann Worldgroup and CAT from Universal McCann. In addition, third-party tool providers also offer this methodology. Going with any of the established names is a safe bet. Start with the agency that you work with and see if they have a capability in this area.

The partner you select will help you execute the research, provide results on the effectiveness of the channels, and provide the channel mix recommendation.

4. Get the Survey Design Right, As This Is Critical   Even though your partner will guide you through the design and execution of the study, be aware of the critical considerations in getting it right, particularly in the matter of identifying the right markets. You should include different markets, especially ones with different dynamics. For example:

- Market where the brand is dominant
- Market with a small number of competitors
- Market where no competitor is dominant

We recommend using a sample design based on cell sizes of about 400, providing enough statistical reliability without making it cost prohibitive. You should rely on your partner to give you expert advice based on your specific marketing factors.

Before the survey goes out to potential customers to the field, an optional in-depth interview on survey design should be conducted to ensure the questions are easily understandable. Keep in mind that an average survey will take a week or so to execute in the field.

5. *Get the Right Cost Data*   One of the most difficult tasks of integration is to capture the right cost data, especially your past spend for all channels that will be included in the study. Getting this information usually requires full collaboration of marketing team members in both your own organization and among your agencies to ensure the quality of the data.

Cost data are also required to determine the costs to reach consumers in the channel (for example cost per thousand impressions/CPMs). This can be collected either from past campaigns or from empirical industry standards. Getting past cost data entails working closely with the media agencies. Make sure you spend enough time reviewing and validating the cost data, because it can clearly affect your optimization results.

6. *Run Several Scenarios*   Several scenarios should be run to determine the channel mix to simulate financial considerations. Once again, your modeling partner should guide you through this. Some scenarios we recommend include:

- Fixed investments in individual channels (that is, sponsorships)
- Minimum or maximum investment in individual channels (optional)
- Different weights for investment levels across marketing objectives

These scenarios will enable you to make practical business allocation decisions.

Conclusion

You now have two proven ways to answer the allocation and attribution questions for channels you use and for channels you may be contemplating. Let's review these two approaches:

True Attribution Modeling provides a precise answer to the channel allocation question by using a sophisticated set of regression models. It uses actual market performance data and requires obtaining the right data from previous use of the channel. This approach, although precise and comprehensive, can be sometimes limiting in its deployment, because it requires data from past campaigns.

When econometric modeling is not possible or when resources or the data are not available, *True Insights-based Allocation* provides answers to the channel allocation by using qualitative and quantitative research methods. *Since this approach is based on consumer data, it can provide recommendations on newer, unused channels.* It is forward-looking, which is a key advantage of this approach.

We have provided you with some practical guidelines in successfully moving forward with implementing true offline and online integration. Although the mathematical concepts behind this optimization are complex and may require a true math geek to understand, the practical guidelines are simple for any marketer to follow and adopt. Use them and you should be well on your way to enjoying offline and online integration bliss!

CHAPTER 11

Digital Dashboards

"The marketing dashboard's purpose is to capture the most critical diagnostic and predictive metrics and visually, at-a-glance, represent performance patterns."
—*Marketing Profs, March 9, 2010*

A dashboard enables marketers to consolidate an abundance of marketing data—pulled from a variety of different information systems—and make it conveniently accessible through visual displays on their computers and/or mobile devices. For example, a dashboard enables you to look at sales by product line and campaign performance compared against goals and across products, markets, and segments, while also allowing you to monitor customer interactions and responses. Importantly, a dashboard can also answer critical questions, such as, "What did I get for the money I spent on my last campaign?" "Which of my key performance metrics are improving?" and "What was the return on my $50,000 or $100,000,000 spends?" Some dashboards will even tell you, "What will I get for my next $50,000 spend?" In fact, it is these predictive capabilities that are really what separates a run-of-the-mill dashboard from an exceptional one.

In this chapter, we will:

1. Explain what a marketing dashboard is and the benefits it provides.
2. Show you how to build an excellent dashboard and what components to include.
3. Show you how to harness the power of a dashboard within your organization.

We all know that marketing in this digital world requires a greater degree of accountability than ever before. But if marketers are going to live up to this accountability mandate, they'll need to keep a close, continual tab on their marketing performance and overall contribution to the organization. This is the only way marketers will remain relevant to the C-suite, which demands to know what is working, what isn't working, and what course adjustments are needed to ensure that marketing investments are allocated appropriately, and ultimately, whether they are paying for themselves.

We've seen plenty of proof that dashboards themselves are a good investment of time and resources. Dashboards help marketers uncover insights for improvement that can lead to increased marketing efficiency, a greater ROI, and expanded influence in the marketplace. Typically, marketers using dashboards can expect to realize insights that yield improvements in ROI ranging from 10 to 35 percent.

Amazingly, despite the fact that most successful marketers view data as a core asset to their efforts, this useful set of tools is often ignored by the very same professionals who lament about the poor quality of insights and the inefficiency of their data infrastructure.

According to a global study by Accenture, conducted in January 2010, a little more than one-third (35 percent) of marketers were planning to devote more resources to implementing a marketing dashboard, with 9 percent expecting to invest "significantly more resources." On a priority basis, this puts dashboards even with investments in building a digital advertising presence (35 percent) and slightly ahead of developing and training marketing teams (34 percent).

Are you ready to realize this competitive edge? Based on a study by the Interactive Advertising Bureau, the Association of National Advertisers, and Booz Allen Hamilton (2007), marketers who are "leaders" in using technology to manage their data are twice as likely as nonleaders to have a dashboard that measures ROI.

With seemingly unlimited computational power and a gigantic explosion in data, information is easily available and online. This proliferation of information has created a new promise for marketing—a transformation that enables real-time access to vital information. There is a greater ability to quickly see patterns and reach deeper insights, all fueled by new tools like the marketing dashboard. And the technology has advanced significantly: modern dashboards provide an easy-to-use drag-and-drop user interface, with rich graphics and the ability to drill down into the details at any time.

Why You Need Your Own Dashboard

You may comfortably assume that agencies and many of your strategic partners, including those in your own organization whose data may reside in some silo, are using a dashboard of their own.

The best dashboards allow you to:

- Easily drill down and get to details, root causes, and more.
- Create personalized views based on a user's domain of responsibility.
- Be forward-looking and predict outcomes.
- Perform data analytics: what ifs, drill-downs, linkages, and comparisons.
- And above all else, generate transformative insights.

Is a dashboard right for your business? In most cases, the time and effort required to build a data dashboard is well worth the investment. Let's look more specifically at the benefits and advantages:

- *Making timely decisions:* Decision makers need the power to recognize data trends and quickly capitalize on market opportunities. Dashboards can dramatically expedite decision making by automating the process of data aggregation, standardization, and dissemination. Looking at a broad array of different media sources, a dashboard enables a marketer to quickly isolate trends that otherwise may go unnoticed.

  For example, a marketer might observe that a week of heavy-up TV spending placed right before a paid search campaign results in a dramatic increase in the effectiveness of the paid search outlay.
- *Making better decisions:* Because dashboards offer a window into the key marketing metrics driving your business, they can help keep you on the right track with your marketing initiatives. Better, more accessible information leads to better decisions.
- *Driving efficiency:* Not only do dashboards deliver information in a timely fashion, they also automate the availability of the data required by stake-holders to support key marketing decisions. Ready access to information enables the marketing department to be efficient, because they can shift their valuable attention toward strategy development and decision making—and away from time spent sifting through disparate data sources in an attempt to formulate a clear picture of the changing marketplace.

  Based on a large number of implementations, we have noticed that a well-designed, automated dashboard can result in a 10 to 20 percent reduction in resources required to get the data ready and organized for conducting analysis.
- *Impacting the bottom line:* Ultimately, a successful dashboard delivers significant impact on marketing performance, establishing a clear link between marketing expenditures and company profits.
- *Motivating higher performance:* Seeing progress is self-motivating! By presenting key points of data in an easy-to-read, intuitive, and highly

visual format, dashboards can focus your attention and motivate you to take concerted action to continually improve campaign performance.

- *Improving communication:* Business decision makers in large corporations are confronted with the daunting task of communicating performance data on a wide variety of marketing inputs and outputs to a large set of stakeholders. Dashboards simplify this communication challenge. All stakeholders can be assisted with their own, often personalized, window into the relevant marketing data and view predetermined key metrics that are driving business results. Dashboards facilitate a culture of learning and sharing best practices across the organization.

- *Answering your most pressing marketing questions:* What are the most important questions a dashboard can answer? Consider the partial list below:

  What is the relative performance and ROI of each medium in the mix?
  How are my campaigns performing against goals?
  What are the potential opportunities for optimizing marketing spend?
  At what point is the creative and message wearing out?
  What are the key trends across the customer funnel stages?
  What are the trends in different communication channels, for example, driving traffic to the company traffic?
  Where is my site traffic coming from?
  How engaged are my visitors in different digital media? How can I better optimize their website experience?
  What are the key drivers of my marketing effectiveness?
  How is our brand doing versus the competition?
  How should I allocate my next set of marketing expenditures?
  Can I differentiate my brand by introducing a smarter media mix?

Now that we've discussed what a dashboard is and what they can do for marketers, it's time to learn how to build one.

Four Steps to Designing Your Own Dashboard

Imagine stepping into someone's new car and finding there is no dashboard. Want to know what speed you're going? Check in the glove compartment for a speedometer reading. Concerned about your fuel level? Ask your friend in the backseat to dig underneath your seat and check the gauge. Want to change the music station? Stop the car, open the trunk, and fiddle with the dial buried under the spare tire. Ridiculous? Of course, but this is what it's like to manage your campaigns and marketing programs without a well-designed digital dashboard.

The good news is that building a dashboard is not as complex as it once was given the availability of many new dashboard tools and products. However, a structured process needs to be followed, so the following four steps are recommended. You will need to carefully align the relationship between your marketing initiatives and the overall business outcomes desired; you may find that this procedure will also raise the role of marketing throughout the organization and establish a framework to help you measure success. If you've looked at the earlier chapters on various online channels, you may already have a clearer idea of which key metrics should be included.

Step 1: Complete the Initial Assessment

We consider this the most critical phase—getting the initial assessment and business context correct. A rigorous assessment should be conducted at the outset of building the dashboard, with the following goals:

- Determining the objective and scope of the dashboard.
- Identifying challenges and knowledge gaps across the business.
- Gaining an understanding of the processes for data aggregation, report generation, and distribution.
- Selecting key metrics that will be used to measure the impact, efficiency, and value of your marketing programs, as well as how these metrics will be used for decision making.

Organize your metrics into the following categories: brand (awareness, ad recall, favorability, purchase intent, etc.); customers (acquisition, retention, customer lifetime value, etc.); product (adoption, frequency of purchase, price, margin, etc.); and competitive frame (market share, share of requirements, brand preference, etc.).

Identify the sources for the data you will need, as well as any data gaps. In the case of gaps, you may need to consider investing in specialized measurement tools to extract the required data. It is worth the time to look at other areas in your organization and speak to colleagues who may have data sets that can be accessed for your own use.

It is also important to define a reporting structure well ahead of time. Specifically, this means deciding who in the organization needs to see what data and how frequently and in what form.

All this information should be inventoried and fed into a requirements document that will help the architect of the dashboard build it to suit your needs. It is important that all key users, especially business owners, are included and that the entire business context for the dashboard be clearly outlined at this stage. We have seen too many instances where this step is skipped, resulting in blotched implementation. Organizations should not jump into dashboard creation without a clear understanding of the objectives and specific expectations regarding benefits, usage scenarios, and ongoing support requirements.

Step 2: Refine Design Requirements

Following the initial assessment, the next phase of the dashboard project is to evaluate design considerations. Don't rush yourself; this requires a good deal of thought even from dashboard professionals. Here are some critical questions to ask yourself and to discuss with your designer:

- Do you have the right Key Performance Indicators (KPIs) spelled out? Are there both primary and diagnostic KPIs, the latter of which can serve as proxies for the former?
- How timely are the data being presented in the dashboard? Can the end user find out when the dashboard information was last refreshed and when the next cycle of refresh is going to be (daily, weekly, monthly)? What's the right frequency for data refresh?
- What is the quality of the dashboard data? Are there ways for the user to know when the data hygiene is not good and the information is only directional?
- Does your dashboard show context to the information so that it can be properly interpreted? Is the source of information tagged to the dashboard so that users can dig deeper into the original source if needed?
- Can you establish data linkages between the various metrics across categories, such as by linking brand preference or intent to purchase with actual purchase behavior?
- Are the right analytics available? Can users access drivers of KPIs?
- Is the dashboard forward-looking? Does it allow for forecasting and/or predicting results or outcomes?
- Are the insights readily accessible with the right context and interpretation?
- How actionable are the insights that are disseminated? Are they approved by subject matter experts?
- What is the appropriate level and type of training required for correct interpretation and utilization of different data views in decision making?
- Can you easily find descriptions for the meanings of each metric, as well as the granularity associated with the metric (in terms of time, geography, product hierarchy, segment, etc.)?

Step 3: Select the Technology

At this stage, it is time to identify the factors that will drive the technology for the dashboard, that is, the right database, hardware, and software tools for building the user interface. Again, this is no trivial task. The factors for selecting the technology are as follows:

- *Access:* Determine the number of users and from which departments, as well as the response time required, information needed for registration, log-in, and password maintenance for different access levels.
- *Navigation:* Conduct a deep-dive on system navigation flows and best paths to get to the required content. How many levels of drill-down will be required?
- *Data review:* Estimate data volumes, including frequency of transmissions and uploads. Complete a review on the data sources feeding into each module and the frequency needed for the data refresh.

Step 4: Design the User Interface

The dashboard needs to have an intuitive User Interface (UI) that retains consistency from module to module. Because dashboards necessitate the compression of large amounts of business information into a small visual area, it is vital to try to get this right the first time. Every data component must effectively balance its share of screen real estate with the importance of the information it is imparting to the user. It is essential to have UI expertise in developing dashboards. There needs to be a standard use of graphics and a structured methodology behind it. Have several members of your team test the interface; everyone should be able to easily find the numbers or charts they will need on a regular basis.

We find that most of the current dashboard interfaces do not provide the rich experience that today's users have gotten accustomed to by interacting with rich media on the web or the numerous applications on mobile devices. We highly recommend getting some digital creative designers brought into the project team to provide expert guidance on the interface design.

Illustrating a Best-in-Class Dashboard   The real power of the dashboard lies in its ability to assemble all the vital information into a single place and to allow the user to access many different views, or slices of information from the various modules, with a mere click. We believe in the one-click rule; that is, only one click is required to get to any of the important functions— insights, reports, views, drill-downs, and pull-ups. This interactive feature of the dashboard requires setting up many filters and buttons. The following screen shots provide a sample list of the comprehensive array of buttons and filters that need to be included; see Figures 11.1 and 11.2.

1. *Geography Filters:* navigate across geographic market views to display data at the desired level of detail.
2. *Time Filters:* navigate between annual or quarterly views.
3. *Module Navigation:* navigate across different modules corresponding to distinct performance areas.
4. *View Navigation:* enables user to access the right data views within a specific module.
5. *Metric Selection:* allows user to select relevant metrics/KPIs for analysis— clicks, engagement, sales, etc.
6. *Benchmarking:* in certain views, allows users to access benchmark data to compare current results with those of past years or quarters.

Figure 11.1
Top menus allow users to select criteria for performance review

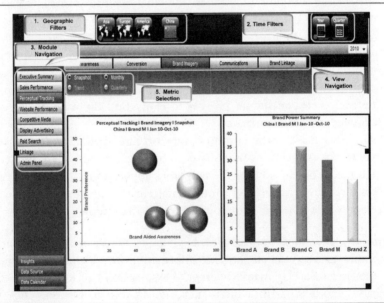

Source: Vipin Mayar.

Figure 11.2
Additional information and documentation can be accessed via tabs

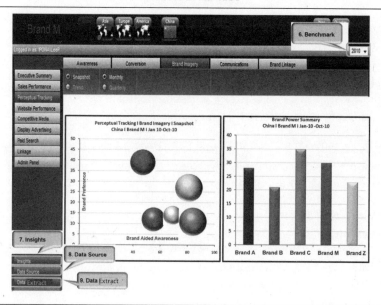

Source: Vipin Mayar.

7. *Insights:* enables users to upload commentary, share these insights with other users, and access the expert opinions of other system users.
8. *Data Source:* enables users to view detailed documentation regarding the source of the data presented—data-gathering process, methodology, and any data deficiencies or biases that would assist interpretation.
9. *Data Extract:* enables users to export the data presented into an Excel document with the click of a button.

Now that we know how to design a one-click dashboard to access all the views, let's look at the key objectives of the various modules.

Executive Summary   No dashboard is complete without an executive summary. This is the area in the dashboard where top-level executives can go and look at the top-line results. Typically, a summary view is created from all the modules. Often the official company marketing scorecard is available online in the executive view.

Exposure Module   This module provides views across the different digital channels, including website, search, display, mobile, and social, to answer the following questions:

- What are the key exposure trends?
- What are the sources of traffic or site visits?
- What is the planned and actual media spend?
- How does my marketing spend align with seasonal variations?
- How does my spend compare with competitors?
- Is the campaign suffering from creative wear-out?

Strategic Module   This module provides views on key consumer perceptions and captures data across brand/advertising attributes, markets, and segments to answer the following questions:

- What are the key trends across all the major customer and brand attributes?
- How engaged are the customers with the brand's Magnetic Content?
- How does the brand perform across the conversion funnel?
- What are the links between the brand attributes, customer attributes, and marketing investment?

Financial Module   This module provides users with views that answer the following important questions linked to financial outcomes:

- What are the key trends across sales, revenue share, and margins?
- What are the sales trends relative to the competition?
- Is there a relationship between sales/share/revenue and marketing investment?

In addition to the Exposure, Strategic, and Financial modules, there is another module you'll want to incorporate into your dashboard: the Analytics Module. This is the module that sets the stage for transformational insights.

Analytics Module   The Analytics Module is a very powerful feature within a dashboard. It can uncover relationships between different variables, especially between driver and outcome metrics. For example, these are all questions that a well-designed analytics module could answer:

- How does marketing investment drive sales?
- How do competitive activities affect sales?

- How do brand metrics drive sales or market share?
- How do display ads affect overall sales?
- How does marketing investment change brand perception?

Without an Analytics Module in your dashboard, these business-driver questions can take weeks to answer. But a proper dashboard can reveal answers instantly!

Another feature to include in your Analytics Module is the ability to examine lag effects, where one variable has an influence on another but there is a gap, or lag, in seeing the effect. For example, there may be a lag between when a display banner campaign is run and when it makes an impact on sales or brand perceptions. Depending on the product or service category, it can take weeks, a couple of months, or longer for the lag effects to take place.

A highly recommended feature that prevents users from making erroneous conclusions is a simple *correlation dial*, which shows the strength of the correlation between the two variables. Figure 11.3 shows two variables side-by-side and their correlation. The two variables are gross margin versus advertising spend, and they have a high correlation of almost 57 percent. In another instance, a marketer investing in brand advertising can quickly look for the correlation between improvement in a key brand attribute and sales. By examining such correlation coefficients, the user can draw conclusions

Figure 11.3
Lag effects and correlations in an analytics module

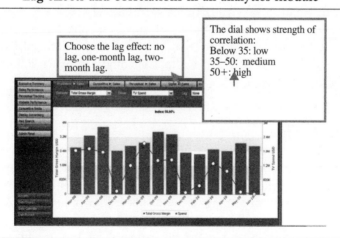

Source: Vipin Mayar.

about whether a variable input (brand metrics) is having an impact on the other (sales). The marketer can get quick feedback and insights on what is working and what's not.

Building and Rolling Out a Dashboard

Now that we understand what goes into designing a best-in-class dashboard, let's shift our focus to build and rollout.

As we outlined earlier in this chapter, selecting the right technology is critical to building an on-time, error-free dashboard. You will need a reliable development partner to complete the build, which may be your internal IT department or an external technology provider or consultant. Make sure you are working with an organization or team that has a proven record of building dashboards. Most of the major agencies have strong dashboard development capabilities, and even smaller agencies may have dashboard providers they use and can recommend.

After a dashboard is built, we recommend a two-phase rollout plan, beginning with a pilot, or "alpha," phase to test things out, validate the data sources, and discover any kinks or problems.

Phase I—Pilot

It's better to walk before you run. Launch your dashboard in pilot form first—typically concentrating on a single campaign, in a single product area or market with a focus on only the key communication channels. The pilot will unearth significant organizational learning relating to the process, as well as the roles and responsibilities for all parties involved in the dashboard's development and use. Make sure that you have fine-tuned and tweaked all processes and design elements prior to launching a broader rollout, where flawless execution is required.

Phase II—Scale

The knowledge captured in the first phase will enable full deployment of a dashboard across all communication channels for all major campaigns. One of the challenges you will face is getting wide-scale quick adoption, that is, getting new users in the habit of turning to the dashboard for results and insights. We recommend, for the first couple of months, sending a weekly e-mail with links back to the dashboard, highlighting some of the key insights and trends from the dashboard. This will encourage reluctant users to get in the habit.

Success Factors and Things to Look Out For

There are many challenges that can thwart the building of a successful dashboard. Keep the following key factors in mind to ensure successful implementation and delivery.

Relevancy   The dashboard must closely reflect the needs of the decision makers. This is why it's critical to involve all of the key stakeholders early in a formal engagement process—before you begin design and implementation of your dashboard. Avoid shortcuts at all cost. We have seen too many examples, for instance, of review sessions being conducted without formal sign-offs or even where key stakeholders are missing altogether. It is very important that the requirements be completed with rigor and that all parties sign off.

Standardization   One particular challenge in creating dashboards for global organizations is standardizing metrics across geographies, campaigns, and communication channels to enable effective benchmarking. A lack of metric standardization will sidetrack interpretation of findings, mire the marketing team in confusion, and prevent action. If you don't have the expertise required to develop standardized metrics, we recommend you hire consultants for this portion of the project.

Breadth and Depth   To generate the insights required for media optimization, a dashboard must have the breadth and depth of coverage required to enable robust analytics. A successful dashboard must support decision making at all levels of the marketing organization. Metrics should be available across multiple campaigns and geographies over time to facilitate effective benchmarking and insight generation. Managers responsible for the performance of a particular campaign or marketing vehicle must have a full drill-down capability to manage performance at a tactical level.

Speed   As information technology drives accelerated change in the marketplace, marketers have the opportunity to outflank the competition through agility in reacting to market trends. Since timeliness of information access has become a competitive advantage, this drives the need for process automation in the channeling of data to the dashboard. Your goal should be to make the data available in as close to real time as possible.

Deploying the Dashboard to Drive Action

If you build a dashboard and nothing material happens, you have failed. The development of a best-in-class dashboard, in and of itself, does not ensure action. Here are some process tips you can use to harness insights from your dashboard that can lead to actual change and improvement.

Regular Review of Analysis   Establish a regularly scheduled process to monitor the key suite of metrics in your dashboard, highlight pertinent insights, and stimulate ongoing action. All stakeholders will need to hold each other accountable; it can be tempting to jump to conclusions, when none may be valid. This is especially true when a set of numbers happens to validate someone's gut or personal beliefs (or their agenda). Often, how a set of numbers is presented can lead to wildly different decisions depending on the order in which the numbers are presented and the context in which they are discussed. It is important to have open, thoughtful discussions and a disciplined, careful review of the numbers.

Individual Accountability   The insights get much more actionable when an individual is assigned responsibility for each metric or an area of the dashboard. A clear metric ownership structure fosters a culture of responsibility and gradually trains people to become specialists who can then be highly responsive to shifts in the data or performance.

Incentive Alignment   Some kind of alignment between incentives and performance is often required to create ownership and speedy resolution among metric owners. The incentive system should be structured in such a way as to motivate people and encourage them to be collaborative as a team.

Dashboards on a Shoestring Budget

A dashboard isn't just a great value proposition for large companies. It's also a very useful tool for smaller companies with smaller budgets. Off-the-shelf dashboards can be customized for specific needs; if you're familiar with the dashboards used in Google Analytics, for example, you can build something to suit. Some tips:

- Look for a simple product that is easy to use and learn.
- Think small and build it out over time. Limit the dashboard to only four or five key views that offer 80 percent of the value.
- Some dashboard products are straightforward, with a drag-and-drop interface. These products can create views with interactive charts, maps, and graphs in minutes.

The popular blog Dashboard Spy is a good source of information for off-the-shelf products, templates for the do-it-youselfer, and examples of best-in-class dashboard designs for various industries. Of course, if your budget allows, you may consider the more sophisticated and popular dashboard tools, such as Business Objects, Tableau, Xcelsius, Cognos, and SAS.

Reliable dashboard suppliers will work directly with a smaller end user to provide a highly customizable, personalized version that can become their default home page on their computer. These small, focused dashboards can also be very nimble and easily accommodate changes as the business grows and selection of KPIs becomes more sophisticated. Typically, it will take four to six weeks to create and install such dashboards without compromising on the quality of the charts, drill-downs, or interactivity.

Conclusion

Developing and rolling out a best-in-class dashboard will require considerable time and effort from a variety of executives from across the organization, but it will pay for itself many times over. If you follow the guidelines we've outlined, and implement well, your dashboard will continually prove the worth of marketing's contribution to the organization and create a key competitive advantage, simply by accelerating and sharpening your ability to make key decisions that drive business results. Regardless of the size of your budget or your company, follow the advice and tips in this chapter and you will be well on your way to dashboard heaven. The alternative is to be stuck having to stop the car and open the trunk to change the music station!

CHAPTER 12

Putting It All Together

"This new marketing model doesn't shout; it listens and learns.
And relevance, interactivity, and accountability are its
essential ingredients."
— *Christopher Vollmer, Partner, Booz Allen Hamilton*

Ifall were well in the land of marketing and media, and most particularly within the exploding digital universe, you wouldn't need this book (and we wouldn't need to have written it!). But marketing, or at least marketing as we have known and used it in the past, is not working so well anymore. The traditional advertising model may not be "broken," but it is certainly less potent now that the Internet has become a primary hub for business and consumer communications. With all the empowering technologies and platforms digital has spawned, both consumers and your business customers have now gained the upper hand with their control over media, content, and advertising.

This Internet-enabled technological revolution has several implications for marketers. First, the digital consumer is more advertising resistant than ever before. Most accept advertising and marketing messages only on their own terms; through use of privacy settings, block outs, opt-outs, time-shifting, and on-demand technologies, there is more individual control over what messages are seen and when they are seen. Ads that are irrelevant, out of context, interruptive, or lacking inherent value will be ignored, clicked away, or otherwise rendered useless to the marketer. Like spent bullets against a superhero's impenetrable chest.

Second, we know the digital consumer is spending more time engaged with the web. The average American now spends 24 percent of his or her total media time online, accounting for 2 hours and 35 minutes per day. That amount of time spent is second only to television, at 4 hours and 24 minutes per day, a medium that commands upwards of $60 billion annually and yet is quickly, inexorably morphing itself toward the properties of the Internet, opening up new possibilities for engagement, interactivity, and measurement.

Finally, the digital consumer is a moving target online. No longer content with just checking e-mail, searching, or surfing portal sites, consumers in every age group are spending increasing amounts of time on social network sites, video platforms such as YouTube, and other, equally immersive digital destinations, often via their mobile phones.

The Two Secrets: A Quick Review

At the outset of this book, and as suggested by the title, we told you there are two essential secrets to achieving online marketing success. Let's review the essential aspects for those two secrets: Performance Measurement and Magnetic Content.

Secret #1: Performance Measurement

In every channel chapter, and particularly in Chapter 2, we've shown you how a select number of key metrics (we recommend seven) can be consistently relied on to gauge the success of online marketing programs.

If you have understood our explanation for the Performance Measurement framework and the associated seven key metrics, you will no longer fall prey to the familiar yet untenable situations of having too many metrics to manage, trying to make the wrong metrics work, or relying too heavily on click-through rates as your sole performance yardstick.

The first step is to identify your most important metrics according to the following three operative buckets: Exposure, Strategic, and Financial:

1. *Exposure*—metrics that capture the immediate impact of your marketing spend, such as the reach/frequency and engagement of digital marketing.
2. *Strategic*—metrics that are forward-looking and help you evaluate strategic marketing objectives related to customer and brand growth.
3. *Financial*—metrics that relate to financial performance and return on investment and that quantify results for sales, market share, and profits.

We also suggest that these three buckets of measurement be viewed as a pyramid, with Exposure metrics at the bottom, Strategic metrics in the middle, and Financial metrics at the top (Figure 12.1) This visualization is different

Figure 12.1

Performance Measurement for marketing is best viewed as a pyramid

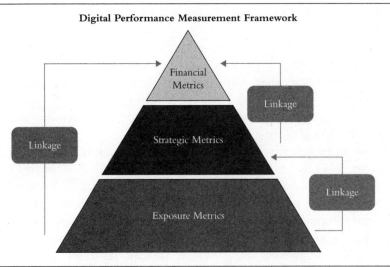

Digital Performance Measurement Framework

Source: Vipin Mayar.

from the typical "sales funnel" but will give you (and your staff) a better handle on developing and analyzing your marketing metrics.

The Top Seven Digital Metrics: A Review

We made the bold assertion that there are only seven metrics that are critical. While countless other metrics are available to marketers, these special seven are the ones that marketers should seek to master. You'll notice that they cover the spectrum of Exposure, Strategic, and Financial metrics. These seven metrics are as follows:

1. *Qualified Reach, or Qualified Visits:* We believe that Qualified Reach is the one critical metric that every marketer should use—specifically because it captures two important dimensions that no other single metric does: both quantity (number of individuals) and quality (the users have performed a desired interaction, which in turn suggests a degree of interest or intention on the part of the consumer). Depending on the channel, the specific metrics you use will vary, but the emphasis is always on actual behavior—a far different approach than typical measurements of raw reach and frequency.

2. *Click-through rates (CTRs):* CTR is the metric most commonly used by online advertisers. Although it is still relied on too heavily, and in inappropriate ways, we believe the CTR should continue to be used, but only as a diagnostic metric, not as a primary metric.

3. *Brand perception lift:* This metric is calculated by determining the change in a brand perception among audiences, with the results compared with those of a control group that was not exposed to the messaging.

4. *Engagement Score (ES):* This represents the degree of magnetism of the content or ad. Based on a flexible value system, the ES works across all digital media, from videos and mobile apps to microsites and social community platforms.

5. *End Action Rate:* End Actions represent the action taken by a user; it is often also referred to as a conversion activity. An End Action can be a sale, a lead generated, a download, a video view, a form completion, and so on. It is the end goal of the content or advertisement and is a critical metric for determining the effectiveness of the campaign.

6. *Efficiency metrics cost per X* (where X can be clicks, impressions, leads, orders, engagement, etc.): These metrics represent the efficiency of your marketing. Are you achieving your goals in a cost-effective manner?

7. *Return on investment (ROI):* ROI is a critical financial metric representing the financial value created by your marketing. The ROI methodologies we have suggested for each of the online channels described in this book are built on the principle of *incrementality*. This is another forward-looking concept and especially helpful when determining ROI of new media. All marketing, whether it is offline or online, should be measured to determine an incremental improvement in some critical consumer activity, such as *acquisition, retention, loyalty, key perception(s), or sales.*

Secret #2: Magnetic Content

The second secret involves nothing less than radically altering the way you are creating and distributing your brand messages and content. Rather than trying to push messages out to consumers who are increasingly resistant to traditional advertising pitches—and typically see them as intrusions or distractions—the goal is to create Magnetic Content that attracts consumers and seduces them into engaging with your brand. Magnetic Content is a powerful form of branded content that directly engages the consumer—so that they willingly choose to interact with it and share it with others. This approach represents a broad shift in emphasis from "paid media," where the marketer places ads that interrupt the consumer's content experience, to "owned media," which is branded content that commands its own attention and interest. It's more about attraction, versus distraction.

Recall the five criteria that define Magnetic Content:

1. Is the content unique?
2. Is the content useful?
3. Is the content well executed?
4. Is the content fun?
5. Does the content make good use of the channel in which it appears?

Not all of your Magnetic Content will be able to meet all five of these criteria. However, the more factors you can address, the more likely your Magnetic Content will be engaging and lead to further interactions with the consumer. In fact, you want to create lots of Magnetic Content, using a variety of formats and channels, to keep consumers moving along a continuum of engagement (reflecting your Engagement Map!) that gradually leads to trial, sales, brand loyalty, and referrals. Each of these five criteria for Magnetic Content needs to be applied to the six digital channels we discuss in this book: search, display, e-mail, social, mobile, and video.

Creating great Magnetic Content is your first, most important task. But to make the most of it, you'll also need to follow our seven strategies for *maximizing* Magnetic Content:

1. Educate and organize your teams around Magnetic Content.
2. Develop Magnetic Content ideas based on behaviors, attitudes, and lifestyles, not your products.
3. Define and own the value proposition. (Ask these two vital questions: "If I were a target consumer, would I use this content?" and "Would people pay for this?")
4. Leverage your existing customer base (as just one example, let them beta test your Magnetic Content).
5. Build an Engagement Map. (Magnetic Content should not be a one-off event, but rather a series of connected, graduated interactions.)
6. Buy media to build reach. (To get scale, you'll still need to buy reach in the form of "paid media" to draw attention to your Magnetic Content).
7. Stay flexible, and remember it's an iterative process: attract, engage, and measure.

Once you understand the key concepts behind Performance Measurement and Magnetic Content, the next step is to apply them across the various digital channels.

Focus on the Highest-Impact Channels to Drive Your Marketing Results

We have identified six key digital channels for their unique marketing benefits and described how to apply the two secrets of Performance Measurement and Magnetic Content to each. But not all channels, and the respective strategies associated with them, are equal in terms of their potential impact. Of the six channels discussed in this book, we believe that four are essential for integrating into your marketing efforts. These select four channels, coupled with a tight focus on the most important strategies for each, will yield the highest possible impact to your business, regardless of whether you are a small business or a large corporation. This does not mean that the other two channels are not important, especially for certain businesses or target consumers, but with limited time and resources, you need to concentrate your efforts on where they will have the greatest impact.

The four channels and their high-impact strategies are discussed next.

Support All Marketing Efforts with Search   Focus on search—both search engine optimization (SEO) and pay-per-click (PPC)—because it is likely to be your biggest driver of traffic and will directly help grow your business. Search is also very cost-effective, particularly SEO. Remember, the reason search works so well is because it allows you to reach hand-raisers—those consumers who identify themselves as being in the market by virtue of their searching behavior. Take into account all the important points we reviewed in Chapter 4. Specifically, it is critical to select the right keywords; acquire the highest quality links; create unique, fresh Magnetic Content that is relevant to your target; solicit buzz from credible influencers in social media; and pay attention to your ROI with paid search. For most businesses, including the smallest firms, we believe search remains the number one tactic for digital marketing.

Use E-Mail as a Proven Workhorse for Acquisition and Retention   This may be seen by some as "old school," but e-mail marketing remains highly effective with a proven ROI and containable costs that your CFO will love. You should pursue it wisely as part of an overall strategy and use the best practices from the chapter, including careful customer segmentation.

Use Social Media to Engage with Your Consumers   The first and most important strategy to master with social media is listening. Consumers are spending increasing amounts of time with social sites, and the conversations held there represent a gold mine of learning that you cannot get anywhere else, and certainly not as cost effectively. It is also critical to focus much of your social media efforts on your core customers—the brand enthusiasts who are passionate about your brand and want to sing its praises to others. Nurture and reward these brand loyalists, and they, in turn, will reward you by serving as your core fan base, defending your brand when it comes under attack, promoting your brand in a more credible way than you could ever do yourself, and providing you with honest feedback about your product or service. It is particularly critical with social media, though, that you be crystal clear on the objectives you want to achieve with this channel.

Importantly, social media demands a fresh, new approach to marketing. You need to talk in a genuine human voice and concentrate on adding real value to the conversation. Standard forms of advertising messaging, such as intrusive banner ads, will not suffice here. Rather, you want to inject Magnetic Content throughout your social media efforts.

Use Mobile as an Additive and Integrated Channel to Supercharge All the Others   The mobile phone is not only ubiquitous—consumers carry them wherever they go—it provides multiple options for consumers and marketers to engage in one-to-one, highly personalized dialogue. With location-based services, mobile lets you add a timeliness and local relevance to your marketing outreach. Location data are key to the future of marketing for the simple reason that this information enables marketers to deliver a compelling offer, coupon, or other reward when consumers are at the point of decision. Even when it takes the backseat role, mobile can serve as a powerful catalyst, accelerator, enhancer, and barometer for an integrated campaign. You can even measure the effects of other media by using the mobile phone as a feedback mechanism. Finally, mobile apps provide rich opportunities for marketers desiring to engage consumers with Magnetic Content that serves a genuine need or want.

Reconsider Your Use of Video and Display   Besides the four must-have channels, video and display also have unique properties and benefits for marketers that should be considered, or reconsidered, as well. With video ads and other forms of branded video content, you can engage consumers in an emotional way—just like with television. There are also countless opportunities for creating rich Magnetic Content that can easily be passed along to others. Display ads, meanwhile, can be a foundation for your other digital efforts, by boosting awareness, strengthening message association, bolstering purchase intent, and specifically directing consumers toward your Magnetic Content.

Implementing What You've Learned Within Your Organization

None of these channel strategies and the many recommendations surrounding Performance Measurement and Magnetic Content can be successfully executed without giving due consideration to a few critical organizational factors. There are, in fact, seven critical factors you should recognize—and perhaps internalize—before passing them on to your colleagues and strategic partners within and outside of your business:

1. Reorganize and educate your marketing teams; put new demand on agencies to support integrated marketing.
2. Break down silos to allow for a free flow of data and integrated measurement.
3. Account for cross-channel effects and proper attribution.
4. Emphasize that targeting is no substitute for an engaged and magnetized customer.
5. Focus on delivering unique content and generating real value.
6. Budget for Performance Measurement and Magnetic Content.
7. Test and optimize continually.

Let's take each of these organization-wide strategies in turn.

1. Reorganize and Educate Your Marketing Teams

Most marketing organizations are evolving their internal structures, processes, and teams for the digital landscape. This includes assigning the right ownership for digital/social marketing or building internal plans and processes to deliver an integrated search, social, and digital content plan to the market. We find this is often still being done in a silo'ed fashion, both within organizations and across marketing service partners. Putting a new demand on your agencies to support integrated marketing will also require a firm hand.

Organizations also need to be reorganized to manage the constant flow of dialogue with consumers via social media. Ambassadors representing each department need to be established and coordinated so that the organization can appropriately respond to consumer requests and inquiries, as well as learn from the interactions that occur continuously through social channels.

There is no substitute for acquiring top digital talent. Regardless of the current state of the economy, digital talent is scarce and demands top dollar. Do not let up in the war to acquire these specialists—especially in the areas of digital analytics, search, social, and mobile. At the same time, you need talent that is experienced in integrating marketing communications, building bridges across offline and online. Very often you will find this scarce even at the leading marketing communication agencies.

Another important dimension to your talent in this new digital age is to have both left-brainers and right-brainers. Typically marketing departments have lacked left-brained people. Left-brainers can manage huge amounts of data, build complex models with databases that talk to one another, and then channel that data into actionable insights. Left-brainers are typically logical, sequential, rational, analytical, and objective. They look at parts, and they tend to look backward as they seek to measure results.

But you also need right-brainers on your team. These are typically the creative types who come up with big marketing ideas based on a thorough understanding of consumer insights. They can also help craft ads and design Magnetic Content that will resonate with consumers in ways that will shape their attitudes and motivate them to engage further with your brand. Right-brainers are random, intuitive, holistic, synthesizing, and subjective. They look at wholes, and they tend to be more forward-looking and visionary.

Both types of people offer critical contributions. Your job is to bring the left-brainers and right-brainers together in ways that will lead to a seamless interplay between backward-looking, precise data measurement and forward-looking creative executions that will engage consumers emotionally as well as rationally. Often, this can be achieved by pairing left- and right-brainers together in teams, and then letting the sparks fly.

Finally, you will need to arrange for training of the key principles of Performance Measurement and Magnetic Content. This training may need to be administered not only to your internal teams but also to your outside ad agency partners. You may also need to enlighten senior management so that they are on board with the new approaches and understand why they're necessary.

2. Break Down Silos to Allow for a Free Flow of Data and Integrated Measurement

The new buzz phrase in the industry is "Data is the new oil," or even "Data is the new sexy." Take this opportunity to develop interest in and support of data across departmental lines. Access to timely, integrated performance data is a critical requirement for successfully optimizing and realizing the returns from these digital strategies. At a minimum, you need to have easy access to brand health metrics, online behavior data across channels, and offline and online spending and sales results. You will also need data from many internal sources to gain the 360-degree view of your customer and to successfully integrate and measure both online and offline efforts together.

Gathering all of this information requires full collaboration of marketing team members, agencies, and vendors. It requires that all these groups work closely and share their data. Unfortunately, very few companies foster this type of collaboration and sharing of data. There is a great tendency for everyone to work in his or her respective silo. A good first step is to appoint someone in your organization as being responsible for driving integration of data, fostering collaboration, and sharing of information. The data dashboard you have created will also be an essential help to you.

3. Account for Cross-Channel Effects and Proper Click Attribution

As a marketer, you need to follow and measure the activity and points of impact all along the consumer's engagement path. Since final conversion to sale is likely the result of cumulative effects from several media, it is important to analyze and attribute sales to all of the channels that contributed, not just the last click. Otherwise you will not be able to spend your marketing dollars wisely.

Many senior marketers we have worked with mention that properly tracking multiple channels is their single biggest challenge with media and marketing. Thus, we argue that you must invest in building out capabilities to understand cross-channel effects. You must also educate your organization to the risk of *not* accounting for cross-channel effects. Many organizations are making this a big focus in the next decade. So should you!

4. Recognize That Targeting Is No Substitute for an Engaged and Magnetized Customer

Given the rapidly fragmenting media landscape and the need for marketers to achieve better efficiencies with their media spending, there is a great deal of effort directed toward reaching narrower and narrower target audiences. In this "hunting" approach to marketing, the idea is to use new digital tools and technologies to more finely tune where the ads are delivered. However, such targeted ads rarely reach the right people at the right time, and they are too often ignored. The other problem is that as you apply better filters in your efforts to refine the target audience, you end up shrinking your reach.

We argue that the "fishing" approach is highly preferable and can be just as cost-efficient. With fishing, the idea is to find the best possible bait to attract your fish. The best bait to use, of course, is Magnetic Content. The best Magnetic Content attracts consumers—the right consumers—toward your brand. It achieves this by being so compelling, entertaining, informative, or otherwise engaging that it attracts promising prospects to your net. It allows you to more efficiently reach your most likely prospects while avoiding wasting money on uninterested consumers. Again, the powerful idea behind Magnetic Content is that you don't so much reach the audience as they reach you.

5. Focus on Delivering Unique Content and Generating Real Value

The consistent creation of Magnetic Content that is unique, relevant, and compelling does not happen by accident. It requires a great deal of organization and forethought. In addition to training and educating stakeholders so that everyone is on the same page with this new approach, you need to readjust your focus, placing less emphasis on paid media and more on owned media assets. You also need to build the right infrastructure, including developing a content management system that will allow you to manage content efficiently and deliver it in a targeted way. This will create efficiencies because you can reuse and repackage core content in a lot of different ways. Magnetic Content will drive social interactions online, and that same content can be shared and linked to, increasing your rankings within search. You also need to create paid advertising programs, online and offline, to alert consumers to your Magnetic Content.

6. Budget for Performance Measurement and Magnetic Content

Over the long run, you will likely end up spending less money on digital marketing programs based on our Performance Measurement and Magnetic Content principles. However, you will need to potentially budget more in the short term as you reorganize and go through what will likely be a long learning curve. The good news is that the initial cost increases will eventually be offset by greater and greater efficiencies due to both better measurement techniques and less waste with your marketing resources.

The cost of deploying our Performance Measurement approach may be more than what you're currently spending to measure your digital efforts, but it's well worth the added expense because it will give you a better understanding of what's working. In addition, the iterative process will inevitably lead to increasingly better business results and efficiencies, thereby helping offset any higher costs.

Budgeting for Innovation: Amazon's Free Shipping

Amazon researched consumer attitudes and discovered that the number one inhibitor preventing many people from buying online was they didn't like to pay for shipping costs. Taking that insight into account, and using out-of-the-box thinking, the e-commerce giant diverted a huge portion of its advertising budget to enable the company to offer its customers free delivery as a service. Amazon's free shipping offer, replicated by many e-commerce sites since, became a magnet to pull in droves of customers who would not have otherwise purchased products that needed to be shipped. Today, that same service innovation is also a profit center: customers can sign up for Amazon Prime, which allows them free, two-day shipping for most products, for an annual fee of $79.

The budgets required for creating Magnetic Content can vary widely. On one hand, the expenses associated with setting up or updating a Twitter account or Facebook brand page can be minimal. On the other hand, the cost of creating a full-blown webisode series using high-production video values and top talent can easily exceed the cost of producing a 30-second television spot. However, while the production costs may be higher with many forms of Magnetic Content, the costs to deliver and distribute it will usually end up being far less than what you would spend on a traditional media buy. This is because you will be redeploying your resources in a more efficient way. You will spend more on creating great content that attracts consumers, and they will help you spread it around to others—at virtually no additional cost to you. You will also spend much less on paid media trying to spray your message across a mass audience that includes a large portion of people who will never buy your product or service. Your marketing dollars will thus go more directly to the very people you want to reach—your most likely prospects.

Investing in the best Magnetic Content resources will help deliver the results you are looking for; you just need to have the measurements in place to demonstrate results and quantify your return on investment. This leads us to the final success factor.

7. Test and Optimize Continually

The key to discovering the marketing tactics that work for your business is to continually learn and test through experimentation. If you need to derive predictive ROI results on unproven tactics—and emerging media channels that may not exist yet—testing can provide the insights, without a lot of investment.

Most companies understand the importance of testing marketing campaigns, whether A/B testing, multivariate testing, or user testing, as a means of improving conversion rates. Many other firms believe that introducing testing into the process is an unnecessary added step, an unwelcome delay to launching a campaign that adds cost.

We strongly recommend that you institute testing as a critical step in your campaign process. Testing is the step that, with a little effort and time, allows you to pinpoint the most efficient tactics to meet your goals.

Conclusion

A few closing, personal remarks from the books' authors:

From Vipin

I made two big resolutions January 1, 2010: run my first marathon and write my first book! I felt much better about accomplishing the book. I had the key concepts outlined and with Geoff as a co-author, I felt confident that we could produce a valuable book with new concepts for marketers.

The two goals together were certainly challenging. Initially, it felt like jumping off a cliff. I had no idea how I would log 400 miles of training runs and write hundreds of pages. Each task by itself seemed overwhelming. As it turned out, running a marathon and combining that with writing helped me a lot. There are a lot of synergies. Both require extreme planning, sacrifices, and time spent alone, away from friends and family. You have to pace yourself so that you have energy for the last few miles or the last few chapters. You cannot give up if your quads are hurting after mile 20 or after your mind is going blank from lack of sleep. Starting early morning runs or starting new sections in the book felt similar. It was very tough to start, but once I got going I could get into a nice flow.

Every time I was discouraged there would be an incident to lift me up—I have a bookshelf at work with more than a couple hundred business books. An impressive collection! So, last year a colleague, a senior marketer, walked into my office and asked me for a recommendation on a digital marketing book from my vast bookshelf, a single, practical book he could apply to his business. I went across the bookshelf, picking up books and then putting them back down. I could not find one that fit the bill. I told him to come back later next year when Geoff and I would have a book written for him!

Such incidents gave me further impetus toward writing *Digital Impact*. It reinforced the need for such a book that marketers could relate to and apply the concepts quickly.

So, why write the book in the first place? The driving force for me was to create a book with all my experiences on a topic near and dear to everyone. Once Geoff joined in I knew, together, we could nail it. At the end of the day, I am hoping people will enjoy the book and get significant value from it and that some will tell me how much they enjoyed the book, which will make the pain and sacrifice worthwhile, just like the smiles and cheering I got running along the route of the New York City Marathon!

From Geoff

When Vipin initially approached me about writing a book together, my first reaction was to politely decline the offer. While I have a great deal of respect for Vipin and his expertise and talents, I was traveling a great deal, helping to run a growing company (eMarketer), and my family life was plenty busy with four children and training for my first half-marathon (yes, Vipin and I are both long-distance runners). With all this on my plate, where exactly was I going to find the time to write a book? Unlike Vipin, giving up sleep for me was not an option! But as Vipin expounded on the key principles he was thinking about—Performance Measurement and Magnetic Content—I eventually became convinced that the book needed to be written and that we should join forces to write it. Not only did I believe in these two powerful concepts, I realized that in my presentations around the country, I had already been talking about the pressing industry needs for better, more streamlined measurement systems and metrics, as well as a creative revolution for how online marketing and messaging should be approached.

Writing this book stretched me. I spent 17 years working in the trenches of New York ad agencies. I've founded and help to build a company dedicated to making sense of the online marketing landscape and its rapidly evolving trends. I have delivered hundreds of presentations and written almost as many reports on subjects related to all forms of digital marketing. But none of these pursuits prepared me for the sheer discipline and monumental focus required to write a book. I've learned that no amount of coffee, or other imaginative distractions, can cure an unexpected writer's block on those bleaker days. Thank goodness for Vipin's organized, insanely logical approach to the book process, which helped keep me on track, even when business trips, board meetings, last-minute presentations, training for my first half-marathon, and the onslaught of daily family life promised to intervene. My training for the half-marathon also provided helpful stimulus and direction for the book. Since I was tracking my weekly miles and the pace I was running at (through a handy mobile app), I was able to see steady progress in my training performance. This in turn motivated me to keep pushing further, and faster. So, too, with the book. I also noticed that my training runs were freeing up the right side of my brain, providing a ripe source of fresh creative ideas for the book.

My hope for the book is similar to Vipin's. I'd like to know that our combined thoughts, organized around the two overarching themes of Performance Measurement and Magnetic Content, resonate with marketers and small businesses and that this will eventually lead to action in the form of better, more successful online marketing programs. In the meantime, I've just signed up to run my first marathon—the 2011 New York Marathon!

INDEX

289